Mar 19
9c
2 60/19
U = 9

BREAKAWAY

BREAKAWAY

FROM BEHIND THE IRON CURTAIN TO THE NHL— THE UNTOLD STORY OF HOCKEY'S GREAT ESCAPES

Tal Pinchevsky

John Wiley & Sons Canada, Ltd.

Library and Archives Canada Cataloguing in Publication Data

Pinchevsky, Tal

Breakaway : from behind the Iron Curtain to the NHL—the untold story of hockey's great escapes / Tal Pinchevsky.

Includes index.

Issued also in electronic formats.

ISBN 978-1-118-09500-3

   1. Hockey players—Czech Republic—Biography.   2. Hockey players—Russia (Federation)—Biography.   3. Defectors.   I. Title.

GV848.5.A1P55 2012   796.962092'24371   C2011-908049-4

978-1-118-09620-8 (ebk); 978-1-118-09622-2 (ebk); 978-1-118-09621-5 (ebk)

Production Credits
Cover design: Adrian So
Typesetting: Thomson Digital
Cover image: Thinkstock/iStockphoto
Printer: Friesens

Editorial Credits
Executive editor: Karen Milner
Managing editor: Alison Maclean
Production editor: Jeremy Hanson-Finger

John Wiley & Sons Canada, Ltd.
6045 Freemont Blvd.
Mississauga, Ontario
L5R 4J3

Printed in Canada

1 2 3 4 5 FR 16 15 14 13 12

To the countless men and women who sacrificed everything in their escapes from behind the Iron Curtain. They hoped for the opportunity to live in freedom, and inadvertently altered the course of history in the process.

Contents

Acknowledgments

Because this project was so contingent on the help of so many incredibly generous people, compiling this list was almost as daunting a task as writing the actual book. I'll do my best to remember everyone.

None of this would have been possible without the time and cooperation of my countless interview subjects, most of whom were incredibly candid in recounting the brave and historic acts in which they were involved. Thanks so much to Mort Greenglass, Peter Stastny, Anton Stastny, Marcel Aubut, Gilles Leger, Slava Fetisov, Alexei Kasatonov, Lou Lamoriello, Dimitri Lopuchin, Jack McIlhargey, Miro Frycer, Michal Pivonka, Lynda Zengerle, Petr Klima, Jim Lites, Nick Polano, Darren Elliot, Neil Smith, Jacques Demers, Frank Musil, Ritch Winter, Lou Nanne, David Durenberger, Glen Sonmor, Petr Svoboda, David Volek, Petr Nedved, Don Luce,

Igor Kuperman, Charlie Pekarec, Mike Smith, Rick Dudley, Sergei Fedorov, Alex Gertsmark, Ken Daneyko, Bill Watters, Craig Laughlin, Jan Filc, Stewart Malgunas, John Whitehead, Turner Stevenson, Alexander Tyjnych, Marshall Johnston, Lev Zarokhovich, Glen Ringdal, Russ Farwell, David Luksu, and Robert Edelman.

Naturally, in my efforts to get in touch with subjects for this book, I encountered several helpful people along the way who were kind enough to point me in the right direction. There are more of these individuals than I could possibly fit onto these two pages but I'd particularly like to extend my thanks to Mark Janko, Todd Sharrock, Kevin Wilson, Louise Marois, Zack Hill, Jeff Alstadtler, Mike Sundheim, J.J. Hebert, Aaron Gogishvili, Jan Rachota, Mandy Gutmann, Sammy Steinlight, Rita Parenteau, Matt Conti, Ian Henry, and Michael Frazier.

I'd especially like to thank Vadim Kostyukhin, my good friend and brother-in-law, who helped tremendously in facilitating my research for this book. Of course, none of this would have been possible without the help of John Wiley & Sons Canada, Ltd., most notably the work of Karen Milner and Jeremy Hanson-Finger. And it all began with the help of my agent, Arnold Gosewich, whose advice and expertise proved invaluable throughout this process.

Finally, I would be remiss, not to mention a bad person, if I didn't take a moment to thank my friends and family. Most notably my wife, Mary, my parents, Marcel and Pnina, and my sister, Sarah, whose belief and encouragement propelled me forward through the most trying times. Love you, guys.

Preface

When you grow up as a hockey fan in Montreal, the Canadiens aren't just the subject of a childlike infatuation, they are the life force that dictates your emotional well-being.

It probably sounds insane, but a bad breakup can be tempered by a lengthy Montreal win streak. Conversely, a productive week at work or school can be undone entirely by a bad loss to the Bruins. This isn't normal. But it's part of the tacit agreement countless people make when they make the Canadiens their favorite team.

So, as a young boy growing up mere minutes from the historic Montreal Forum, you can be sure I vividly remember the first time I saw a Canadiens player in the flesh.

I was about 12 years old, it was Christmastime, and the shopping mall located across the street from the Forum was absolutely bustling. I don't remember who I was with or what I was shopping for or even what I was doing. But I remember seeing Petr Svoboda there. Not on the ice, but in a normal, real-world setting, doing everyday things that everyday people do. I was in awe, frozen in place, incapable of approaching him for an autograph.

Considering he was already one of my favorite Montreal players, crossing paths with Svoboda was a huge thrill. And as I began to share the experience with more and more people, I learned about the unique circumstances that had brought the fleet-footed Czech defenseman to Montreal. How he had escaped from Czechoslovakia before the Canadiens clandestinely brought him to Montreal and hid him in a downtown hotel for a few days before selecting him in the draft. For a kid whose political consciousness was shaped mostly by the Rocky Balboa-Ivan Drago fight in *Rocky IV*, it was something of an awakening.

Learning about how Petr Svoboda had come to Canada so surreptitiously really was the first time I developed any sort of political consciousness at all. By the time I learned about the Stastny brothers, who through my childhood had tortured the Canadiens as members of their provincial rival, the Quebec Nordiques, my first curiosities had developed regarding the convergence of sports and global politics.

After moving to New York following university to work as a journalist, I heard a variety of these stories, each one more compelling than the next. As I learned more about the subject, I was shocked to find that no one had attempted to compile these incredible hockey tales into a single narrative.

Equipped with a mental list of people to approach for interviews, I finally decided it was time to pursue this idea for my first book. I knew I had something after spending an hour on the phone with Petr Klima. He was incredibly candid and gracious when it came to discussing his particularly fascinating story.

That same week, I was able to get a corroborating perspective courtesy of Jim Lites, who demonstrated a palpable excitability and charisma in telling a story he admittedly hadn't shared in many years. Every indication was that I had a book.

Over the next two years, I tracked down roughly 50 other players, coaches, scouts, and assorted individuals in my research. Nearly everyone I spoke with quickly adopted an energetic tone when I asked them to share their own unique perspectives on these fascinating stories. When I was fortunate enough to speak separately with Peter and Marian Stastny, however, I noticed something more in how they described their experiences to me. A visceral, stirring passion that was undeniably powerful, even 30 years after the events in question took place.

I'd like to say I was surprised by the candor that all these fascinating people demonstrated, but the truth is I had no idea what to expect. I had little experience asking people to share the darkest details of the most trying periods of their lives. I'd never asked anyone to describe their thought process in making a decision that would alter their lives forever, possibly at the expense of the well-being of their family and friends.

Having heard and researched these incredible stories first-hand, my only hope is that I've adequately and honestly translated it all onto the pages of this book. And if I've done that, then I've done some measure of justice to the countless people who made these unthinkably brave decisions during what was a truly compelling period in modern history.

1

The Prague Spring

It was much more than ice hockey, of course. It was a replay of a lost war.

It started with an uprising, but it ended with a hockey game.

Around 4:30 on the morning of August 21, 1968, a black Volga limousine, its bulbous, large headlights leading the way, sped from the Soviet embassy in Prague toward Czech Communist Party headquarters. Over the years, the black Volga limousine had become mythologized throughout Eastern Europe as the vehicle commonly involved in the abduction of citizens. In the early morning, this particular Volga was trailed by a convoy of Soviet tanks.

When the convoy arrived at Communist Party headquarters, operations forces sealed the premises and cut off all phone contact with the outside world. With that done, a group of Soviet troops armed with machine guns entered the office of Alexander Dubcek, who just six months earlier had been selected as first secretary of the Communist Party of Czechoslovakia.

Although a Soviet colonel had initially entered the office, where Dubcek was meeting with members of his cabinet, it was two plainclothes officers—one old, one young—sporting tweed jackets and open-neck shirts who initiated the dialogue as soldiers stood by the door, machine guns in tow.

"Comrade Dubcek," they respectfully addressed him. "You are to come with us straight away."

"Who are you, what do you want?" Dubcek replied.

By the time Dubcek and his colleagues were placed under arrest and escorted by KGB agents to a barracks in the Carpathian Mountains in what is now Ukraine, Operation Danube had overtaken Czechoslovakia.

Earlier that evening, two Soviet aircraft touched down at Prague's Ruzyne airport, where several armed troops proceeded to take over the main terminal. From there, about 500 tanks rolled into the country as airships dropped leaflets from the sky explaining the peaceful intentions of these forces. In total, 27 divisions, including 5,000 armored vehicles and 800 aircraft coming from the Soviet Union, East Germany, Poland, and Hungary, swept through the country in a single day. Czech military were ordered to avoid armed resistance, and all of Czechoslovakia was overtaken within 24 hours. The Prague Spring had effectively been crushed.

The winds of change had officially begun earlier that year, when Dubcek became the first Slovakian to lead the Communist Party of Czechoslovakia. A month later, in a speech marking the 20th anniversary of the Communist seizure of power in Czechoslovakia, Dubcek laid out his intentions for his country. Despite being ordered by new Soviet leader Leonid Brezhnev to make changes to his speech, Dubcek still boldly proclaimed, "Today more than ever, the important thing is not to reduce our policy to a struggle 'against' but, more importantly, to wage a struggle 'for.'"

From there, Dubcek initiated a variety of wholesale changes in Czechoslovakia, including the abolition of censorship, freedom of the press, and the rehabilitation of citizens unjustly persecuted during the 1950s.

When the "Two Thousand Words" manifesto was published in three Czechoslovakian newspapers on June 27, the Czechoslovakian people's wishes for change were made bare. The manifesto was written by author Ludvik Vaculik, but it was also signed by 70 prominent Czechoslovakian citizens, including writers, cultural figures, scientists, and, in a new approach to revolution, athletes. Among them was Olympic gymnast Vera Caslavska, whose participation in the manifesto forced her to flee to the mountain village of Sumperk.

In an effort to end these calls for revolution, the invading troops had wasted no time making their demands on the Czechoslovak people. In the western village of Trencin, Colonel Nikolai Shmatko wrote an occupational decree, which was posted conspicuously in spots around town. Locals were forbidden from leaving their homes between 8 p.m. and 5 a.m. Soviet troops were to occupy "important military offices, radio and television stations, teleprinter installations, and institutions of the press." Locals were forbidden from carrying firearms or "weapons that can be used for stabbing." They were also forbidden from leaving the town, and foreigners were banned from entering. Anyone who disobeyed these rules was "liable to sanctions under military law."

Within days, the Soviets formally established an occupational presence throughout Czechoslovakia that would remain, undisturbed for the most part, for the next 20 years. But there would be one more overwhelming display of defiance against the Soviets seven months later. The demonstrations in March 1969 remain to this day among the most revered moments in Czechoslovakian history. It was a historic moment inspired by, of all things, two hockey games.

Numerous civil liberties were quashed by the 1968 invasion. Another unfortunate by-product of the occupation was the loss of the 1969 World Ice Hockey Championship. Scheduled to be held in Czechoslovakia for the first time in a decade, the annual international tournament was forced to move to Stockholm, Sweden, in the wake of the invasion, which had killed 25 people, seriously wounded 431, and left countless buildings damaged by gunfire. Although the people of Czechoslovakia couldn't attend these games featuring the world's finest amateur hockey players, they could still rally in full force behind their national team.

"It was like a new chance for the whole republic," says David Luksu, a sports reporter on Czech television who has written multiple books about Czechoslovakian hockey. "Hockey is the Czech national sport."

In the world's foremost amateur hockey tournament, Czechoslovakia would be pitted twice against the Soviet national team. The recent political context made these two games more than just a simple on-ice rivalry. These were two games against a nation that had crossed Czechoslovakia's borders and imposed its military will. They were also two games against by far the most dominating amateur hockey team on the planet.

After Canada had dominated international hockey for three decades, the Soviet Union wrested away the championship mantle by 1969, winning the two previous Olympic gold medals, as well as four consecutive World Championships. By the time Czechoslovakia faced the mighty Soviets in Stockholm on March 21, 1969, the entire nation was riveted by a match that could hopefully salvage some sense of national pride following its squelched rebellion.

Dubcek, who still served as first secretary after his release from the Ukrainian barracks, commented on that game years later, recalling, "The whole country watched [on TV] as Czechoslovakia played the Soviets; it was much more than ice hockey, of course. It was a replay of a lost war."

Czechoslovakia sported a 3–1 record going into the first game against their hated rivals, but the Soviets had gone 4–0, dominating by a combined score of 34–6. Playing in what was inarguably the single most important sporting event in their country's history, the Czechoslovakian nationals came out flying. They carried an overwhelming physicality throughout the game, a style enabled by the recent rule change allowing full-contact body checking in all three sections of the ice. With ample opportunity to engage in rougher play, the ultramotivated Czechoslovakians were a difficult matchup for the fleet-footed Soviets.

Before the game even started, the Czechoslovakians had taken their first shot against the Soviets. Veteran national team member Jaroslav Jirik had covered the red star on his jersey with tape, expressing his opposition to the Communist Party. By the opening face-off, other players had done the same.

After a scoreless first period, defenseman Jan Suchy opened the scoring for Czechoslovakia on a power play halfway through the second, putting a rebound past Soviet goaltender Viktor Zinger, who lay prone on the ice following a flurry of action. The moment the puck hit the back of the Soviet net, star Czechoslovakian winger Vaclav Nedomansky, in an unbridled outburst against his opposition, lifted the Russian net off its moorings before dumping it on the ice. As Suchy rushed to his team's bench and was mobbed by his countrymen, Czechoslovakia's Jaroslav Holik could be seen pointing his stick at Zinger and repeatedly calling him a "bloody Communist."

If anyone had reason to show his bitterness against the Soviets, it was Holik. Among the most outspoken athletes in Czechoslovakia, he occasionally turned his stick around during games and fired it like a gun as an act of social commentary. For years he had engaged in bloody confrontations with Soviet players in international competition. And especially with Alexander Ragulin, a hulking Soviet defenseman who outweighed Holik by 40 pounds. These bloody battles against the Soviets hadn't gone unnoticed. In fact, they had angered Czechoslovakia's Communist Party so much that Holik, whose brother Jiri also played on the national team, was held off the 1968 Olympic team that won silver in Grenoble.

Almost halfway through the third period, Czechoslovakian star Jan Cerny added to his team's lead when he finished an improbable rush. Taking the puck at the blue line, Cerny turned to his backhand to blow by a Soviet defender before outwaiting the goaltender just long enough to put the puck into the net. With a two-goal lead late in the game, Czechoslovakia rode a flawless performance from goaltender Vladimir Dzurilla to top the Soviets 2–0. Finally, after months of feeling as if the Soviet republic had been stepping on their collective neck, Czechoslovakians could enjoy a remarkable, if fleeting, victory over the Soviet Union. When the siren sounded, both teams ignored the customary handshake that traditionally followed games at the World Championships. Years later, team captain Jozef Golonka was quoted as saying, "We said to ourselves, even if we have to die on the ice, we have to beat them."

When the two teams played again a week later, this time sporting matching 7–1 records, the energy in Czechoslovakia seemed uncontainable. After entering the third period tied 2–2, quick goals from Josef Horesovsky and Jaroslav Holik were enough to spearhead a 4–3 Czechoslovakia win. For a brief moment in time, Czechoslovakia had defeated its occupiers.

The awesome energy this second victory sparked in Czechoslovakia was captured days later in a *Time Magazine* article that read: "Overcome by a vicarious sense of triumph, a huge and excited crowd swarmed into Prague's Wenceslas Square. One happy hockey fan carried a poster that read BREZHNEV 3, DUBČEK 4. The crowd chanted, 'We've beaten you this time!' Someone shouted, 'The Russian coach will go to Siberia!'"

On Czechoslovakian state television, television announcer Milena Vistrakova was unable to contain her excitement over her country's victory against the Soviets. "Normally, I drink herbal tea, but today I will toast our hockey players with wine," the state TV veteran said. "Because this is not only a victory in sports, but also a moral one."

For her comments, Vistrakova was abruptly banned from television, ultimately pursuing a career in theater before returning to Czechoslovakian airwaves more than two decades later. Although her comments halted her television career, they reflected the sentiment of a proud nation whose populace was poised to flood the streets in celebration.

With 70,000 Soviet troops still occupying the country, a reported half million Czechoslovakian citizens took to the streets in a celebration that quickly morphed. Starting out as nationwide festivities, the mammoth gathering soon took a more violent turn.

Within minutes of the final horn sounding on the 4–3 win, Czechoslovakian citizens stormed the streets in droves, making sure to target any and all representations of the Soviet occupation. The same *Time* article describes a brick being smashed through the plate-glass window of the office of the Soviet airline, Aeroflot: "A small group [then] dashed through the opening and began heaving furniture and filing cabinets onto a bonfire in the street."

In Bratislava, thousands of citizens stormed the streets with signs that read "Occupiers," "Fascists," and "Brezhnev is a hooligan." In other cities, barracks housing Soviet troops were surrounded by protesters, who proceeded to smash windows and destroy vehicles. In the town of Olomouc, rows of demonstrators were headed by military personnel. In Ostrava, machine-gun fire could be heard in the streets while mobs in Pardubice surrounded a Soviet tank and painted a swastika on a Soviet flag before setting it on fire. While the Soviet airline's headquarters were attacked, someone reportedly spray painted "Long live the victory of Athens over Sparta" on a wall. For the short time that this celebration-turned-uprising took place, obscenities and Molotov cocktails hurtled through the air across the country.

Seeing the violent demonstrations as another counter-revolutionary threat, the Soviet Union looked to finally behead the reformist movement once and for all. Dubcek was forced to resign as first secretary, saying that if he didn't, "the Soviets would set up another provocation that could lead to further public turmoil and even a bloodbath."

Dubcek would eventually be dispatched to Turkey to serve as ambassador, but he was not allowed to take his children with him. And with that, the democratization movement in Czechoslovakia was done. But the power of sport and its innate ability to unite people and perhaps plant a seed for eventual political change wasn't lost. For the next 20 years, hockey players in Eastern Europe would look to this unique precedent in utilizing their on-ice talents to overcome the restrictions placed on them by the Communist state.

Perhaps drained by their two historic victories over the Soviets, the 1969 Czechoslovakian national team lost their final game 1–0 to Sweden to post a record of eight wins and two losses, which was matched by both the Soviets and the Swedes. Based on goal differentiation, Czechoslovakia would have to settle for the bronze medal. But the seismic, if momentary, shift the players caused back home had shown the kind of force their talents could inspire. And for one shining star on that bronze-medal team, it would lead to a courageous decision that inspired a generation of like-minded athletes to pursue freedom.

• • •

Not only had Czechoslovakia beaten the Soviets twice at the 1969 World Championship but they also boasted three of the six tournament All-Stars, compared with only one for the Soviets. Dzurilla and Suchy led the team through the tournament, particularly the games against the Soviets. But the tournament also saw the emergence of All-Star forward Vaclav Nedomansky, whose size and strength had made him an impossible matchup for any team.

With nine goals in eight games, the six-foot two-inch, 210-pound winger epitomized the spirit of the upstart Czechoslovakian team. Though not as individually skilled as any of the superstars on the Soviet team, the native of Hodonin was an immovable object in the offensive zone, imposing his will on even the most physical of defenses.

He had already established himself as a young star playing for HC Bratislava, but the 1969 World Championship had been something of a coming-out party for Nedomansky. His overall performance in the tournament established him as one of the top power forwards in the world, and the inability of other national teams to contain him quickly made "Big Ned" an idol in a country looking to rebuild its morale in the wake of the Prague Spring.

"I just admired him," remembers Miroslav Frycer, a young hockey star who was establishing himself in junior hockey in the early 1970s. "He was a big idol for every hockey player."

Perhaps more importantly, Nedomansky was a Czech star playing on a Slovak hockey club, making him a uniting figure in a country that could occasionally pit Czechs against Slovaks, even if they were playing on the same team. That ongoing conflict between Czech and Slovak hockey players is probably best demonstrated by a conversation American hockey coach Lou Vairo once had with Bratislavan legend and Czechoslovakian national coach Ladislav Horsky.

"You want to beat the Soviets more than any other country?" Vairo asked Horsky, whom he had befriended through years of international competition.

"No, we want to beat the Czechs more than any other country," the Slovakian Horsky replied.

In his conversations with Vairo, Horsky had even said that for Bratislava, the lone Slovak team in the Czech Elite League, winning the national title was far more important than Czechoslovakia winning a World Championship.

"Even though they were one country, it was instilled. They were different. The Czechs were more like Germans and Slavs. They were more Protestant, more industrious, highly educated, serious," Vairo says of the difference between the two peoples.

"The Slovaks, they were Catholics, farmers, more people of the earth, so to speak. More like Ukrainians or even Hungarians. They were poorer and less educated. They always felt like second-class citizens to the Czechs."

With a united Czechoslovakia hanging on every box score, Nedomansky's national team followed up their bronze medal in 1969 with another bronze in 1970. The performance hadn't inspired Czechoslovakian demonstrations, but it was another showcase of Nedomansky's tremendous skills. Big Ned finished second in tournament scoring behind Russian Alexander Maltsev at the 1970 tournament, again being named a tournament All-Star. The 1971 tournament saw the Czechoslovakians improve on the podium, winning silver as the Soviets won their ninth consecutive World Championship gold. Nedomansky posted an impressive eight goals in a prelude to a performance at the 1972 tournament that would establish him as arguably the best hockey player not playing in North America.

In 1972, with the tournament taking place in Czechoslovakia for the first time since 1959, the hope was that the hometown crowd could will their national team to a championship win at the expense of the still-hated Soviets. This wasn't a particularly realistic goal, considering how dominant the Soviets had been in the international arena, but after tying their first matchup 3–3, Czechoslovakia and the Soviet Union entered their second game on April 20, 1972, with matching 3–0–1 records. In light of their previous tie, this game could very likely decide who would win the gold medal. With the scars of the Prague Spring still relatively fresh, hope remained across Czechoslovakia that the local team could halt the Soviets' championship streak.

After causing a turnover that would lead to the Soviets' first goal, Jaroslav Holik redeemed himself when he scored later in the game to give Czechoslovakia a 3–1 lead. The goal, to this day considered among the foremost moments in the history of Czech sports, would prove the eventual winner in a 3–2 Czechoslovakia win that put the Soviets on the precipice of losing out on World Championship gold for the first time in a decade. An 8–2 Czechoslovak win over Finland coupled with the Soviets' 3–3 tie with Sweden on the last day of the tournament would give Czechoslovakia their first world title in 23 years and earn the entire country a great measure of honor and respect. As an athletic accomplishment, the win was surely of incredible importance for Czechs and Slovaks, but culturally it was a landmark.

Holik may have been the hero in the big game, but it was Big Ned who firmly established himself as one of the world's elite players with nine goals and six assists in 10 tournament games. He may have missed out on the 1972 tournament All-Star team, but Nedomansky was beginning to appear on several scouts' radars across the Iron Curtain.

"He was very good. He was an international star for sure," says Marshall Johnston, a winger for the Canadian national team who transitioned into coaching in the NHL in 1973. "A big guy, highly skilled. Didn't have a lot of speed, but [a] very good shot, very smart."

Regardless of his shortcomings, Nedomansky was an established star in a global hockey landscape that was about to change. Although European hockey players, especially Russians and Czechoslovakians, rarely left the continent to play hockey, the emergence of a new North American hockey league was arousing a race to find new international talent. When the World Hockey Association (WHA) began play in 1972 as a rival to the established National Hockey League, the untapped European talent pool became of far greater importance.

"In the seventies at the height of the Cold War, there was a second battle going on," says Gilles Leger, a former scout for the WHA's Toronto Toros. "It was a war for hockey talent between the National Hockey League and the World Hockey Association."

By 1974, one WHA team in particular, the Winnipeg Jets, was leading the charge in recruiting European talent. As Eastern European players were strictly off-limits, Winnipeg general manager Rudy Pilous courted two Swedes, Anders Hedberg and Ulf Nilsson. After arriving in Winnipeg in 1974, the two young Swedes teamed up with legendary winger Bobby Hull and produced immediate results, with Hedberg scoring 53 goals and Nilsson setting WHA rookie records with 94 assists and 120 points.

Swedish players instantly improved the Jets, but Gilles Leger, who had just been named general manager of the Toros, was paying close attention to the Czechoslovakian national team. Acquiring Soviet players seemed impossible, but Leger had noticed the rift between Czechoslovakian players and their Communist government.

"At that time, the players in Czechoslovakia were basically a propaganda tour. They were dominating the European and World Championships," says Leger. "They would get to travel and they saw what the Western players had. They were then forced to go back to their bland workday as amateur athletes in the East. The equipment was poor quality and they played in an open ice rink in the winter there."

The atmosphere seemed ripe for a Czechoslovakian star to contemplate playing in the West. And by then there was no bigger star in the East than Vaclav Nedomansky. After leading Czechoslovakia to bronze at the 1973 World Championship, Nedomansky came back in 1974 with his best tournament performance yet. The Soviets had steamrolled their way to another gold medal, outscoring the competition by an astounding 64–18 margin, but Czechoslovakia made their mark with a convincing 7–2 win over their hated Soviet rival. The 7–2 win, since referred to by hockey historians as "the Perfect Game," was the worst loss the Soviets had ever sustained in any official international competition. As he did countless other times, Vaclav Nedomansky opened the scoring that day for Czechoslovakia.

With a torrid scoring pace, Nedomansky led Czechoslovakia to a silver medal and was named the tournament's top forward with a World Championship performance so dominating that WHA teams started frothing at the mouth at the thought of adding the skilled star to their roster. For front-office figures like Leger, the prospect of bringing Nedomansky to the West was suddenly becoming something more than a pipe dream.

"They had become big assets for the Communists because when they traveled they always had the military with them, they had their phones tapped. I think this pushed the players even further, being oppressed like that. They felt like they should give it a chance to play over here. There was a tremendous strain on them," remembers Leger. "I had scouted him [Nedomansky] and I told my owner that we need this guy. We had stars, [Montreal Canadiens great] Frank Mahovlich was playing for us. I said, 'We've got the Big M, we want the Big N.' Let's go after this guy."

By the time the hulking forward had established himself as one of Europe's best players, Leger had some competition in luring Big Ned overseas. In the previous couple of years, a number of WHA clubs had attempted to make contact with Nedomansky and persuade him to sign a contract to come to North America. But they didn't have two of the major advantages that the Toros possessed. For one thing, the Toros had established contact with agents within Eastern Europe who could help them contact Nedomansky and discuss the prospects of his coming to Toronto. They also had one of the more flamboyant owners in all of hockey.

A junior tennis champion in his native Canada, Toros owner John F. Bassett was born into one of his country's most prominent families. Bassett's father, John W.H. Bassett, didn't just have wealth and influence. After fighting in World War II and running unsuccessfully for a parliamentary seat in the 1954 Canadian federal election, John Bassett Sr. had become among the most politically connected men in Canada.

"Bassett had a direct line to the government. John Bassett's father was one of the most important movers and shakers in Canadian politics: one of the stalwarts of the Conservative Party," says Morton Greenglass, a Toronto lawyer who later represented Nedomansky. "If you wanted anything done anywhere in Canada, you called John Bassett Sr. Johnny [Jr.] pulled the strings, all cloak and dagger. Next thing you know, Ned is in Canada."

John Bassett Jr. didn't just have familial political connections, either. Having cultivated an eye for flair and showmanship in the world of sports, Bassett was also owner of the Toronto Northmen—later the Memphis Southmen—of the World Football League and had offered large contracts to former NFL greats like Larry Csonka to join his team. Before attempting to bring Nedomansky to the Toros, Bassett spent more than $2 million to bring two of Canada's most iconic hockey players—Frank Mahovlich and Paul Henderson—to Toronto.

In the years leading up to his defection, the Czechoslovakian team captain had managed to meet with NHL general managers, including Punch Imlach of the Buffalo Sabres. Meetings were facilitated by George "the Baron" Gross, a longtime Toronto sports writer who had defected to the West in 1949 after the Communist takeover of Czechoslovakia. Having been previously imprisoned by the incoming Communist regime in Czechoslovakia, Gross pretended to be a kayaker in training and paddled with a friend across the Danube and into Austria before resurfacing in Toronto. A founding sports editor of the *Toronto Sun*, Gross always entertained Czechoslovakian hockey players during their trips to Toronto and had developed a pleasant relationship with Big Ned, who bided his time before coming to North America.

"I was only 27 years old then. Czechoslovakia still needed me," Nedomansky told *Sports Illustrated*'s Mark Mulvoy in 1974. "When you become 30, that's when they don't need you anymore. I had to wait."

Shortly after turning 30 in 1974, Nedomansky began planning his clandestine trip to North America. Both the Toros and the NHL's Atlanta Flames, who had obtained Nedomansky's negotiating rights from the Sabres, had attempted to negotiate Nedomansky's legal release with the Czechoslovak government. When that acquisition failed to materialize, the quest to bring Nedomansky to the West took a more secretive turn.

In July 1974, Nedomansky acquired a travel visa and packed his wife, Vera, and son, Vaclav Jr., into their Chrysler, along with three pieces of luggage. More than three bags would have aroused suspicion among government officials that the Nedomanskys might not return. They arrived in Bern, Switzerland, where Nedomansky met up with Richard Farda, a national team teammate who had also successfully requested government clearance to travel to Switzerland. It was then that Nedomansky contacted the Toros' and Flames' front offices, both of which immediately sent representatives to Bern. In the end, Ned sided with Toronto, signing a five-year, $750,000 contract. With the deal freshly signed, Toros general manager Buck Houle immediately ran to the Canadian consulate to acquire a visa for Nedomansky and his family.

After arriving in Toronto as a landed immigrant, Nedomansky instantly became Toronto's newest sports star. What's more, he had also touched off a fiery political back-and-forth between the WHA and the International Ice Hockey Federation. In bringing Nedomansky to Canada, the Toros had not compensated the federation: cash was supposed to be paid to member nations in exchange for their players' services. Excited to have his new star player in Toronto, Houle would only say that the Toros were "not compelled to pay anything to anyone."

Having arrived in Canada wearing a yellow sports shirt and a pair of faded blue jeans, Nedomansky told the Toros that he would need to buy some new suits. Fortunately, Bassett's Toros co-owner, John Craig Eaton, was the owner of one of Canada's largest department store chains.

Although technically he had come to Canada legally, Vaclav Nedomansky had escaped from behind the Iron Curtain with his wife and young son with no idea when, or even if, he would ever see his friends and family again—though Farda eventually joined him in Canada. Nedomansky was effectively erased from the local history books back home. Despite having served for more than a decade on the Czechoslovakian national team and leading Czechoslovakia to its most enduring sporting triumphs, it was almost as if Big Ned had never existed.

"He just disappeared. Everybody was afraid. If somebody defected, afterward you wouldn't even mention their name. Because you were afraid that someone was listening. Somebody was trying to catch you and give away information to the KGB or Czechoslovakian police," says Frycer, who himself defected in 1981. "You couldn't talk about people like Nedomansky.

There was rumors he betrayed his country and all these things. People were really afraid."

Once in Toronto, transitioning to Western life wasn't terribly difficult for Nedomansky. In Bratislava, he had been pursuing dual degrees in physical fitness and biology, so he had the intellectual capacity to learn a new language and adopt a new culture. But there were still anxieties born out of his experiences in Czechoslovakia.

"We trained one year in Sweden and I can remember that we had some exhibition games in Finland. He did not join us for those games in Finland because he was still worried. It was so close to Russia, they [KGB agents] might still come and get him. There was a fear factor there for sure," says Leger. "There's a lot of horror stories of people who have defected and they get them sooner or later. I remember traveling at that time and seeing many KGB agents in Zurich and those kinds of places. They had agents everywhere."

As one of the first players to arrive from behind the Iron Curtain, it was important that Nedomansky set a strong precedent for the countless countrymen secretly following his exploits back home on Radio Free Europe. Transitioning to Western life may have taken Nedomansky some time, but he was an instant hit on the ice. He scored three goals in his first five games with the Toros and in his first game at Toronto's Maple Leaf Gardens, 14,000 spectators—the largest crowd in Toros history—serenaded him with a chorus of "Big Ned, Big Ned." But adversity would soon arise in Big Ned's Canadian adventure.

In his second season with the club, despite Nedomansky's astonishing 56 goals, the Toros finished with the worst record in the WHA. With Toronto's "other hockey team" struggling to attract fans, change was in order. So, as he had with the Toronto

Northmen of the World Football League, Bassett decided to move the team southward, taking the Toros to Birmingham and renaming them the Bulls. Just two years after abandoning everything he had ever known in coming from one hockey-mad country to another, the prospect of playing ice hockey south of the Mason-Dixon Line wasn't particularly appealing to Nedomansky. "He didn't want their mint juleps and their bully beef," Greenglass says of Nedomansky's response to the move. "That didn't fly."

Nedomansky was also unsure how his landed immigrant status would transfer to the United States and unhappy with the move to Birmingham. That displeasure was evident in his play with the team formerly known as the Toros. After he scored 56 goals the previous season in Toronto, his production dipped to 36 goals in Birmingham. Halfway through the team's first season down south, *Sports Illustrated*'s Peter Gammons captured the affair succinctly, writing: "The Bulls regularly fill about half the seats in the 16,753-seat Coliseum, but so far they lead the WHA in only two departments: payroll and losses."

Noting how Birmingham consistently sold out their World Football League games, Bassett hoped he could capture the hearts and minds of Alabamans in creating a new hockey hotbed. The team even conducted a hockey seminar for students at the University of Alabama. But despite their best efforts, hockey wasn't winning over Alabamans, nor vice versa. While Nedomansky had his reservations about the move, Bulls' defensemen Jim Dorey and Barry Long refused to make the trip, and other Bulls' players publicly expressed their skepticism.

Unable to piece together wins, the 1976–77 Birmingham Bulls finished ahead of only the Phoenix Roadrunners and the Minnesota Fighting Saints, who folded barely halfway through the season. For the most part, the maiden campaign in Birmingham was a disaster. On a Thanksgiving night game against the New England Whalers, Whalers coach Harry Neale was heckled so mercilessly by Birmingham fans that he eventually grabbed a stick and went into the stands. Local police broke up the confrontation before taking Neale to the local station for questioning. At the next home game, Alabama state troopers were stationed behind the visitors' bench. "No hockey crowd in the world can drink beer with these fans," Bulls executive vice president Peter McAskile told Gammons.

For a player of Nedomansky's background, these kinds of hysterics weren't amusing. His second season with the Bulls didn't fare any better. Nedomansky started the 1977–78 campaign with a pedestrian two goals and three assists in 12 games before being traded to the Detroit Red Wings of the National Hockey League in the first-ever interleague transaction.

"I asked for a trade before we first moved to Birmingham but he [Bassett] wouldn't let me go," Nedomansky told reporters after the trade. "At the beginning, Quebec and Winnipeg were interested in me, but Bassett wouldn't trade me to another WHA team."

But Detroit wasn't exactly an ideal location either for a 33-year-old athlete who likely had only a few years left in his career. Although he was moving from a franchise in severe financial straits to an NHL team with greater security, the man who had played for a single team in Czechoslovakia for over a decade was nervous about the move. He and his family, which now included a second child, were also applying for Canadian citizenship, which compelled Nedomansky to consider commuting to Detroit from across the border in Windsor, Ontario. "We tried to explain to Vaclav that this was a good move for him to go to Detroit," says Leger, who was Birmingham's general manager when Nedomansky was traded. "He would be sure that he was getting his money. But it was really traumatic for him."

Just a few weeks after arriving in Detroit in November 1977, Nedomansky was reminded of his previous escape from his old national team. Scheduled to play against the Red Wings on January 2, HC Kladno, one of Czechoslovakia's best-known hockey clubs, was suddenly expressing deep reservations about facing off against their former comrade. The contest was part of an eight-game exhibition series between NHL and Czechoslovakian club teams. But not long after Nedomansky's arrival in Detroit, the Czechoslovakian Ice Hockey Federation told NHL president John Ziegler and the NHL Players' Association that it did not approve of Nedomansky, whom it considered suspended under International Ice Hockey Federation rules, suiting up for the Wings against his former countrymen. In response, Ziegler told the Czechoslovakian Ice Hockey Federation that it could either accept Nedomansky's participation in the series or not bother coming to North America at all.

After the Red Wings' players agreed that they wanted their new teammate to take part in the exhibition game, it became more apparent that the series was on. Considering that the Czechoslovakian Ice Hockey Federation stood to earn $200,000 from the series, everyone expected Kladno and the other Czechoslovakian club, Pardubice, to come. "We notified the Czech federation that the Detroit game is part of an eight-game series we planned," Players' Association head and Nedomansky's agent Alan Eagleson told the press. "If they intended to not go through on the game between Kladno and the Red Wings, they should forget the series entirely."

The resurfacing of tensions with his home country had been a difficult exchange for Nedomansky. But the most painful part of Vaclav Nedomansky's NHL career was still on the horizon. And his agent would be squarely involved.

• • •

"This was the biggest there was," remembers Nedomansky's lawyer, Mort Greenglass. "[Bill] Watters did a great job negotiating the deal."

After a difficult season spent transitioning to life with the Detroit Red Wings, Vaclav Nedomansky had a tremendous bounce-back campaign in the 1978–79 season. Although the team was a loser, Big Ned led the Wings in goals and points at the age of 35. Entering that off-season as a free agent, Nedomansky was due a nice raise in what would likely be his last professional contract.

And so, in the summer of 1979, Red Wings general manager Ted Lindsay and Watters, representing Nedomansky's agent, Alan Eagleson, negotiated the basic framework of a deal that would make Big Ned among the world's highest-paid hockey players. With his days in the NHL waning and still no chance of returning to his home country in the foreseeable future, the 15-year deal would offer Nedomansky the security he had hoped for since leaving his life in Czechoslovakia five years earlier.

The deal supposedly awarded the star forward a $250,000 salary in each of the first four seasons before reverting to a $60,000 salary that would increase annually by $10,000 until 1993–94. What's more, the guaranteed deal also assured Nedomansky of a front-office job with the Red Wings once he retired. With the contract just needing to be signed, Watters called Eagleson with an update. After Eagleson directed Watters to wait until the next morning to close the deal at a prescheduled press conference, the group woke up the next day only to find Wings owner James Norris Jr. refusing to sign.

"During the night, other people heard about the deal. News like that doesn't stay secret," says Greenglass. "Other owners apparently got on the phone and started to put the pressure on Norris because it would cost them gazillions. At the press conference the next morning, Norris said, 'I'm not signing.'"

After playing the following season without a contract before signing what Greenglass characterized later as a "compromise contract," Nedomansky sued his agent, Alan Eagleson, seeking in excess of $1 million in damages. The case, which came to trial in the Ontario Supreme Court in 1984, was unprecedented. For one thing, no hockey player, particularly one who had played for the authoritarian Czechoslovakian government for over a decade, had ever questioned the integrity and authority of his agent. And this wasn't just any agent; it was the most powerful man in hockey.

"He could call all the players off the ice and the owners would go bankrupt. Or at least lose a shitload," Greenglass says of Eagleson. "Keeping in mind that Ned was a unique property. He wasn't from this continent. It was a crime what happened."

Arguing in front of Judge M.A. Catzman, Greenglass charged that Eagleson's negligence had misled Nedomansky into believing that the initial 1979 contract had been signed, a message that was "allegedly confirmed" in a telex sent from Eagleson to Lindsay. Instead of this long-term contract, Nedomansky was ultimately sold what Greenglass characterizes as a bill of goods.

"It was just a fraction [of the original deal]. None of the guarantees. Which was a big thing," says Greenglass. "The guy defects from another country with his wife and kid. It's not like he can go back. He can never go back behind the Iron Curtain. So he's stuck."

The scaled-down deal also included a buyout clause that, were the Wings to exercise it, would absolve the team of any responsibilities to Nedomansky so long as it paid 60 percent of the total money owed. After signing a contract in 1980 that was to pay Nedomansky $1.4 million over four years along with an option year, Detroit exercised its buyout in 1982. For the first time in his life, Nedomansky was essentially unemployed.

As the investigation into Eagleson intensified, more allegations of misrepresentation surfaced. Shortly after arriving in the West, Nedomansky had hired Eagleson to be his manager. Two years later, Eagleson, who was authorized to manage all of Nedomansky's financial affairs, invested some of his client's money in a mortgage held partly by a company called Nanjill Investments Ltd. Nedomansky didn't learn until later that Nanjill was run partially by Eagleson and his wife and had even been named after Eagleson's wife (Nan) and daughter (Jill).

"He's coming from another country, he was raised to depend entirely on the authorities," says Greenglass. "He was quite sincere and dependent. That was one of the problems. He was dependent on Eagleson."

Nedomansky may have been the first hockey star to question the integrity of one of hockey's most powerful figures, but there was another iconic player paying very close attention to the proceedings in the Toronto courtroom. Over the course of a legendary career, former Boston Bruins defenseman Bobby Orr had granted Eagleson control over his personal business affairs for more than a decade. But in 1978, after knee injuries had forced him to retire, Orr was in dire financial straits. Despite signing a five-year, $3-million deal with the Chicago Blackhawks in 1976 that was supposed to guarantee him $1.5 million, Orr was forced to pursue legal action just so he could collect less than $1 million in salary. By 1980, after legal battles with the government over back taxes and with Eagleson over assets, Orr was broke. Once the Nedomansky-Eagleson battle began playing out, Orr was only too happy to contact Greenglass about his own experiences with Alan Eagleson.

"He was giving me so much information. I was tape recording it, he was talking so fast. About what he's doing and how he got fucked by Eagleson," says Greenglass. "I wasn't really interested in how Bobby was screwed by Eagleson, except as a background as to the way Eagleson operates."

After his deal with Detroit was terminated, Nedomansky had short stints playing with the St. Louis Blues and New York Rangers before retiring from hockey in 1983 at age 39. The claim called for damages on the basis of loss of income, collective-bargaining agreement benefits, and pension, as well as mental anguish Nedomansky had suffered both during and after the negotiating process. The first witness called to the stand was Nedomansky's wife, Vera, who testified that she and her husband had thought the original deal was done and were looking forward to enjoying financial security, the loss of which placed a great strain on her husband.

As the case proceeded, Greenglass revealed that Nedomansky had also turned down a three-year, $1-million offer from the Rangers in order to sign a long-term deal with Detroit. He also claimed that his client's lack of familiarity with the English language and North American economic system had played a part in negotiations. While being questioned by Greenglass, Watters testified that the original contract would have paid Nedomansky $19,250 annually once he turned 50 as part of a pension plan.

Instead, Nedomansky was collecting a $5,250-a-year pension at the time of the trial. "I always felt his future would be involved in hockey," Watters said of Nedomansky while on the stand. "The plan from day one was to provide Vaclav with long-term security."

When Vaclav Nedomansky took the stand, he revealed that it was not until a full year after the initial agreement had been discussed that he was told there were problems sealing the deal. By the time of the trial, he was making a living teaching at hockey schools and doing promotion for Pripps, a Swedish sports drink. He claimed that on June 29, 1979, he had been contacted by Watters, who had just finished speaking with Lindsay, and was told that "no matter what happens, you are definitely going to get this money." The trial instead revealed that final negotiations were stalled by a disagreement over the inclusion of a one-third buyout clause that would have allowed Detroit to buy out Nedomansky's contract at one-third of its amount were the player to pass through League waivers.

Donald Anderson, an actuary Greenglass called to the stand, later testified that Nedomansky lost almost $1.8 million in total earnings by agreeing to the watered-down version of the contract in 1980. In one of his final testimonies, Nedomansky would admit that he was "shocked by what happened. I couldn't really understand the situation, but I did understand it wasn't the deal I made a long time ago."

After Eagleson admitted that he did not seek arbitration in the 1979 dispute over fears that Nedomansky's victory would lead to a long court battle that would hurt his career, Judge Catzman rendered his judgment in September. Claiming Eagleson acting negligently "gives rise to no liability in law," he rejected Nedomansky's damages claim, ordering him to pay Eagleson

$71,000, along with additional undisclosed fees to cover his legal costs. Despite assurances from Greenglass that they would win an appeal, Nedomansky ended the legal battle immediately.

"He [Catzman] found against Ned, who had to pay his [Eagleson's] costs, which was disgusting. The Nedomanskys refused to appeal. I was really upset about it," says Greenglass. "Keep in mind the culture from which they came. The government says do this, you do this. Judges are part of the government and nobody in the government is wrong. They were born into that."

Whatever the reason, Nedomansky earned a reputation for being dour and standoffish as his NHL career wound down. Blues scout Bob Plager even joked to *Sports Illustrated* in 1983 about Nedomansky, who was then playing with the Rangers. "A bar in Chicago asked him to leave," Plager reportedly said. "Because they wanted to have Happy Hour."

Big Ned faded from the public eye after his lawsuit against Eagleson. He eventually resurfaced in Villingen-Schwenningen, West Germany, where he coached the local hockey team for the 1987–88 season. Not long afterward, the Cold War ended and Vaclav Nedomansky returned to Czechoslovakia for the first time in almost two decades. He had divorced Vera, which Greenglass attributes at least partly to the stress of the Eagleson trial. Upon returning to his birthplace, Nedomansky worked as a scout for both the Blues and Los Angeles Kings, all the while becoming reacquainted with the land he captained in countless international hockey tournaments before effectively being erased from the local history books.

Nedomansky eventually returned to Slovakia and has since worked with the Slovak national team. He refused countless requests to be interviewed about his career and has earned a reputation for shying away from his on-ice accomplishments.

"He doesn't want to speak about his hockey career," says Luksu, who interviewed Nedomansky for one of his books. "I don't know why, because he was one of the best forwards in the history of Czech hockey. It's a little bit strange."

Regardless of his unwillingness to discuss his contributions to Czechoslovakian history, Nedomansky, along with his national-team teammates, planted the seeds of a new kind of revolution through Eastern Europe. Even before Nedomansky left the Eastern Bloc, his place in the international game was assured. His 65 World Championship goals remain the most of any Czech or Slovak player and the fifth-most of all time, while his six goals and eight points in a game against Poland in 1972 both remain single-game records in the modern era. For succeeding generations, Nedomansky and his teammates would inspire Czechs and Slovaks long after the Warsaw Pact dissolved. That includes players like Jaromir Jagr, arguably the greatest Czech player in history, who wore the number 68 throughout his career to honor the sacrifices of the Prague Spring.

It may have been reluctantly, but in the end, Big Ned became a symbol of Czechoslovakian defiance as well as confirmation that Eastern European amateurs could come out from behind the Iron Curtain and dominate in the National Hockey League. And for one talented Bratislavan family who had witnessed firsthand Warsaw Pact tanks entering the country, the seeds of defiance would grow into a historic exodus.

2

The European Project

I heard from hockey people that there was a mother in Czechoslovakia who gave birth to three hockey stars. One played left, one played center, one played right. I said "Impossible."

While Vaclav Nedomansky was confronting new challenges in North America, his former national team was enjoying a new golden age without him. After winning silver at the World Championships in 1974 and 1975, the Czechoslovakian national team would go on an exemplary streak that its countrymen hadn't seen in a generation. It started with an incredible gold-medal game against the Soviets at the 1976 Olympics in Innsbruck, Austria.

The Czechoslovakian national team had confronted daunting obstacles throughout the tournament. Much of the team had suffered with influenza, and captain Frantisek Pospisil failed a random drug test, forcing the team to forfeit a win over Poland in the medal round. The failed test was attributed to a dosage of codeine that team trainer Dr. Otto Trefny had given Pospisil to combat the influenza outbreak that had wreaked havoc in the Czechoslovakia locker room. Despite it all, the Czechoslovakian players found themselves on February 14 playing the mighty Soviets, winners of four of the previous five Olympic tournaments, with the gold medal still a faint possibility.

After taking an early 2–0 lead over their hated rival at Olympiahalle Innsbruck, Czechoslovakia allowed the Russians to tie the game before Edouard Novak gave the team a 3–2 lead with eight minutes remaining in the game. With Czechoslovakia poised to defeat the Soviets for Olympic gold, two goals in one minute by Soviet snipers Aleksandr Yakushev and Valeri Kharlamov dealt Czechoslovakia one of their cruelest defeats since the Prague Spring. But the national team would learn from the shocking loss.

Two months later, at the 1976 World Championship, Czechoslovakia would turn in one of the greatest performances in international hockey history. In winning their first World Championship since 1972, Czechoslovakia rampaged through the tournament's opening round, winning all seven games by an astounding 54–7 margin. Most importantly, they defeated the Soviets 3–2 in their opening matchup. In the four-team medal round, the Czechoslovakians opened with a 5–1 win over the Americans, which they followed up with a 5–3 victory over the Swedes. With gold all but assured, Czechoslovakia tied the Soviets 3–3 in the tournament's final game, completing a dominating undefeated World Championship performance. But the magical 1976 international hockey season wasn't over just yet.

In September, at the first-ever Canada Cup tournament, a six-team battle staged in both the United States and Canada, the world's best amateur teams faced off against a Team Canada that was essentially a collection of NHL All-Stars. In their opening game, the world champion Czechoslovakians beat the Soviets 5–3, casting doubts on whether the Russians were really the world's best amateur team after all. Days later, thanks to a stout goaltending performance by Vladimir Dzurilla and a late goal by Milan Novy, the Czechoslovakians dealt the Canadians a shocking 1–0 loss at the Montreal Forum. For a moment, at least, the Czechoslovakians were the world's best hockey team.

While much of the world had anticipated a USSR-Canada final, Czechoslovakia had extended their dominant play from the World Championship to qualify for the best-of-three final round at Maple Leaf Gardens against the host Canadians. But it didn't take long for Team Canada to bring the defending world champions back to earth, racing out to a 4–0 first-period lead against the upstart Czechoslovakians, eventually winning game one by a 6–0 score. The second game would go to overtime, when Canadian winger and Maple Leaf legend Darryl Sittler raced down the wing and froze Dzurilla momentarily with a fake shot before putting the puck into an open net and handing the host nation a 5–4 win and the tournament title. Despite playing with only one good leg, Bobby Orr was named tournament Most Valuable Player.

At the 1977 World Championship, Czechoslovakia would return to Austria, the site of their humbling Olympic loss the previous year. In Vienna, the team rebounded from an ugly 6–1 loss to the Soviets in the opening round with a 4–3 win over their rivals in the medal round. The victory led Czechoslovakia to their second consecutive World Championship. Perhaps most importantly, they knocked the Soviets, who had won 10 of 11 World Championships between 1963 and 1975, off their perch as the world's best amateur team.

It wasn't a coincidence that this incredible stretch of stellar play coincided with the emergence of three talented brothers from Bratislava who played with a synchronicity that no Czechoslovakian team had previously seen. Before long, the Stastny brothers were known worldwide. "The three of them were different types of players. Peter was the talent and Marian was probably the toughest and Anton was the artist, who would come along and put it in the net," says Leger, who as a WHA scout and general manager spent years watching the brothers play. "They complemented one another and supported one another. Plus all three were bright guys."

Coming from a large family, Marian, Peter, and Anton Stastny grew up with two distinct memories. The first was Warsaw Pact tanks rolling into their home country and quelling political reform. The other was seeing Vaclav Nedomansky dominate the ice playing for their hometown team, HC Slovan Bratislava. By the time they were starring for the Czechoslovakian national team, the Stastny brothers were spearheading a dominant run that had been seen only once before in Czechoslovakia's history. Of course, the last time Czechoslovakia won consecutive World Championships, it ended in a tragedy that the country would not recover from for over a decade.

• • •

The first Czechoslovakian hockey dynasty didn't just symbolize a rebirth for a troubled country. It marked a sea change in international hockey. In 1947, in what would prove to be a familiar refrain 22 years later, Czechoslovakia's morale and pride were shattered by an occupying power that had pierced its borders.

It began in 1938, when Czechoslovakia's northern and western borders were annexed to Nazi Germany as part of the Munich Agreement. From there, Germany invaded the remainder of Czechoslovakia in 1939, while southern Slovakia was ceded to Hungary, and Poland invaded the Zaolzie territory, a region that Poland and Czechoslovakia had been disputing for years.

With the Nazi surrender in 1945, Czechoslovakia was whole again, but recovering from almost a decade under the Third Reich proved difficult for a nation that saw countless ultimately failed coup attempts against the Germans. As they did in the wake of the Prague Spring, the Czechoslovakian people rallied around their national hockey team in an effort to rebuild a formerly defeated nation.

After halting all operations during World War II, the International Ice Hockey Federation brought back the World Championship tournament in 1947. The event took place in Prague, making it the perfect opportunity for a recovering Czechoslovakia to demonstrate its rebirth in an event that had been previously dominated by Canada. Before the war put the World Championship on hiatus, the Canadians had won seven of eight tournaments, as well as gold in three of four Olympic Games. Their only Olympic silver came in 1936, when they lost to an upstart British team made up primarily of Canadian expats.

With Canada poised to maintain its dominance in inter-national hockey, the Czechoslovakians, unbeknownst to most of the world, had developed a considerable pool of talent heading into the 1947 tournament. After opening the World Championship with a convincing 23–1 win over Romania, the upstart national team, who just a few years earlier had been living under an oppressive Nazi regime, proceeded to dominate the tournament in a way no European team had previously done.

In rolling to a record of six wins and one loss, Czechoslovakia outscored their opposition by an astonishing 85–10 margin. Their only loss coming at the hands of the Swedes late in the tournament, Czechoslovakia posted emphatic victories over the competition, including wins of 13–5 over Austria, 12–0 over Poland, and 24–0 over Belgium. In running roughshod through the tournament, a reinvigorated Czechoslovakian team became the first European squad to win the World Championship.

The win had been facilitated by an unlikely Czechoslovakian ally. An Austrian 2–1 upset of Sweden on the tournament's final day practically handed the gold medal to Czechoslovakia, winning high marks for the country that had ruled unfavorably over Czechoslovakia for hundreds of years. The sudden Czechoslovakian adulation for all things Austrian was captured in *Time Magazine* shortly after the tournament:

> Cheering wildly, Czechs in the grandstands threw their silver cigarette lighters to the Austrians. So many gifts of butter, meat, poultry, chocolate and liquor piled in on the Axa Hotel, where the Austrians were staying, that the management turned the lobby into a temporary warehouse. Flags flew in Brno. Pilsen begged the Austrians to visit its best hotel. And in two coal mines of Ostrava, miners promised to work two extra shifts digging coal for Austria. In hockey-happy Czechoslovakia the joke of the week was a cartoon showing a man carrying a bag overflowing with rare food. "Stop him," cries a woman. "He's a black marketeer." "Oh, no," comes the answer. "Just an Austrian."

After earning silver at the 1948 Winter Olympics in St. Moritz, the Czechoslovakians came to Sweden in 1949 looking to repeat as world champions. Fielding mostly the same squad that dominated in 1947, the Czechoslovakians opened the 1949 tournament with a 4–2 loss to the host Swedes. But with an awe-inspiring 19–2 win over an overmatched Finnish squad the next day, they were able to qualify for the medal round, which they opened with an important 3–2 win over Canada before avenging their previous loss to Sweden with a 3–0 victory on the tournament's final day. And with that, the Czechoslovakian national team had won their second consecutive World Championship, establishing a new global hockey power and instilling national pride in their adoring people. But a colossal shift in global politics made the celebration short-lived.

While the Czechoslovakian national team was winning silver at the St. Moritz Olympics, a Soviet-sponsored coup back home had installed a Communist government and established Czechoslovakia as a prominent part of the Eastern Bloc. All non-Communist government ministers in Czechoslovakia were immediately dismissed from their posts, and one prominent politician, foreign minister Jan Masaryk, was found dead in his home under what many people considered suspicious circumstances.

As the new Communist government placed strict restrictions on the movement of most citizens, Czechoslovakian athletes took advantage of the travel opportunities their physical gifts afforded them. That opportunity for defection may have extended to the world champion Czechoslovakian national team. According to a *Time Magazine* article published shortly after the tournament, the morning after celebrating his team's second consecutive World Championship, Czechoslovakia coach Antonin Vodicka noticed that forward Zdenek Marek was missing. According to an article in *Time Magazine* the following month, "What made matters sticky for Vodicka was that he had unwittingly helped

Marek to desert. Usually he kept the team's passports locked up, but when Marek asked for his 'to change some foreign currency,' Vodicka handed the passport over. Moaned Vodicka: 'This will break my neck.'"

This story may be inaccurate, as the International Ice Hockey Federation record books do not have a Zdenek Marek listed on that 1949 championship team. But there had been tales of defection among the Czechoslovakian hockey team. In the previous four months, eight other Czechoslovakian hockey players had deserted their team and country. Two ran off in Switzerland; six others fled to Paris before ending up in London. At the Summer Olympics the previous year, two members of the Czechoslovakian Olympic swim team and one of their team managers hadn't returned. Understanding that a rash of desertions by some of their most beloved athletes was no way to win hearts and minds, the Czechoslovakian Communist Party took swift, deliberate action. By the time the triumphant hockey team returned home, their next game against a club in France had already been canceled. The government's reason, as outlined in *Time*: "Too many of our finest sportsmen sent out to represent the national flag remain abroad."

The team spent the rest of the year preparing to defend their world title in 1950, but the defections only further troubled the Communist government. On March 11, 1950, as the national team waited to board a flight to the World Championship in London, the entire squad was rounded up by police and imprisoned.

"They [the Czechoslovakian government] suspected they would leave the country. That was the reason. They didn't want them to leave," says Jan Filc, current head coach of the Slovakian national team and a former Czechoslovakian team member. "Some of those players probably corroborated police information, because they knew a lot about the discussions they had. It was a very difficult time for those guys. I spoke with a couple of them much later on, who had a really bad time in prison. It was the beginning of Communism."

By all appearances, at least one member of the team had worked with the Communist government. According to discussions with former Czechoslovakian national coach Dr. Ludek Bukac, every national-team player but one was arrested. The lone exception was forward Vladimir Zabrodsky, leading to speculation that the star player may have been working with the KGB. Bukac says there were also rumors that the order to indict these players had come from Moscow, in an effort to eliminate competition to the developing hockey program there.

The better part of the team remained imprisoned until October, when they were trotted into a courtroom and charged with treason, with many of the team's players accused of plotting to defect. In the end, 12 national-team players were given sentences ranging from six months to 15 years. One player who received a 10-year sentence, Vaclav Rozinak, would later describe the scene in a 1968 radio interview:

In London, we wanted to prove that the team was good, that the world title we won in 1949 had not been a coincidence. But, then some people appeared and said that we would not be going because visas for the reporters had not been obtained. Two days later, it was clear we would have to stay. Of course, we were annoyed. The whole thing peaked at a pub when undercover secret police showed up. Somehow a fight broke out and we ended up at the police station. We thought it was all a joke and thought we'd only stay there overnight. Even in court, when we were suddenly found guilty of treason and espionage, we laughed and didn't take the charade seriously. But the fun was over when we ended up in prison with our hair shaved off. We realized then they truly were not going to let us go.

It was the team's best player who received the harshest treatment. In leading the Czechoslovakian charge, Bohumil Modry had quickly established himself as the best goaltender in Europe. He was even captured in a historic portrait taken by photographer Mark Kauffman, which appeared in *Life* magazine in 1948. Perhaps looking to make an example of the star goalie, the government trial reserved the harshest judgment for Modry, handing him a 15-year sentence.

"The whole team, besides a couple of players, was sent into jail and they spent about five years in the uranium mines," says Luksu, who has interviewed some of the team's surviving members. "They were in mines in a little town. They dug materials for atomic bombs for the Soviets."

Even though many of the players given lengthier sentences were released after five years, their time away from their countrymen had not been easy. They returned to a decimated state hockey program. Modry had the greatest difficulty readapting to civilian life. Not only had Modry returned to a very different country but his health had declined steadily while working with radioactive materials. He never regained the status or adulation he enjoyed before the Communist coup and died in 1963 at the age of 46. "The relationships were broken because nobody could trust any other guy on the team," Filc says. "Because everybody was suspicious."

The systematic persecution of a World Championship team set a dangerous precedent in Communist Czechoslovakia. Any citizen, no matter how beloved, would encounter significant government attention if suspected of plotting to defect. The Prague Spring would eventually inspire some Czechoslovakian athletes to muster the courage to escape, but by the time the Stastny brothers began toying with the idea of leaving, the government response would result in a historic sports saga.

• • •

The year Bohumil Modry returned to Czechoslovakia's civilian population, the Stastny clan added a new member to their brood. A family of leaders and thinkers, the newest addition was named Peter. Like his siblings, he would pursue the highest standards in both academics and sports. By the time he and his older brother, Marian, and younger brother, Anton, were competing together on the national team, they would spearhead a Czechoslovakian international hockey power not seen since the ill-fated postwar team.

Before long, the Stastny family would swell to five boys and one girl. During the winter, the Stastny boys would spray the field outside their postwar apartment building with water, turning it into their own personal hockey rink. Maybe it was their shared DNA, perhaps it was the familiarity born out of sharing a home growing up. Whatever the reason, the Stastny brothers demonstrated a Zen-like connection on the ice. The result was an offensive barrage so potent that it captured the hearts and minds of a new generation of Czechoslovakians.

"There was a bond with them off the ice but they were completely different personalities. As brothers, they always stood up for each other, and on the ice they were unbelievable," says Miro Frycer, who played junior hockey with Anton Stastny before joining Peter and Marian on the national team. "On the top was

Peter, a natural leader off and on the ice. Marian was the oldest one, so he was supporting them and giving them advice. Anton, I think a lot of people didn't give him much credit because he was the youngest. It was three different personalities. Peter and Marian were the natural leaders and Anton was the quiet guy."

Since Anton was not old enough to play on the 1976 and 1977 World Championship teams, it was Marian and Peter who first mythologized the Stastny name across Czechoslovakia. In their first World Championship tournament together in 1976, 24-year-old Marian and 20-year-old Peter combined for an astounding 10 goals and 18 points. They matched that output a year later, when their combined 10 goals and 19 points led Czechoslovakia to its second consecutive World Championship. Almost like clockwork, Marian and Peter continued their impressive output in the 1978 tournament, although their 9 goals and 20 points were only good enough for silver.

By the 1979 World Championship, the Stastny brothers had established themselves as a formidable world-class force. They were now joined by their youngest brother, Anton, who at age 19 registered an impressive five goals in eight games playing alongside his two older brothers. That year, they also led their Slovan Bratislava club to the Czech League championship, the first time a Slovakian club had ever won the league title.

"They were just pushing each other hard on the ice. It was incredible. They were yelling and screaming at each other a lot, but they were helping each other," says Frycer, who played on a line with Peter and Anton for a short period of time when Marian got hurt. "If you were in a wheelchair, you could play with them and score a few goals."

That awesome talent would not go unnoticed by Western scouts, especially with Vaclav Nedomansky establishing himself as an offensive threat in both the WHA and NHL. By the time four WHA teams were absorbed into the National Hockey League in 1979, one front-office figure was keeping a close eye on the Bratislavan brothers.

In a few short years, Quebec City lawyer Marcel Aubut had furiously climbed the ranks with the Quebec Nordiques from team lawyer to team president. The team's merger into the National Hockey League secured the franchise's long-term viability, but the details of the merger also hurt the four merging teams (the Nordiques, Jets, Whalers, and Oilers).

"WHA teams had to make a lot of compromises as far as players we had on our team [were concerned]. Some of the NHL teams had drafted some of the WHA players, which means the four teams coming in were becoming very weak starting in the NHL," says Aubut. "What was left to me was to find a shortcut to improve my team. I heard from hockey people that there was a mother in Czechoslovakia who gave birth to three hockey stars. One played left, one played center, one played right. I said, 'Impossible.' Then I looked closer and realized it was true. From that day, I vowed to find ways to get them out."

Fortunately for Aubut, there was a new Quebec Nordiques employee who was keenly familiar with Eastern European hockey. With the Birmingham Bulls having dissolved along with the rest of the World Hockey Association, Gilles Leger was hired by Aubut to become the Nordiques' director of player development. Leger's hiring was a calculated one. During his time with the Toros and Bulls, the former WHA scout and general manager had spent countless hours watching the Stastnys. And by now, Aubut had been eyeing the Stastnys long enough that Czechoslovakian government agents recognized his face at international tournaments. "We were the most wanted guys in the whole of Czechoslovakia," says Aubut. "They knew we were after their players."

But these weren't just any players Leger and Aubut were targeting. They were national heroes, cult-like figures who had ushered in a new golden age of Czechoslovakian hockey. In an effort to keep them in Czechoslovakia, the Communist Party offered the Stastnys incentives to remain in their home country. Each brother was offered a car, albeit a cramped Fiat—a luxury that could take years for most Czechoslovakians to acquire. Apartments too, which could take 10 to 15 years for a regular citizen to get. As national team members, they earned around 1,000 korunas for a win, roughly $100, or a week and a half's wage for a typical Czechoslovakian worker. But the government concessions weren't enough to cure a toxic locker-room environment. Upset with their coach in Bratislava, Peter complained publicly that the club suffered from a lack of leadership. In retaliation, the coach threatened to keep him off the Czechoslovakian national team. When the coach, Ladislav Horsky, sold six of the team's best players to other clubs in an apparent cash grab, the Stastny brothers were ready to leave.

"I was being threatened by people from management and they guaranteed me I would never play for the national team," remembers Peter. "When you hear this, it's like threatening your life. Threatening your dreams and everything. We had problems there as a whole team. Management was rotten and corrupt."

Before long, Aubut and Leger outlined their plan to help Peter, Marian, and Anton escape from behind the Iron Curtain. They called it the European Project. The Czechoslovakian government would not be cooperating.

As the Czechoslovakian national team continued to pile up victories, Aubut continued to explore ways to bring the

Stastnys to Quebec City. After hiring Leger, Aubut started by using the 83rd overall pick in the 1979 NHL Draft to select Anton. The youngest Stastny had been taken 198th overall by the Philadelphia Flyers the previous year but failed to sign with the team, making him again eligible for the draft.

As the Nordiques' pursuits and the Stastnys' troubles converged, the scene was set for Aubut to make contact with the brothers at the 1980 Winter Olympics in Lake Placid, New York. Just 275 miles from Quebec City, the event would be the perfect opportunity for Aubut and Leger to spirit the Stastny brothers, as well as their wives and families, into Quebec. But the government attaché trailing all the Czechoslovakian athletes was ready. Known among players as the *očko*—the Czech word for eye—the government presence was watching over the Stastnys. Given the increased speculation that the brothers might defect in Lake Placid, the tension surrounding the national team was palpable.

"I was in the locker room at every practice. Because they [the Stastnys] knew that I was friends with their coach over there, they were afraid. There was a certain fear, a certain stand-offishness. The Stastnys were very uncomfortable with me because they were afraid I might say something to Horsky," says Charlie "the Czech" Pekarek, an expat who served as host for the Czechoslovakian hockey team at the 1980 Olympics. "With the national team, they came as a delegation. The people that came with them, there were at least two or three of them from the secret police, they wanted to make sure that whatever happened, whatever was communicated, had to go through them. They didn't want to have players, the best players in the country, all of a sudden starting to defect. They were worried about the political implication of the situation."

Thanks to the formidable police presence around the team, Aubut's plan to leave Lake Placid with his coveted players went nowhere. This first plan, just one of many, had been far too simplistic. Bringing Czechoslovakia's most famous family to Quebec City would be far more difficult than just grabbing them and heading for the border. "It didn't work. It was very risky," Aubut says of the plan. "That was the toughest time of the Cold War, and those players were the pride of the country. They [the Czechoslovakian government] were willing to do anything to fight people who wanted to get them defected. Losing the quality of the players plus losing the perception of the value of the Communist regime, they were losing on the politics side and sports side and that is why there were so many people [agents] to make sure it would never happen."

The tension surrounding the Stastnys' anticipated escape hurt the Czechoslovakian national team. Despite Peter being the tournament's second-leading scorer, Czechoslovakia finished a disappointing fifth at the Olympics, the lowlight being an embarrassing 7–3 loss to an upstart American team that would go on to win Olympic gold. The Games in Lake Placid were best remembered for Team USA's "Miracle on Ice," but it was also a turning point for the Stastny brothers, whose dreams of defection would intensify with every succeeding game.

• • •

In the coming months, the government watch grew increasingly suffocating for the brothers, especially Peter, who had begun secretly learning English to facilitate his escape. But on August 21, 1980, with the Czechoslovakian team in Innsbruck, Austria, the site of their silver-medal performance at the 1976 Olympics, Peter

Stastny saw an opening. After four failed attempts to defect, the Stastnys saw their best opportunity to come to Canada.

The Stastnys' club team, HC Slovan Bratislava, was in Innsbruck participating in a tournament against three other European clubs: the Soviet Union's CSKA, also known as Central Red Army; Finland's Tappara Tampere; and Sweden's MoDo Ornskoldsvik. A few days before their final game, Peter skulked away from his teammates at the Innsbruck Holiday Inn and found a nearby payphone. As Anton stood guard to make sure no one was watching, Peter Stastny dug out the phone number he had copied from an NHL *Media Guide* and placed a call to the Quebec Nordiques. "The decision was by far the toughest decision I ever had to make and it was the best decision in my life too," says Peter. "There were so many ways it could have gone wrong."

A flabbergasted Leger took Peter's call. By the next afternoon, he and Aubut were checked into Innsbruck's Europa Tyrol hotel, situated about two blocks from the Holiday Inn. After meeting with an intermediary known as Mr. Bond and making contact with the Stastnys in their hotel, Aubut and Leger arranged a series of clandestine meetings. It was here that the brothers outlined the details of their defection while also negotiating separate six-year contracts that would pay them each around $250,000 a year. But negotiating these contracts would be the easy part. This definitely wouldn't be a simple escape in the dark of night.

Not only would Anton be joining the group but the escape would also include Peter's wife, Darina, who came to meet him in Innsbruck despite being eight months pregnant with their first child. But the eldest Stastny would not be making the trip. Marian would be taking far too many risks were he to defect, given his wife and three children back in Czechoslovakia. So in one of the most heart-wrenching acts of his life, Peter decided that he, along with his wife and Anton, would leave without their older brother. The inherent dangers of including Marian and his family were just too great. With a house, a family, and a potential legal career at stake, he simply had too much to lose.

"Marian did not know. I knew with [his] wife and three children it was impossible. They [the Czechoslovakian government] would let the wife go but never the children. They kept them as insurance," says Peter. "We thought maybe bringing in a chopper to get them, but they [Czechoslovakian soldiers] shot people crossing the border. They got three weeks off from the military service when they shoot somebody. That was the rule. You had maybe one week a year if you behaved well. But if you shoot somebody, you get three weeks. It was a mean way to motivate."

Aubut and Leger pleaded with Peter and Anton to leave immediately, but the two younger brothers wouldn't have it. There was still one game left to play in the tournament, and they weren't about to miss what could be their last opportunity to play alongside their older brother. That this final match pitted Bratislava against the Soviets certainly was an added incentive to stay just one day longer.

While the Stastnys played in what would ultimately be an embarrassing, if inconsequential, 11–1 loss, Darina grabbed Peter's and Anton's bags, throwing them in the back of one of the red Mercedes-Benzes Aubut had rented, this one driven by Ludovit Katona, a Toronto-based expat who worked as a go-between with the Nordiques and the Stastnys. The team scheduled to go back home immediately after the game, Peter and Anton joined their teammates for postgame drinks and a final meal before meeting with Aubut and Leger. "After the last game of the tournament, the team was going home by bus and leaving by midnight. We just said goodbye to our teammates and it was very emotional," says Peter.

"It's very special, because when I said goodbye to my parents, they didn't know. I didn't want them to know, so when they got interrogated [by government agents] they wouldn't know [anything]."

Unsure when, or even if, they would see Marian again, Peter and Anton moved ahead with their escape plan, but it did not start off smoothly. As the Czechoslovakian team bus idled outside the hotel, Peter and Anton went separate ways through the hotel before meeting Aubut, Leger, Darina, and Katona. But something had been lost in the planning: when Peter emerged at the hotel side exit, the Mercedes was there with his wife sitting inside, but Anton was nowhere to be found. After waiting for some time with his very pregnant wife, Peter again had to decide to leave without a brother. With the team bus leaving and the window for the Stastnys' escape closing, various morbid thoughts went through Peter Stastny's head. "Something screwed up. He [Anton] wasn't there. I was nervous. Maybe he was kidnapped. by [the] secret service or forces. There was a Russian rower who defected after the Olympics in Munich and was drugged and kidnapped and woke up in the Soviet Union," says Peter. "Around 1:30 a.m., it [the waiting] felt like three years in my life, I decided to go to Vienna without my brother."

Fortunately, they weren't on the road long before a silhouette emerged in the distance. Sure enough, it was Anton, who had gone to visit Aubut and Leger's hotel, thinking that was their meeting place. By now, Marian Stastny was alone in the back of the Czechoslovakian team bus being reprimanded for his brothers' escape and coming to terms with the end of his hockey career. But back in the red Mercedes, with tragedy narrowly averted, the real adventure was only beginning.

With Leger and Aubut racing ahead in a separate Mercedes, the Stastnys and Katona sped through the Alps on their way to Vienna. For Peter, Anton, and Darina, the drive through the mountains afforded them plenty of time to contemplate several questions. Would they be followed, maybe even captured? Would they be allowed into Canada as refugees? What would become of Marian and the other family members left behind in Czechoslovakia?

This last question was of utmost importance. The Stastnys' parents would surely be targeted and Marian's hockey career could be abruptly halted as a result of his brothers' defection. There was also another older brother, Vladimir, deeply involved in Czechoslovakian hockey, and a younger sister, Eva, who was only 14 years old at the time. After six hours of asking themselves several harrowing questions that might never be answered, the Stastnys arrived at the InterContinental hotel in Vienna, where they quickly ran up to Aubut's top-floor suite and tried their hardest to catch up on some sleep. As Aubut and Leger headed to the nearby Canadian embassy to expedite visas for their band of refugees, it wasn't long before the Stastnys realized they weren't alone.

Shortly after the Stastnys arrived at their Vienna suite in the early morning hours, their hotel room phone began to ring. There was no doubting who it was. Czechoslovakian agents had tracked them down. The resulting phone conversation made it perfectly clear that, despite abandoning their national team, the Stastnys weren't free just yet. "They [agents] called the room. Threatened their parents, about how they were going to lose their job. They threatened them like you could not imagine. It shook them up," says Aubut. "They were shaking a lot, very much shaking. But we acted quickly to help them."

While the Stastnys fielded these phone calls, Aubut and Leger left the hotel for the embassy, instantly recognizing the covert agents around their hotel. After years of scouting foreign players at international tournaments, they were both familiar with the dark sunglasses, tinted car windows, and other calling cards of Communist agents. They had been identified. "It was very, very dangerous. We were followed," says Aubut. "We saw them. There were 10 of them. Right around our car at the InterContinental."

"That was quite hectic. We had to hustle and get out of there," says Leger. "We saw the cars that these people had, the black sedans that aren't built as well as ours."

Just driving through Vienna to the embassy would be no easy task. They were barely 20 minutes away from the Czechoslovakian border and the severity of the situation was dawning on Aubut and Leger. Journalist E.M. Swift described the short trip in a 1980 *Sports Illustrated* article: "Quite undone by this chance meeting [with security forces], Aubut and Léger started to drive the Mercedes at high speed to the Embassy at 10 Dr. Karl Leuvering Strasse, but Léger's hands were shaking so badly that he was unable to read the map he had carefully prepared. He hopped out of the car and flagged down a taxi, instructing Aubut to make his own way to the Embassy."

Upon arriving at the embassy, both Aubut and Leger were greeted by a woman named Schallgruber, to whom they frantically shared their terrifying tale and stressed the importance of bringing the Stastnys to Canada as soon as possible. Before long, they took a moment to peek outside and saw several Czechoslovakian agents stationed just beyond the embassy entrance. Noticing the dangerous scene beginning to materialize, Schallgruber acted swiftly.

"Do you have a gun?" she asked the men.

From there, two Viennese police officers were called in to escort Leger and Aubut back to the InterContinental while embassy officials immediately started working on visas for the Stastnys.

Long before booking their last-minute flight to Innsbruck, Aubut had retained Toronto lawyer Michael Bukovac to help with immigration. From the embassy, Aubut called Bukovac, who had aided in Vaclav Nedomansky's defection, before contacting his wife, whom he asked to track down Gilles Lamontagne, the former mayor of Quebec City who was now Canada's acting defense minister. Upon hearing from Aubut, Bukovac got on the phone with longtime friend and Member of Parliament Douglas Fisher, who relayed the Stastnys' story to Canadian Immigration Minister Lloyd Axworthy. From there, Axworthy called an emergency Sunday-night meeting at Toronto International Airport. After taking a last-minute flight from Winnipeg to Toronto, Axworthy met with Bukovac and senior immigration officials, who had been summoned collectively from their Sunday dinners, in the Air Canada first-class passenger lounge.

Even with the visas approved, getting the Stastnys to the embassy would not be easy. By the time the police escort returned Aubut and Leger to the hotel, the situation had escalated. Now aware of where the Stastnys were hiding, Czechoslovakian security forces had begun storming the hotel. In light of the sprawling government presence, two Viennese police officers wouldn't be enough to help the group get back to the embassy, which was legally considered Canadian territory.

While the Stastnys collected their things for their upcoming trip, a squad of additional policemen mobilized around the InterContinental. Once ready to return to the embassy, the group crept behind a secure wall of police, who ushered them to their car.

"We had some commandos who escorted us. They wouldn't let anybody within 50 feet of us. They were ready to shoot. Gilles and Marcel went there with a stack of 100 dollar bills, handing them to officers. They were trigger happy," remembers Peter.

"They cleaned up the lobby, they cleaned up the elevator. It was very high security."

By 10:30 a.m., the Stastnys had a multivehicle police escort leading them to the embassy. With another busy Vienna day now in full swing, the motorcade didn't bother being inconspicuous. "We were driving on the walkways. The streets aren't very wide. We had police in front of us, behind us [with] sirens," says Peter Stastny. "When they couldn't move, they went onto a one-way street in the wrong direction. Driving on the lawns, among the trees. It was an adventure. Looking back, you just kind of smile and enjoy, but it was very tense."

Visas in hand, the group then made its way to the airport, where they boarded a 747 charter plane with first-class tickets to Amsterdam. The embassy officials and police escort even boarded the plane alongside the Stastnys, staying with them until takeoff. Still coming to terms with the situation they had just evaded and with Dutch police forces escorting them around the Amsterdam airport, it was only once their connecting flight to Montreal took off that the group felt truly safe. Apparently Aubut and Leger had come prepared for such a triumphant moment. "They pulled out cigars," says Peter Stastny. "[It was the] good old days when you could smoke on the plane."

Despite much of Quebec City being thrilled by Peter and Anton Stastny's arrival, their defection prompted a backlash among some Canadians. One column published in the *Globe and Mail* immediately following the defection read: "The episode even borders on farce; now that the players have been spirited away from Czechoslovakia, the Nordiques will be paying $50,000 to that country's hockey federation, according to the NHL's guidelines. Forget the cloaks and daggers; it's business as usual."

The column proved inaccurate, but the difficulties Peter and Anton endured in adapting to their new lives would go beyond the occasional salty newspaper column. They were also expected to improve an NHL team that had cast much of its hopes on their broad shoulders. Back in Czechoslovakia, Marian Stastny's problems were just beginning.

• • •

Despite not speaking a word of French, Peter and Anton Stastny were immediate media darlings in Quebec City, an insulated French Canadian hub that neither was familiar with. The two brothers provided an injection of scoring the moment they suited up for the Nordiques, who the previous season had posted a conference-worst 44 losses and 61 points. When Peter Stastny scored in his first game at Quebec City's Colisée, the city became enraptured with les boys from Bratislava.

Either because of troubles with translation or the overwhelming arrival in Canada, the press conference had been an awkward affair for the brothers. When asked what upset him most about Czechoslovakia, Peter cited his club team's recent tendency to sell their players. When a reporter asked the Stastnys if their childhood dream had been to play in the National Hockey League, Peter answered no. But any conversation with Anton and Peter inevitably turned to the brother they left behind. The most succinct answer to the Marian question came from Aubut near the end of that first Stastny season in Quebec, after the subject was broached by a *New York Times* reporter: "Marian is only 27. He has many good years ahead of him. Is he playing hockey at all now over in Czechoslovakia? He is practicing with the junior team in Bratislava," Aubut said. "Other than that, what is Marian doing? Waiting."

After returning to Czechoslovakia, Marian Stastny was banned from both his club team and the national team, effectively making him the unemployed father of three children. While Aubut started planning Marian's own escape the moment he brought Peter and Anton to Canada, the eldest of the family's three hockey stars was living an increasingly isolated life in Czechoslovakia. As the brother of the two most high-profile defectors in the country's history, Marian carried a debilitating target on his back everywhere he went. "Marian had a really tough time. He was angry about it," says Jan Filc, who was also kicked off the national team after his older brother, a world-class figure skater, defected. "He [Marian] didn't tell me too much about it, but I had that feeling that he was preparing to join them."

Until Marian could find an opportune moment to leave Czechoslovakia, he would have to find new ways to fill his vacant days under the watchful eye of the government. Difficult as the situation was for Peter and Anton, they still had the daily distraction of playing hockey; Marian didn't.

Before Peter and Anton's escape, their parents had been waiting for years to receive a new apartment from the government—an upgrade that would allow them to enjoy their impending retirement. No sooner had their two boys left than Mr. and Mrs. Stastny learned that their request for the new apartment had been rejected by the Communist Party. As Peter and Anton learned more of Marian's difficulties, their feelings of guilt only worsened.

"Difficult is an understatement. They immediately suspended him. His hockey career was over. His life was over. He was watched 24/7. It was psychological terror. He lost every friend in that country. Somebody talks to him, they were called for interrogation. People were running away from him next time. That was the police regime. The main motivator was fear," says Peter Stastny. "I knew I had no future there. After hockey, there would be nothing for me. Either I adapt to them, which I considered impossible, or I would end up as a laborer. When somebody was threatening my hockey career, it was worse than threatening my life. They made the decision easy for me and I am eternally grateful."

Peter and Anton did their best to keep in touch with their family, calling them every Sunday. At one point, Bell Canada even called to make sure Peter's $1,300 monthly phone bills weren't the result of clerical error. The overall stress of their flight to Canada even caused Darina to go into labor early. Fortunately, her and Peter's first child, a girl they named Katarina, was born healthy in Canada. With Peter and Anton spending much of their time away from home at practice or games, Darina attempted to raise a child in a strange land with a foreign language. To their credit, her Quebecois neighbors tried their hardest to make her transition easier. Whenever she was unsure of something and Peter was away, she would visit a neighbor with a barrage of questions. "It was so emotional. My wife was already with child and she needed help but she didn't speak the language," says Peter. "They [Darina and neighbors] tried with dictionaries and both ended up crying. But it forged some very nice friendships."

The transition was made easier by the fact that their first season with the Nordiques was an unmitigated success. Early in their rookie season, the line of Peter, Anton, and Jamie Hislop scored all six of the team's goals in a home-and-home weekend series against the Colorado Rockies. They set a league record when they became the first set of brothers to each score a hat trick in consecutive games. They set another record for brothers when they combined for 16 points in a win over Washington, breaking the record of points in a game for two brothers previously held by Max and Doug Bentley.

After finishing last in their conference the previous season, the Nordiques enjoyed a remarkable 17-point improvement, making the play-offs and coming within one win of beating the Philadelphia Flyers in the second season's opening round. While Anton's 85 points were an impressive showing for a 21-year-old, Peter almost immediately gained cult-like status in la Belle Province. His 109 points ranked sixth in the entire National Hockey League, and the total remains among the highest ever for a first-year player. The performance would earn Peter the Calder Trophy as the league's top rookie and turned the Nordiques into a province-wide infatuation. Peter was also able to adopt the NHL's more physical playing style that first season. In his first game against Philadelphia, Peter was tripped roughly by the Flyers' Mel Bridgman before skating away in pain to his bench. The next time the two teams met, Bridgman tripped Peter again. But by then, Stastny had learned about his new league's rough-and-tumble play, dropping his stick and gloves and going after Bridgman.

Despite their incredible success in Quebec, any evidence of the Stastnys' existence in Czechoslovakia was wiped out by the Communist Party. As they had done with Vaclav Nedomansky after his defection, the Czechoslovakian government refused to acknowledge the Stastnys in any shape or form unless it somehow cast a negative light on the brothers. That trend continued throughout their career, especially when Peter played for Canada at the 1984 Canada Cup. Peter's games against his former home country were televised in Czechoslovakia, but the state broadcaster refused to make any mention of one of their all-time greatest players. Even when Peter Stastny scored a goal against

Czechoslovakia, the Czechoslovakian broadcaster was forbidden from uttering his name.

Although Stastny was condemned by the Czechoslovakian government, his defection had changed the way Czechoslovakia's governing sports body addressed its older players who wanted to leave. Within a year of Peter and Anton's defection, the Czechoslovakian government and the NHL came together on an agreement to make four players available to the West in a special draft. For roughly $175,000 in salary, not to mention a $50,000 transfer fee to the Czechoslovakian government, NHL players could acquire the services of Ivan Hlinka, Bohuslav Ebermann, Vladimir Martinec, or Jiri Bubla. By the time of the draft, all four players were 31 years old and on the downslide of their careers. This international agreement became irrelevant once the Vancouver Canucks ignored the draft entirely and signed Hlinka and Bubla to contracts that caused an uproar among league executives. Ebermann and Martinec never played in the NHL.

In the year after the brothers' arrival, Aubut helped bring over Anton's girlfriend, Galina, who like the rest of the Stastny clan hadn't been warned about Peter and Anton's defection. Her presence in Quebec City eased the brothers' transition, but through it all Marian's absence hung over them, making their successes difficult to enjoy. Fortunately, Marcel Aubut had never given up on the prospect of bringing Marian to Canada.

• • •

Most of the Stastny family was spared serious government harassment and persecution in the wake of the brothers' defections. But Marian's life was forever altered. He had been blindsided when his two younger brothers told him, just hours before their final game in Innsbruck, that they would be leaving.

"We need to talk," Anton told Marian as they ate lunch the day of their final game.

"Can it wait a few minutes? Maybe after lunch?" asked Marian, who at that moment had other things on his mind.

"I have to be alone with you and it is quite important," Anton replied.

"What could be more important than the match tonight?" Marian asked.

"We are leaving," Anton said.

Marian Stastny was more shocked than angry. While he had noticed Gilles Leger around the tournament, seeing Nordiques representatives like Leger or Marcel Aubut had by now become a common occurrence. It rarely meant anyone would be leaving for Canada. Just months earlier, Marian had earned his law degree and, with his two younger brothers about to defect, it likely spelled the end of both his hockey and legal careers. "I never imagined that my brothers would do something without me or I would do something without discussing with them," said Marian. "It was an immense shock to me. I didn't have time to be angry. Anger came a little bit later."

Sure enough, the day Marian Stastny returned to Bratislava, he was told by his club team that he would never be allowed to so much as lug his equipment around the team arena. His hockey career effectively over, it wasn't long before Marian Stastny realized that he was being followed 24 hours a day by government agents. The same dark sedans parked by his home every day, eventually following him any time he got in his car to drive around town. Soon, he was commanded to make twice-weekly visits to the local police station to report to the police chief.

"Marian, don't drive the car 120 km per hour in downtown," the chief once instructed Marian. "Only 60 km per hour is permitted. We lost you for about two hours."

Any long-term prospects Marian Stastny had for himself or his family were effectively crushed following the escape of his two brothers, which he had nothing to do with. He was informed that his children would never be allowed to attend university in Czechoslovakia, their best hopes for careers being as apprentices in various industrial fields. In the year following Peter and Anton's defection, Marian's only distraction was building his new Bratislava home. "The house helped me a lot. During the night, I was thinking about the situation. I was trying to pinch myself. I don't play hockey anymore? Is this reality or am I dreaming?" said Marian. "When I was trying to clean something or build something or help my workers, my thoughts were somewhere else. It helped me calm down. It was a good escape for myself."

Within a few weeks of his brothers' defection, Marian was offered something resembling a lifeline by his government. He would be able to play for his club team again and potentially renew his legal career, but there was a catch. In exchange for increased freedoms, Marian would have to publicly denounce his brothers. Despite the opportunities he was offered in exchange for this gesture, he rejected his government almost immediately. "I simply told them, 'I don't appreciate what my brothers did to me but I'm not ready to denounce them. They are and they will forever be my brothers.' I couldn't denounce them," said Marian. "After I renounced the denunciation, everything was gone. They told me I had no chance to play hockey anymore and I won't be able to travel abroad. I got mad and I decided to write a letter to the president of Czechoslovakia."

Within days of writing the Czechoslovakian president Gustav Husak, Marian reported to the local police station, where the chief read him passages from the letter, assuring Marian that the president would never receive it. "When I went home, I simply said to myself there is no other way than to escape the country to save my family and save a few of the years of my hockey career," said Marian.

"It was really a terrible time. Everybody was scared to talk to somebody like Marian," says Frycer, who was secretly planning his own defection at that time. "There were spies from KGB everywhere, watching you closely. You had to be careful who you were talking to, what you were saying to people."

In the spring of 1981, as Peter and Anton completed their first NHL season, Marian Stastny had mapped out his escape: a route through Hungary into Yugoslavia and then Austria. Still unsure exactly how closely he was being watched, Marian successfully took his wife, three children, and mother-in-law to a popular spa in Hungary. When they returned home without incident, Marian realized that following this route to freedom was a distinct possibility.

These trips to Hungary, simple sojourns between two Eastern Bloc countries, were partially inspired by a chance meeting during a soccer game with friends. One of the players, an officer at the local police station, informed Marian that he was now being monitored only part of the time rather than on the 24/7 watch he had grown accustomed to. "I had less people around my house, and when I went somewhere I didn't see the car always behind me," said Marian. "So when I went to Hungary I realized I wasn't watched."

Twice more Marian made the trip and twice more he returned without being confronted or interrogated by authorities. By the time Peter was named the NHL's best rookie, Marian had made all the arrangements to finally leave. After entering Hungary, Marian approached the Hungarian-Yugoslavian border, where he was stopped by border police. "It was just 15 minutes," Marian's wife, Eva, told the *New York Times* in 1982. "But it was a year."

After being waved into Yugoslavia, Marian and his family spent the night in Zagreb. The next morning, Marian visited the Austrian consulate, looking for a three-day transit pass into Austria, unsure if three days would be nearly enough to find a way into Canada. When his visa request was rejected, Marian and his family spent the night in Zagreb contemplating their future. The next morning, a determined Marian visited the consulate again, set on getting his family into Austria. "I verbally fought with the consulate of Austria to have the transit visa. At the beginning they didn't want to give it to me. The next day, I explained to them the situation," remembers Marian. "The lady [at the consulate] said 'I won't give it to you for three days, I will give it to you for seven days.' She was a super lady. Two days later I went to Canada with Marcel Aubut and Gilles Leger."

After receiving Marian's call from Vienna, Aubut and Leger immediately revisited their connections in the Canadian government, including Lloyd Axworthy, who was able to expedite a Canadian visa for Marian and his entire family. Within 72 hours of entering Austria, Marian, his wife, and his three children were on their way to Quebec.

"I was the happiest guy in the world when Marian showed up. It was the biggest boulder off my shoulder. What a relief," says Peter, who was attending an NHL Players' Association event in Las Vegas when he first heard about Marian's safe escape. In the 30 years since Marian's arrival in Canada, the brothers have still never discussed his defection. "He didn't tell me, I didn't ask him. I don't want to know, and he doesn't want to tell," says Peter. "My suspicion is the money helped him. I knew we moved a lot of money there for him."

The next season, with all three brothers playing on the same line in Quebec, the story of the Stastnys came full circle. The first trio of brothers to play on the same team in a generation, Peter, Marian, and Anton immediately delivered results on the ice, leading a Nordiques' offensive charge that scored an impressive 137 goals in the team's first 30 games. With the three brothers and Frycer, who defected a month after Marian, making for a prominent foreign contingent, the team put up a sign that read "locker room" in three languages: English, French, and Slovakian. Frycer was so excited when he scored his first goal in Quebec that he celebrated by kissing his stick and doing a few pirouettes at center ice. Two months into his first season in Quebec, Marian was the team's second-leading scorer. Not bad considering he hadn't played hockey in a year. He even established roots in Quebec City when he opened a restaurant in the area. All together, the three brothers combined for an astounding 300 points despite Anton missing 12 games due to injury. Leading the Nordiques with 139 points, the third-highest total in the league, Peter was now a bona fide hockey superstar.

Thanks mostly to secret rallies around the radio to listen to Radio Free Europe, tales of the Stastnys' NHL exploits began coming into Czechoslovakia. Before long, their countless accomplishments in Quebec motivated other Czechoslovakian hockey players, whose missions west rarely resulted in the same kind of success the Stastnys enjoyed. In Poprad, about 200 miles east of Bratislava, another family was struggling to attain their own dreams of freedom.

• • •

Even though Czechoslovakia's performance in Lake Placid in 1980 was mostly forgettable, Peter Ihnacak would have loved to be on that team. One of the top players in the country, Ihnacak was initially named to the Olympic team by coach Ludek Bukac but was removed shortly before the tournament began. Bukac confirmed that the move was forced by the Communist Party. Following their maternal grandfather, who had emigrated legally to New York in 1930, three of Ihnacak's nine siblings had defected to the United States between 1967 and 1969, during the time of the Prague Spring and subsequent siege of Czechoslovakia, when Peter was just a child. As a result, Ihnacak was considered a flight risk by the Czechoslovakian government for most of his life. By the time Ihnacak was a valued member of the national team, government forces began clamping down on his movements. He was allowed to participate with the team in a pre-Olympic tournament in Lake Placid, where he saw his siblings, Magdalena, John, and Maria, for the first time in over a decade. But upon returning home to Czechoslovakia after the Olympic prep, Peter Ihnacak received a phone call the night before the team was scheduled to depart for the Olympics. He would not be making it back to Lake Placid. The same thing would occur the next year when Ihnacak was without warning removed from the national team roster before the Canada Cup tournament.

From that point on, Ihnacak was free to travel with the national team east of the Berlin Wall but was strictly forbidden from any tournaments west of the Bloc. After being denied a visa for the 1981 Canada Cup and then having his passport confiscated, Ihnacak deserted the Czechoslovakian hockey program and returned home to Poprad. But it wasn't long before his parents received a letter warning them that Peter's desertion could lead to his imprisonment. By then, Peter Ihnacak was ready to leave.

Ihnacak returned to the national team and played well enough to be included on the roster for the 1982 World Championship in

Finland. After getting his passport back, Peter hid it, along with other important documents and money, in his hockey pants so as to avoid its confiscation. As the tournament approached its conclusion, Ihnacak made a collect call to his brother in New York and arranged a specific time and place to meet. They found each other by a back exit at the team hotel and boarded a boat that would take them to Sweden. On his way to Europe, John had summoned Leafs general manager Gerry McNamara and coach Mike Nykoluk, who accompanied the brothers on the long boat ride to Sweden. "All that night I didn't sleep. I just kept thinking and thinking. In that minute, when I stepped on the boat and left the harbour, I had lost everything," Ihnacak told the *National Post*'s Joe O'Connor in 2006. "I was scared for my mother and my father, because I know when my sister escaped the police came and raided our house, and asked questions."

As with the Stastnys, there was another hockey-playing Ihnacak left in Czechoslovakia whose life was about to change drastically. While Peter was being fitted for a uniform to play with the fabled Toronto Maple Leafs, his younger brother, Miroslav, was coming to terms with life as a government target. Immediately following Peter's defection, Miro Ihnacak had his passport seized and was banned from attending any hockey-related activities outside Czechoslovakia and the Soviet Union. When Peter was finally able to call home to offer something resembling a proper goodbye, Miro's plight wasn't the only unwelcome news. Their father, Stefan, was dying from a lung condition. The Stastnys' arrival in the NHL may have appeared seamless, but for Peter Ihnacak, coming to Toronto wasn't nearly as easy. His fiancée, Deborah, soon joined him in Toronto after defecting during a vacation in Italy. After they were married, they had a son who, in a tribute to their new home, they named after then Canadian prime minister Brian Mulroney. But adapting in Toronto was still a challenge. "With Peter, we tried to help him when they put him on our line [in Toronto]," says Frycer, who was traded to the Maple Leafs during his first NHL season. "But it was too much pressure on him in Toronto. Poor kid, such high expectations and the pressure bit him a little."

While with his junior national teammates in an airport waiting to board a flight to the World Junior Championships in Minnesota, Miro was approached by team officials, who coldly seized his team jacket and handed it to another player who would take Miro's place at the tournament. From that moment on, Miro was determined to join Peter in Toronto. He tried several times to approach government officials and legally pursue his mission to Canada. But each time, he was told to go home and keep quiet. Miro even went as far as to marry a Yugoslavian student and try to leave Czechoslovakia with her. But his exit visa was denied and the marriage was annulled.

Four years after the Leafs drafted both Peter and Miro in the 1982 NHL Draft, following yet another denied request to emigrate to Canada, Miro and his new fiancée, Eva, fled to Vienna from a tournament in West Germany, where they met McNamara. The timing couldn't have been better, as two weeks earlier Miro had been told that he would have to serve a two-year stint in the army, making him all but untouchable to the Maple Leafs. After a week of hiding out in Austria, Miro and Eva gained legal clearance to come to Canada. But it hadn't been easy. After unsuccessfully lobbying the embassy for a visa, the Leafs' front office pestered Ottawa for a special permit. All this with Miro and Eva hiding just 45 minutes from the Czechoslovakian border.

The finer details of Miroslav Ihnacak's defection have never been discussed publicly, but they were likely facilitated by funds, reportedly $150,000, the Leafs sent to Czechoslovakia to bribe officials. McNamara's flight was momentarily diverted while in the process of landing in Vienna due to a terrorist shooting at the airport, but there was never any connection made between that incident and Miro's defection. "Five days, and I never slept," is how Leafs owner Harold Ballard described his experience of the events to a *New York Times* reporter. "It was like one of those movies you see."

"It was very hectic," was all John Ihnacak, then 39, would tell Sherry Ross of the *Bergen Record*. "Let's just say it was a very spectacular escape."

Trying to adapt to a new life while coming to terms with his persecution in Czechoslovakia, which allegedly included a KGB kidnapping, Miro immediately encountered high expectations from the Maple Leafs faithful, who had been awaiting his arrival for years. Those expectations were elevated even further when the Leafs assigned Miro the number 27. The same number had been previously worn by Darryl Sittler, one of the most popular players in Leafs history until he was dealt to Philadelphia in 1982 after a standoff with team management.

"It was too much pressure on him [Miro Ihnacak]. He was a skilled hockey player, but in my eyes, he just couldn't handle the pressure with the Leafs," says Frycer, who occasionally played on a line with both Ihnacak brothers. "Poor kid, I think the pressure killed him. Everybody was saying, 'Well, he is the next Sittler.' Me and his brother, Peter, were trying to help him as much as possible. The poor kid, he just couldn't handle it. He was trying so hard to do his best all the time."

The Ihnacaks never enjoyed the same success the Stastnys did, but their stories created a furor among the hockey-mad Toronto media. In 1987, both brothers admitted to the *Toronto*

Star's Rick Matsumoto that they still had nightmares about being pursued by government agents. Both brothers eventually returned to Europe, where they played well into their 40s.

As for the Stastnys, in the years since their harrowing adventure, the brothers have established strong roots in the province of Quebec, where Marian still lives and operates a golf resort in St. Nicolas. Posting the second-most points of any player through the 1980s, behind only Wayne Gretzky, Peter would eventually document his story in a best-selling autobiography before becoming a leader in the European Parliament. To this day, he still credits his success to something that was a monstrous liability in Communist Czechoslovakia but became an asset in his escape to Canada.

"I feel very blessed. My religion is the only way I can find the explanation. I don't have the slightest doubt that God had something to do with it. I am a man of faith and I prayed a lot for my brothers and my family. I never asked for anything special. We were protected and I was blessed with four children. I prayed to live in freedom," says Peter, who was restricted from practicing his faith freely in Czechoslovakia. "A lot of people died, tens of thousands were sentenced to multiple years in prison for nothing, for having a different opinion than the regime had. Some families were split up. My fellow citizens and colleagues in Slovakia now enjoy the same freedom I did when I ended up in Canada."

3

The Beginning of the Czech-sodus

We started to drive on the autobahn. We weren't even sure where the heck we were going. We just wanted to get away from there.

It may have seemed sudden, but Nick Polano's short, sad tenure with the Detroit Red Wings had come down to this. After only one year behind the Wings' bench, his head coaching career practically hinged on the 1983 National Hockey League Entry Draft in Montreal.

Things had seemed so promising just a year earlier, when Detroit offered Polano his first NHL head coaching job. It had been a meteoric rise following just one year on the Buffalo Sabres coaching staff under the legendary Scotty Bowman, but there were certain red flags surrounding the Detroit job. Like how the Red Wings team Polano inherited was now known throughout the hockey world as the "Dead Wings."

After winning four Stanley Cups in the 1950s, the Detroit Red Wings made the play-offs just twice between 1967 and the day Nick Polano was hired in 1982. Considering longtime owner Bruce Norris, the son of James Norris, the man who refused to sign Vaclav Nedomansky's 15-year contract, had recently been convicted on fraud and tax-evasion charges, any change was good for the Wings. But despite renewed confidence courtesy of new owner Mike Ilitch, the losing continued under coach Polano.

"I think it was very clear from day one. Mike Ilitch wanted to win," says Jacques Demers, a Stanley Cup–winning coach who was then riding the rails with the Fredericton Express of the American Hockey League. "They were tired of losing. They had bought a franchise that was going nowhere. There was nobody in the building and they wanted to get on track."

That wouldn't happen with Polano behind the bench. In his first season as their head coach, Detroit won just 21 of 80 games and finished last in the Western Conference. Desperate to turn things around, Polano immediately went off the grid the moment his disastrous 1982–83 season ended.

Hoping to find talented players off the conventional hockey radar, the struggling coach traveled to the 1983 World Championship in West Germany. It was there that Polano looked to begin the process of saving his historic franchise, and maybe even his job.

To no one's surprise, the 1983 Worlds saw the Soviet Union convincingly win their fifth straight championship. Their only sizable competition came from another Communist hockey powerhouse, the second-place Czechs. Polano was spellbound by both teams, even if he couldn't get anywhere near them.

As was the standard for most international tournaments, Czech and Soviet agents were keeping a watchful eye. For Polano, approaching Eastern Bloc players to chat between games was out of the question. "There was always a presence," says Darren Eliot of the Communist watchdogs.

A Cornell University student who spent that summer tending goal for Canada, Eliot was shocked by the military escort at games behind the Iron Curtain. "The stadium wasn't huge, maybe 6,000 to 8,000 seats. Take one section, the closest to the locker rooms, [it was] all military people."

Although Polano couldn't engage these dominant players, he did meet a number of Soviet and Czech expats posing as agents and scouts who offered to smuggle hockey players into North America for the right price. "There were a lot of shady guys," says Polano. "They wanted money and they tried to convince me that they would do whatever we wanted."

These "shady guys" included Ludovit Katona, the Czechoslovakia-born restaurateur who had become world renowned for his role in the defection of Peter and Anton Stastny. "We didn't trust him," Polano says of Katona. "I just felt they [all] were shady because this was what they were doing for a living; busting people out of countries."

After returning to Detroit, Polano immediately notified Red Wings general manager Jim Devellano about a special player. His name was Frantisek Musil, an imposing six-foot three-inch, 200-pound slab of Czech bedrock considered one of the world's best young defensemen. Devellano had his reservations, even if bringing Czechoslovakian players to North America was becoming easier.

Following the Stastnys' 1980 defection, the NHL and the Czechoslovakian Ice Hockey Federation began negotiating the transfer of Czech players to North American teams. In 1981, the Vancouver Canucks bypassed a proposed special draft and brought over established Czech players Ivan Hlinka and Jiri Bubla. Miroslav Dvorak and Milan Novy soon followed, transferring legally to the Philadelphia Flyers and Washington Capitals respectively. But these players were well past the prime of their careers when they landed in the NHL. Younger players like the 18-year-old Musil were strictly off-limits.

Despite Ilitch and Devellano's trepidation, Polano was able to convince them that Musil was their guy. By the day of the 1983 draft, Polano's coaching future partially rested on Musil's incredibly broad shoulders. But the Red Wings weren't willing to spend too high a draft pick on a player who might never make it beyond the Iron Curtain.

Polano's former team had made that mistake two years earlier. With their first pick in 1981, the Sabres drafted Jiri Dudacek, a Czech winger whose father was a high-ranking member of the Communist Party. The prized recruit never played in the NHL. "Scotty Bowman drafted him in the first round not having a clue about his background. His dad was pretty involved in the party," says Michal Pivonka, a Czech junior star who played with Dudacek. "He was one of the kids who would never, ever leave. That was a wasted pick."

The Red Wings weren't about to make the same mistake and so decided to wait until the draft's middle rounds to select Musil. With their first pick, the Red Wings selected center Steve Yzerman, immediately identifying him as a star player they could build around. After selecting winger Lane Lambert in the second round, Polano and company prepared to pick Musil. That was until the Minnesota North Stars snatched the defenseman with the draft's 38th pick. While Minnesota general manager Lou Nanne was promising to bring Musil to North America, Nick Polano was crushed.

"We lost our guy," the generally mild-mannered Devellano said angrily. "What are we going to do now?"

Poring over his scouting notes from the World Championship, Polano suddenly remembered another young Czech with star potential. He had never seen this winger play but had heard about his fiery temperament and raw skills. Desperate to tap into the Czechoslovakian talent pool, Polano took a shot in the dark.

"Well," he told Devellano. "There's a kid."

• • •

Growing up in Chomutov, Czechoslovakia, Petr Klima was groomed for hockey stardom practically from birth. His father, Joseph, had played for the national team and his older brother, also named Joseph, was an accomplished player in his own right. With that impressive bloodline and an array of open-ice skills, it wasn't long before the young Klima was competing internationally for his country. But as he developed a freewheeling spirit on and off the ice, clashes with his government started to emerge. That could mean trouble considering how Czechoslovakia's Communist government had a history of arbitrarily arresting its citizens.

Following the Prague Spring, the 1971 national assembly elections had sparked a new wave of mass arrests in the country. In the six months after an election decried by many as rigged, Czechoslovakian police arrested more than 200 protestors, imprisoning 40 for distributing leaflets. By the time Petr Klima was a young hockey prodigy, his people understood that even the faintest protest was grounds for imprisonment.

Due to constant fears of defection, Czechoslovakian teams traveled with a perpetual presence. Players' passports were seized, and their salaries, while competitive compared with the rest of the country, were miniscule by NHL standards. "Usually there were two or three people watching the players. Who they talk to, where they go, how much money they spend," Klima remembers. "If you spent too much, they asked where you got the money. We were not allowed to take any more money [on trips] than they gave us."

Despite these rules, the industrious Klima found ways to subsidize his annual income of roughly $7,000. Mostly by smuggling valuable Czech crystal out of the country and selling it on the black market. That kind of defiance drew the attention of not only his government. There were also agents lurking in the wings. Associates of the "shady guys" Nick Polano had encountered at the World Championship. "There was a lot of agents, not real hockey agents," says Klima. "They said, 'If you sign with me I will give you a couple of thousand dollars.' Which was a lot of money back then. [They said,] 'I will talk to your team, whomever you were drafted by.'"

Klima couldn't help but consider the offers from these so-called agents. He had traveled to tournaments abroad and witnessed the open, comfortable lives of North American players. In stark contrast, government restrictions and the allure of potential NHL riches made life on the Czechoslovakian national team difficult for a young upstart like Petr Klima.

Through radio and magazine coverage banned by the Communists, Czechoslovakians followed the NHL exploits of players like the Stastny brothers, who by now had become fully embraced in Quebec. Back in Czechoslovakia, Klima found his frustrating situation magnified by the intense, if one-sided, rivalry with the Russians. After the Stastnys' defection, Czechoslovakia almost never beat the neighboring Soviets.

A merciless team, the Soviet Union won eight gold medals in 10 Winter Olympics between 1956 and 1992. The Czechoslovakian

Olympic team never finished ahead of the Soviets in that span, winning three silver and three bronze medals.

That nasty rivalry wasn't simply born out of the agony of defeat. Almost 20 years after the Prague Spring, the on-ice feud between the two countries remained one of the bloodiest in sports. In the 1970s, Vaclav Havel's dissident movement galvanized enmity toward the Soviets, turning any match against the Russians into an absolute battle. "It was hell. It was a war. It doesn't matter if you were going to lose to Poland or Germany or Hungary. Who gives a fuck?" says Miroslav Frycer. "If you're going to play against Russians, you had to give it back 110 percent. Even if you have to die out there, you wanted to beat them. You wanted to kill them on the ice, pay them back for what happened to us, the whole country, in 1968."

Frycer continues: "Usually after the game you shake hands. I know that half of us didn't shake their hands. We would just stare in their eyes. We hated them. They were good guys off the ice, but in the moment they were Russians first. We just walked past them and told them, 'This is for 1968.' It was a stupid thing, but for us it was big. They were so powerful. We were just a toy."

All these factors shaped Klima's dreams of playing in North America. By the time an unknown Czech family visited Klima's parents in the summer of 1983, he was seriously considering defection.

Petr was away that day serving in the military, but his family assumed that these strangers were sent by the Red Wings. Just days earlier, the Klimas had heard on the radio about the Wings selecting Petr in the fifth round of the recent draft. "The Red Wings sent some Czech family. They just stopped by our house and left a jacket and all the books about Detroit. Just souvenir stuff from the Red Wings," remembers Klima, who knew that the Red Wings' logo may as well have been a giant bull's eye that could hurt his career. "We couldn't wear anything. They gave me a sweater, jacket with the logo, and everything, but we kept it in the closet. If I put it on I would be done."

The family explained that the Wings would be in close contact with Petr via a series of covert European intermediaries. But they would first have to wait for him to complete his military service. Ignoring that obligation would make Klima a deserter and an enemy of the state. That label could make obtaining a visa to enter the United States even more challenging. The offense alone could land him in prison.

Klima's frustrations slowly worsened as he balanced his military service with playing hockey for both his club in Litvinov and the Czechoslovakian national team. He eventually confided in two teammates. The first was Petr Svoboda, a prized defenseman who, unbeknownst to Klima, was planning to defect from Czechoslovakia. The other was Frantisek Musil, who so greatly anticipated his own escape that he had secretly started learning English.

All three continued to represent their country while having secret conversations on the bench or in the locker room. Considering the lengths the government went to in tracking their players, authorities were bound to find out about their flirtations with defection.

"I got very upset and maybe sometimes I would make a comment in the dressing room, where players were spies," says Klima. "They were spying for the government. I made probably a few too many comments."

Czechoslovakian officials were on high alert when their emerging star traveled to North America in 1984 to compete in the Canada Cup. Knowing Klima was on his way, Nick Polano scrambled to make contact with his prized recruit. He started by finding an interpreter through a Czech cardiologist at Henry Ford Hospital in Detroit. From there, Polano eventually made contact with Klima in Vancouver and Buffalo, the sites of Czechoslovakia's games.

In momentary meetings held in hotel rooms, Petr expressed to Polano his intentions to defect, Frantisek Musil, with his improving English, serving as translator and consultant. In the end, these backdoor discussions and secretive phone conversations during the Canada Cup yielded the basic framework of a 10-year, $2.5-million contract. By September 10, 1984, Polano had Klima's contract done and Mike Ilitch's private jet at his disposal. So when the final horn sounded that evening on Czechoslovakia's 4–2 loss to Sweden, Polano hoped to have his young star in Detroit by morning. But it wasn't that simple. Only 19 years old, Klima had given no word to his family and not yet fulfilled his military obligation.

"We must be careful. I am ready to defect but I cannot until after I am released by the army," he explained through Musil. "If I leave now I will be a traitor, I could be shot."

There was also the issue of his girlfriend, Irina, who became a crucial part of the deal. Klima returned home a few steps closer to defecting, but his meetings hadn't gone unnoticed.

Whereas Musil and Svoboda handled their business with subtlety, Klima quite literally wore his intentions on his sleeve. Upon returning to Czechoslovakia, he began wearing popular Western clothing brands. He invested in a house and car to give the impression he was staying, but his Puma and Adidas track suits gave away his true intentions.

That the Czechoslovakians finished last at the Canada Cup hadn't helped. With his lackluster play showing that his focus lay elsewhere, Klima was left off the 1984 Olympic team that won silver (behind the Russians, of course). With that, Petr Klima was ready to make his escape.

In February 1984, while Klima served out his military service and struggled with Czechoslovakian authorities, his close friend, teammate, and confidant Petr Svoboda defected. A month earlier at the World Junior Championship in Stockholm, he shared with Klima and Musil a plan for all three to stay in Sweden and defect. But Musil and Klima declined the offer and the plan was ultimately abandoned. Weeks later, while his Czechoslovakian teammates celebrated a championship at a tournament in Munich, West Germany, the 18-year-old Svoboda walked out the door with nothing but the clothes on his back to meet a friend who drove him to a Munich hotel. "About three months before I defected, I spoke to a couple of [NHL] scouts," says Svoboda. "I knew there might be an opportunity for me, but there was nothing in stone. I was still very young so I was ready to do whatever it took to live on this side of the world."

Officially a refugee, Svoboda contacted two Czechoslovakian expats playing in West Germany, who in turn got Svoboda in.touch with an agent. From there, NHL general managers began flocking to Munich to woo Svoboda. "The procedure started right away. In those three months [in Munich], there was a lot of general managers flying in to have interviews with me," says Svoboda. "So I knew I was going to be drafted."

Svoboda managed to call his parents to alert them of his decision to defect. He continued to try to make contact with them, though the news back home got progressively worse. In the aftermath of his defection, his father lost his job as the general manager of a hockey team; his mother lost her work status.

His father would remain unemployed for the next 30 months. Once the government efforts to retrieve Svoboda intensified, he could no longer risk calling home. "I couldn't call. The line was tapped and they got interrogated," says Svoboda, who was well aware of the consequences of returning to Czechoslovakia. "If I had to go back, I would have been done. My career would be over for sure. I would be on trial for leaving the country, but it never came to that."

One of the most compelling pitches came from Montreal Canadiens GM Serge Savard, who dispatched a team representative to Munich to impress the young Svoboda with tales of the team's majestic history. After making arrangements with Svoboda and his agent, Savard did his best to throw his NHL contemporaries off the defector's trail. That summer, Svoboda shocked the hockey world when he unexpectedly joined Canadiens' brass onstage at the NHL Draft on June 9. "They [the Canadiens] brought me to Montreal about five days prior to the draft. Basically hid me in the Ritz-Carlton," says Svoboda. "They claimed they hadn't heard from me and then drafted me fifth overall."

While Svoboda quickly starred in the NHL with the Montreal Canadiens, Klima and Musil could only stew in anger. That rage would seep to the surface when the Russian national team came to Prague that spring for an exhibition match.

At the game, Eastern Bloc agents and military were liberally sprinkled around the arena. Players had been warned that the game was not to get out of hand, and so the competition was typically fierce yet civil. Then, suddenly, Klima and Musil lost control. In the midst of an on-ice scrum, Musil dropped his gloves and went after Russian stars Slava Fetisov and Vladimir Krutov. Almost immediately, a number of players, including Klima, jumped into the fray. The melee demonstrated the obvious. Klima and Musil had reached their breaking point.

It may not have been politically motivated, but Petr Klima's hatred for the Soviets always seethed on the ice. "They were very dirty and they still are dirty players," he says of the Russians. "It was very hard to play a clean game if the opponent is very dirty and cheap."

Czechoslovakia would finally beat the Russians to win the 1985 World Championship that summer. But by then, Klima and Musil were both close to making the fateful decision that would change their lives forever.

• • •

Despite being left off their 1984 Olympic team, Petr Klima and Frank Musil were establishing themselves as Czechoslovakia's best young players. Their developing skills gained them even more attention after Czechoslovakia won gold at the 1985 World Championship in Prague, the country's first world title in eight years.

Whereas Musil contributed two points and stout defensive play to the championship effort, Petr Klima wouldn't showcase his skills at the 1985 World Championship. This time it wasn't government interference keeping him on the bench but a wrist injury sustained just days before the tournament during an exhibition game against Sweden.

Relegated to spectator status, Klima entered the locker room during a team practice to find Czechoslovakian agents combing through his locker. Throwing around his brand-name clothes, they joked about how comfortably these valued Western labels fit before carrying them past Klima and out of the locker room.

"Communists don't have to explain anything," Klima says of the incident. "They didn't have to have a reason."

In the meantime, Nick Polano's office with the Red Wings was becoming an increasingly hostile place. Still a perennial NHL doormat, the Red Wings had only a lone sign of hope: the play of Steve Yzerman. An All-Star in his first full NHL season, the explosive young center was drawing fans back to the arena, but it wasn't enough to save Polano, who was fired after three mediocre seasons as the Wings' coach.

Instead of exiling Polano entirely, the team decided to retain his eye for talent and named him assistant general manager. In doing so, they clearly outlined his top priority in the new job: getting Petr Klima out of Czechoslovakia. "You wanted this guy," Devellano reminded Polano. "Now you better get him."

By now, other teams were noticing Klima's play. The Calgary Flames even approached Devellano about a possible trade. But the trade talks ended the moment Nick Polano received a phone call from a Czech contact on August 15, 1985. "He's in Rosenheim with the Czech team," the voice said. "Come now."

Czechoslovakia's national team would be competing in a tournament in Rosenheim, West Germany. That's all Polano was told. Lacking any concrete details, Polano prepared to find Klima, grab him, and make a mad dash to the nearest embassy. It was a crude plan, but a plan nonetheless.

Suspecting he might defect, Czechoslovakian officials left Klima off their tournament roster. For Klima, the repeated benchings weren't simply a slap in the face; they were an attempt on his livelihood. The Czechoslovakian national team made only three or four trips across the Iron Curtain each year. Banning Klima from these tours could effectively end his dreams of joining the Wings. Fortunately, the national team was coached by

Frank Pospisil, a Czech hockey icon who also coached Klima's club team in Litvinov.

Wanting one of his best players on the ice, the coach pleaded with authorities to let his star join the team. After Pospisil promised there would be no defections under his eye, Petr Klima was on his way to Rosenheim. "We went out, they took your passport, your driver's license, everything. So we had no ID," Klima remembers of the trip. "Frank Pospisil did guarantee to the government that I would come back. That didn't happen."

In Detroit, Polano commandeered Ilitch's private jet while his interpreter—ironically also named Petr Svoboda—made his way to Germany. But Polano needed a partner within the organization to help break Petr Klima out of the Eastern Bloc.

• • •

Detroit lawyer Jim Lites was 30 years old when he helped his father-in-law, Mike Ilitch, negotiate the purchase of the Red Wings' home, Joe Louis Arena. Now the team's executive vice president, Lites jumped at the opportunity to help Polano in Rosenheim.

The two had originally gone on a mission to Prague in 1984 with the intent of finding Klima and bringing him to Detroit. That plan crumbled the moment they witnessed the national team's formidable government entourage.

That initial trip to Prague had really been a dry run to see what Lites and Polano could get away with behind the Iron Curtain. When it was over, Lites understood that the Czechoslovakian government would never negotiate Klima's release.

To curry some favor behind the Iron Curtain, Lites engaged the Czechoslovakian Ice Hockey Federation and purchased the contracts of two older players. The hope was that the transfer fee for these players, Milan Chalupa and Frank Cernik, would help the Wings get Klima. Other than that, Lites had no real use for either player. "They [Czechoslovakian officials] would tell you they were 33 or 34 years old, but they were probably 37, 38," Lites says of the two transfers. "They couldn't play. Cernik tried, Chalupa was scared. They performed very little for us."

A year later, with Klima headed to Rosenheim, the two men saw an opportunity and took Ilitch's jet to West Germany. Simply finding Klima would prove difficult. Besides the military escort and passport confiscation, Russian and Czechoslovakian teams also lodged in secret, out-of-the-way locales. Through Polano's contacts, they tracked the Czechoslovakians to Nussdorf am Inn, a wooded village south of Rosenheim.

Once the flight from Detroit landed, Lites drove the group to Nussdorf in a rented red Mercedes SLE. It was a conspicuous vehicle for such a covert mission, but an obvious choice for the Michigan-born, car-loving Lites.

The team's lodging had been shrewdly selected. Except for a large hotel, Nussdorf was barren. A reclusive village surrounded in every direction by thick woods. For Lites, Polano, and Petr Svoboda (the interpreter, not the hockey player), finding a proper place to meet Klima wouldn't be easy. With the hotel teeming with government agents, their only option lay deep within the treacherous woods.

That night, sometime between midnight and 12:30 a.m., 20-year-old Petr Klima risked everything and tiptoed through the hotel parking lot into the forest. If a member of the government contingent found him, he could be arrested on the spot. The dark woods were scary for Klima, but the thought of abruptly ending his hockey career in prison was terrifying.

Jim Lites waited inside the rented Mercedes as Klima, Svoboda, and Polano came together in the woods, where Polano hatched a plan to get Klima to the U.S. embassy in Frankfurt. "It was very scary. They were scared too," says Klima. "When we decided to do it, there was no turning back."

But despite the preliminary jostling and secret meetings, Petr Klima still wasn't ready to leave. He was concerned for his family and wanted Polano's word that his girlfriend would meet them in Detroit. Polano blindly agreed to the demands, even if he couldn't guarantee Irina's safe (and very much illegal) passage beyond the Eastern Bloc. Still not ready to move, Klima asked to meet again in 24 hours. The next night, Klima did the exact same thing.

With a third meeting planned for the next evening, Polano was running out of time. They were mere miles from the Czechoslovakian border, and there was a long precedent of Communist agents entering neighboring countries to apprehend escapees. "He really got nervous," Polano says of Klima.

Meeting for a third time in Nussdorf wouldn't be easy. The team had a game that night and would not be returning from Rosenheim until late. What's more, Polano and Svoboda were getting tired of hiding out in the woods.

After a stirring victory that third night, the team was in high spirits and enjoyed a late meal together in the hotel. While Polano and Svoboda waited in the woods, Klima conversed nervously with his teammates. As dinner became postmeal drinks, Klima excused himself to go to the restroom, where he squeezed through a small window and ran to the forest to meet Polano—and his destiny.

"He said he was ready to go," says Polano, who was blind-sided by one final Klima request. "[But] he wanted more money on his contract."

Polano tried to explain that negotiating player contracts was not part of his job description. But Klima insisted on money for his family, who would be targeted by Czechoslovakia's government once he left. Only one person could settle these last-minute financials, and he was sitting in a red Mercedes. Feeling exposed in the open parking lot, Lites was willing to do anything to get Klima in the car. After a few minutes, he had an idea.

"I think I'd like to get him enough money to get him a new Corvette," he calmly told Polano.

For a fellow car-lover like Klima, Lites's promise settled the stalemate. Everyone moved into the Mercedes for an all-night ride to Frankfurt. Then Klima revealed one last surprise.

"I left some stuff in the hotel," he said through the interpreter Svoboda. Already in the car, Polano was shocked when Klima ran back into the lion's den, where teammates and an untold number of government agents were waiting.

"Hey," Polano blurted. "You can't go back in there. We got you out of there."

"They don't know I'm gone," said Klima. "They're all sleeping."

It felt like days to Nick Polano, but it was really only a couple of minutes before Klima reemerged with some photos and other assorted reminders of the family he was leaving behind.

He hadn't told his parents that he was defecting. There had been no goodbyes, no phone conversations, no promises to meet in the future. For all he knew, Petr Klima would never see his family again.

"He came back and just had a ripped T-shirt, some photos, and a little bag. He really had nothing," remembers Polano. "We started to drive on the autobahn. We weren't even sure where the heck we were going. We just wanted to get away from there."

With the possibility that Czechoslovakian agents were already after them, Lites barreled down the highway, while Klima and Svoboda sat tensely in the backseat. Still incredibly anxious, Polano eyed Klima and Svoboda as they talked.

"What's he saying?" Polano asked Svoboda.

"He said he can't believe how slow this car is," Svoboda responded.

"So he likes speed?" Polano asked.

"He likes speed," Svoboda confirmed while Klima smiled nervously.

"Well, I'm scared shitless," Polano said candidly as the vehicle approached 90 miles per hour. "We can't go any faster than that."

Making only occasional stops for gas, food, and bathroom breaks, the group drove all night. Eventually, Polano took a moment in Stuttgart to make a quick long-distance phone call.

It was the middle of the night in Detroit when Mike Ilitch received the call explaining that Petr Klima was on the run. Tired from driving all night, Polano and Lites also explained that they needed help expediting Petr's visa to enter the United States.

"Call me back in twelve hours," Ilitch told them. "I'll see what we can cook up."

Ilitch first contacted his good friend Max Fisher, a local millionaire, philanthropist, and political financier. Considered one of the most connected men in the country, Fisher in turn phoned the most influential person he knew: Leonard Garment. Garment was best known for acting as special counsel to Richard Nixon when he was president, but he made his mark in 1973 when he defended then vice president Spiro Agnew against tax evasion charges that ultimately led to Agnew's resignation. After hearing about Mike Ilitch's hockey-playing political refugee,

Garment called Lowell Jensen, the U.S. deputy attorney general. By then, Petr Klima was in Frankfurt, coming to terms with how drastically his life was about to change.

• • •

By his own admission, Petr Klima was happy to have escaped Czechoslovakia's Communist regime. Still, that first waking realization that he was a fugitive was among the worst moments of his life.

"The hardest was the first couple of days. The shock, literally in shock. It's almost like somebody died in your family, that first moment. You're walking around in your body like you want to not breathe," says Klima. "I woke up and I could not believe it. I couldn't get up, I couldn't walk. We went downstairs for breakfast and there was Jim and Nick eating and reading the paper and smiling and I want to kill myself."

After arriving in Frankfurt, Nick Polano and Jim Lites rushed Klima to the U.S. embassy. But without a passport or proper ID to help identify him, getting Klima's visa would be difficult. That anonymity wouldn't last long.

Word traveled fast from Nussdorf, and local newspapers featured a prominent story about the Czech hockey star's flight. The photo accompanying the articles made it easier for embassy officials to identify Klima, but despite Lowell Jensen and Leonard Garment's work in Washington, processing the visa would take time. Until it came through, Klima would be continuously shuttled from hotel to hotel under assumed names. Staying in one place only meant risking capture and imprisonment.

Like clockwork every morning, Lites and Polano visited with U.S. embassy officials. And every morning they found themselves with the rest of their day to waste. These short visits became so frequent that both men soon knew embassy officials by name.

"At nine o'clock, we'd show up at the U.S. embassy and at 9:05 they would say, 'Come back tomorrow.' We would literally have the rest of the day with nothing to do," remembers Lites. "Nick and I would go play golf. We had the whole day to kill."

If the days felt long for Polano and Lites, they seemed to never end for Klima. Trying to maintain a low profile, he mostly worked out, watched television, and engaged Svoboda in aimless conversation. Occasionally, he would escape to the local movie theater, a dark, neutral venue where he could watch Sylvester Stallone's *Rambo* and Arnold Schwarzenegger's *Commando* leave a trail of carnage. But movies were only a passing distraction, especially with no word yet about Irina.

As days turned into weeks, the strain started to show on all four men, and particularly the 20-year-old Klima, who began hearing of the propaganda spreading back home, stories about how he was a traitor who chose wealth over his country and deserted his family and team.

He couldn't call his family, who had been broadsided by news of his defection. Frank Pospisil, who had guaranteed Klima's return to Czechoslovakia, told state media how Petr was "lured by the money of the NHL" and had "betrayed the collective of his teammates."

Even the national team was affected by his escape. Days after Klima's defection, the Czechoslovakian government announced it would no longer train west of the Berlin Wall. All this turmoil was a lot for any 20-year-old to process.

"The second day we had him, he knocked down about five vodkas in a row," says Lites. "He was a kid, you know? He wanted to watch *Rambo* movies and go out and run around."

Looking for anything to help pass the time, Klima eventually persuaded Svoboda to accompany him to the annual Frankfurt Motor Show. It started as a grand experience. But Klima soon noticed a young German man staring and pointing at him. The man had clearly recognized him from stories in the newspapers. Terrified, Klima grabbed Svoboda and left.

By American Labor Day, Lites and Polano were still paying daily visits to the embassy in search of Klima's paperwork from Washington. Since the embassy was closed for the holiday weekend, both men boarded a plane for Zurich to attend an international hockey tournament. For his trouble, Klima got the car for the weekend.

Enjoying the perfect diversion from life on the lam, Polano and Lites eventually struck up a conversation between tournament games with Russian star forward Igor Larionov. Larionov was one of the world's top players, and his familiarity with English made him an attractive NHL commodity. Half in jest, Polano mentioned how good Larionov might look wearing Red Wings' colors. "He makes this 'slit their throat' sign," Lites says of Larionov. "[As if to say,] 'That's what happens if we defect.' It was almost a joke. No way, no one even bothered to draft Russian players."

Slightly unsettled by the exchange with Larionov, Polano and Lites had another surprise waiting for them upon their return to Frankfurt. Klima had been driving home with Svoboda from a nice dinner when the Mercedes caught an embankment and crashed. Both men were fine, but the car was totaled. Terrified that local officials would race to the scene, the two Petrs fled on foot from the wreckage.

When Lites returned from the tournament in Zurich, Svoboda handed him a piece of paper. "That is where you can find the car," Svoboda explained.

Maintaining his cool, Lites visited the Hertz rental office in Frankfurt and quietly handed them the paper. "[It was] a Mercedes, brand new. I remember . . . handing them the keys and saying, 'The car is here, there has been an accident,'" Lites says. "I bought the insurance. Thank God!"

Lites was able to laugh off the incident, but Klima was rattled by it. After more than two weeks on the run, he didn't appear any closer to playing in the NHL. Using broken English picked up from the action movies he'd been watching, Petr Klima pulled Polano aside.

"Are you having thoughts of going back?" Polano asked Klima as he looked out their 40th-floor hotel window.

"Going back," Klima started in his fractured but improving English, "would be like falling out that window."

Klima wasn't the only one feeling the strain. Svoboda had been employed under the expectation that he would be back with his family in Vancouver within a few days. After a few weeks on the run with Klima, he missed his wife and young children and worried that officials might come after what family he still had in Czechoslovakia.

A new interpreter was on the way when Lites decided to head back to Detroit to work on Petr's visa. Without openly admitting it, Lites was thrilled to be going home. He had left his wife, Denise, with their one-year-old child, and Polano agreed they could accomplish more by splitting up. Besides, there was only so much golf they could play. "We were bad golfers," Lites remembers.

Klima stayed and waited in West Germany.

• • •

After three weeks of moving between U.S. embassies in Frankfurt and Cologne, Jim Lites was working with Immigration in

Detroit while Nick Polano moved forward with the plan to spirit Petr Klima's girlfriend across the Iron Curtain. To do so, he went back to the sources that had helped him track down Klima.

The Red Wings had already paid these go-betweens $25,000 cash, which Lites had brought to Germany in a briefcase. Sensing he would need their help again, Polano contacted Ilitch about wiring him more money. "In those days, people would do a lot of jobs if you paid them some money," says Polano. "That's one thing we had a lot of."

One of Polano's Toronto contacts referred him to a jeweler in Vienna familiar with the Czech-Austrian border. Leaving Klima with his new interpreter, Polano traveled to Austria to meet this short, shadowy gentleman.

The terms were simple. For $25,000, the girl would be smuggled into Vienna. That was it. Nick Polano didn't ask any questions. Neither did Mike Ilitch, who wired Polano the money within a couple of days. After agreeing to the jeweler's terms, Polano was told he would find the girl on an agreed-upon date in the lobby of Vienna's Marriott hotel.

"How will I know if it's the right girl?" Polano asked Klima days before the meeting.

"There's a mole on the right side of her neck," Klima responded.

With the cash courtesy of Ilitch and a physical profile to go by, Polano returned to Vienna. Sure enough, an anonymous group approached him in the Marriott lobby with Irina. "They brought her into the lobby and I went in, got the money, gave them the money, and never saw them again," says Polano. "They were diplomats, but I didn't care who they were. I just wanted to get rid of that money and get the girl."

After Irina's escape, the government campaign against Klima intensified. Czechoslovakian agents were believed to be looking for him along the German countryside, and he was tried in absentia and sentenced to 18 months in prison. "They [the Czechoslovakian government] were saying she [Irina] was on her way to see me and she was pregnant and I killed her," says Klima. "They wanted Interpol to look for me, because *they* couldn't find me."

Irina wasn't dead or pregnant; she was stuffed in a secret compartment in the trunk of a car headed toward Vienna. Polano reunited the young couple in West Germany and didn't see them again for days. "She moved into the hotel room with him and I never saw them," says Polano. "I'd get up every morning and the 'Do Not Disturb' sign was on [their door]."

Polano didn't ask too many questions about how Irina had arrived in Austria; nobody did. Foreign diplomats had been involved, most likely bribed to bring her across the border. Lites makes reference to Portuguese diplomats, while Klima mentions Japanese. Klima also mentions Ludovit Katona as a collaborator. The same world-renowned hockey smuggler Polano had encountered at the 1983 World Championship. Retired and still living in Toronto, Katona declined to comment on his work with NHL players.

After becoming reacquainted, the couple visited the embassy to confirm that Irina was alive. As life on the lam suddenly became more bearable, they began discussing their new life together in America. He would play hockey, she would get a job and go to school. They would marry, maybe even try to bring their families to Detroit. After five days together in Frankfurt, those conversations were put on hold.

On September 20, five weeks after helping Petr Klima flee the team hotel in Nussdorf, Nick Polano found that Petr's visa had finally come through. Immigration classified him as a refugee who demonstrated "a well-founded fear of persecution." With that, Petr Klima would finally become the first Czechoslovakian hockey player to defect to the United States.

"Mike Ilitch made contacts with the Reagan administration," Jim Lites remembers. "He laughs to this day about how he still makes a $25,000 contribution to the Republican Party every year because they helped us."

But Irina's visa hadn't been granted yet, as she had just arrived in West Germany. And so once again Petr would have to leave her. "That was tough, to leave her there, because obviously I didn't see her for a long time and she was scared. That was the hardest," says Klima. "I came over here [to the United States] and I didn't speak the language and she was over there crying on the phone. She wanted to go back home because she didn't think she was going to make it."

Klima knew that Irina returning to Czechoslovakia wasn't an option. "She would have gone to jail," he says. "They had a hearing in front of a judge. She got three and a half years. Once you go back, you've got to go to jail and serve the time."

On September 21 at 5:15 p.m., Petr Klima and Nick Polano landed at Detroit Metro Airport. Hiding his longing for Irina, Klima told the press in a prepared statement that he was "very happy to be in Detroit and the United States."

With Klima officially a member of the Red Wings, Polano went home to find a number of phone messages from American Express asking about a $35,000 European spending spree. Apparently he and Klima racked up quite a bill during their month abroad. The credit card bill was impressive, but now that Klima was in Detroit, Polano's most pressing priority was the upcoming hockey season.

"Petr got here and ended up on his own, whether it was right, wrong, or indifferent," remembers Lites. "He [Klima] was pretty wild, and once I got him here he stopped being my problem. It was the hockey guys' problem in the short term."

Arriving in Detroit just in time for training camp, Klima had never felt more alone. Irina moved in with German friends of Klima's former interpreter, Petr Svoboda, while Klima was housed temporarily with a local Czech family. Lites eventually helped him buy a car.

Feeling abandoned and lonely, Klima soon learned that, because of his defection, his father had lost his job managing a local hockey team. His new government-assigned job was as a janitor sweeping floors in a nearby factory.

It all weighed heavily on Klima, who had a hard time absorbing the gritty urban landscape of 1980s Detroit. The young hockey player had grown accustomed to Europe's cosmopolitan, classical architecture. Detroit in September 1985 was, by contrast, a decaying urban network that provided the crime-riddled backdrop for popular action films like *RoboCop* and *Beverly Hills Cop*.

"I was five weeks in Germany, with all their beautiful clean cities. But from the airport in Detroit, they drove me through downtown," Klima remembers. "I said, 'Oh my God, what is this?' All the buildings were abandoned, there was nobody there but homeless [people]."

Petr Klima had evaded Czechoslovakian agents, abandoned his family and country, and even smashed up a perfectly good Mercedes. Now, with the National Hockey League season approaching, his life was about to truly change.

• • •

In the fall of 1985, nobody expected the Stanley Cup to return to Detroit for the first time in 30 years. Despite his lackluster three-year coaching tenure, Nick Polano had helped compile an exciting corps of young Red Wings. Along with Klima, they included young superstar Yzerman and fellow rookies Gerard Gallant and Adam Oates. But perhaps most visible among the group was Bob Probert, a hard-living 225-pounder selected in the 1983 draft alongside Klima.

In an effort to fine-tune these young, rowdy Wings, Jim Devellano signed veteran free agents to expensive contracts. Most notably Warren Young, a journeyman forward who parlayed one successful season with the Pittsburgh Penguins into a four-year, $1.2-million contract. Between these and Yzerman's mammoth seven-year, $3-million deal, Devellano spent over $10 million on eight players in a single summer.

Red Wings fans were right to be skeptical about these dollar figures. Especially after Detroit finalized a five-year, $1.4-million contract with college star and rookie free agent Ray Staszak, who played four games with Detroit before sustaining a career-ending shoulder injury.

One thing was for certain. Detroit's young team needed a whip-smart disciplinarian to coach this eclectic bunch into contention. The team instead settled on Harry Neale, a congenial, warm man who hadn't coached in almost five years. To no one's surprise, Detroit's 1985–86 NHL season started with a streak of prodigious losing that was unfamiliar to Petr Klima, who just months earlier had won a World Championship. Despite the team's horrible start, Petr did experience the odd flash of brilliance. In his 10th NHL game, he scored the clinching goal in a 6–3 win over Pittsburgh, one of only two victories the Wings enjoyed in their first 15 contests.

"Our start could have been worse," Devellano told the press. "But not much."

With six goals in those first 15 games, Klima performed respectably, but he had difficulty gelling with teammates. After two months in the NHL, he still couldn't speak English and was struggling to integrate into Western culture.

Difficult as the transition was, Klima appreciated his new life. He even wore the number 85 to commemorate the year he came to America. In the winter, Lites served as guarantor when Klima bought his dream house, its cavernous halls and countless rooms ultimately making him feel more alone. When he wasn't playing, practicing, or on the road, Klima sat at home watching television, hoping to pick up a few words of English. He occasionally called his family in Czechoslovakia, but their phones were tapped and they would just plead with him to come home. When his phone rang, Petr often let it ring.

Life on the road wasn't easier. "My roommate [on the road] was [veteran goalie] Greg Stefan my first couple of years. Whatever he ate, I ate. Whatever he drank, I drank," Klima remembers. "Because I couldn't talk. We went to the restaurant and he would ask, 'What do you want?' I didn't know what he was saying, so whatever he ate, he [ordered] two."

The disastrous stretch for the Red Wings wasn't confined to the ice. In the first few months of the season, Devellano had his car stolen four times, and the team experienced numerous airline engine failures while traveling to games.

Klima's difficult first NHL season became more bearable in December, when Irina finally received her visa. After clearing her immigration hearing, she arrived in Detroit in time to celebrate the Christmas holidays. She immediately enrolled in a nearby school to learn English and got a job working as a hostess at the Fox Theater, a local venue owned by the Ilitch family. But adjusting to Western life remained difficult, particularly when Petr called his family, who begged him to return to Czechoslovakia.

"I can't," he would agonizingly tell them. "I have a life here."

Still working as a factory janitor, his father was taunted by employees who intentionally dropped trash on the floor. "He had to work every day sweeping the floor in the factory," says Klima. "The good thing was I had in my contract that the Red Wings were sending them money."

Fortunately, Klima had a friend who could appreciate his situation. Petr Svoboda (the hockey player, not the interpreter) had been playing in North America for over a year and was slowly adjusting to NHL life. "He was giving me advice: 'Read the books, learn the language,'" remembers Klima.

Life gradually got easier for Petr and Irina, but the Red Wings' 1985–86 season was an unsalvageable mess. After winning just 8 of 35 games, Neale was fired. His replacement, Brad Park, had recently retired as a player and was out of his element as a coach. With Steve Yzerman battling injuries, the Red Wings finished the season with 57 losses, by far the highest total in team history.

But before the season ended, veterans Reed Larson, Ron Duguay, and Greg Smith were jettisoned out of town. Warren Young was traded back to Pittsburgh shortly thereafter. Their replacements, hard-nosed defensemen Darren Veitch and Mike O'Connell, represented a philosophical shift among the Red Wings brass.

Lacking a physical presence had left Yzerman vulnerable and unprotected. That was a problem for a team playing in the rough Norris Division, known league-wide as the "Black-and-Blue Division." Following another lost season, Devellano decided to change course and surround his young, talented core with a battalion of all-elbows thugs.

From now on, stars Yzerman and Klima would be shadowed by bodyguards Probert, Veitch, and eventual off-season additions

Lee Norwood and Tim Higgins. "They were a bunch of characters. But working hard every night," says Darren Eliot, a Red Wings goalie who was then playing for their farm team in the Adirondacks. "It was a whack-and-hack crew if there ever was one."

When Brad Park was asked to not return, Devellano made it his mission to find a tenured coach. His search ended when he heard about a contract squabble involving a Black-and-Blue Division rival.

In 1986, the functionally illiterate blue-collar hockey brat who once supported his younger siblings by driving a Coca-Cola truck finally made it. The son of a Montreal police officer, Jacques Demers had inherited a no-name St. Louis Blues team and coached it within one win of the Stanley Cup Final. After finishing second in the 1986 coach-of-the-year balloting, Demers was ready for a pay raise.

He shared that sentiment with Blues owner Harry Ornest, a hands-on overseer notorious for running the team on a shoestring budget. Formerly a coach with the Blues, Jim Devellano saw an opportunity.

"I had four kids, I was a divorced father, I wasn't making enough money," says Demers. "The Red Wings offered me an opportunity to buy a house. That wasn't offered by Mr. Ornest."

Demers jumped at Devellano's four-year, $1.1-million offer and the chance to rebuild the Red Wings. He married his second wife on August 29, 1986, and opened the Red Wings' training camp a week later. Almost immediately, he targeted Petr Klima as a linchpin to the Wings' success.

After committing to learn English during the off-season, Petr Klima felt reenergized. Although he was criticized for his sometimes selfish play, 32 goals in 74 games had made Klima's rookie season a statistical success. Detroit felt more like home, but there were still occasional overtures from his parents, who continued to plead with him to return home. Klima hadn't seen his family since fleeing Nussdorf a year earlier, though he knew his father was still working as a janitor. But a familiar face was arriving from Czechoslovakia.

• • •

On a warm night in July 1986, the phone rang at the Edmonton home of 27-year-old agent Ritch Winter. His girlfriend, Tracy, had finished work at a local nightclub and was just falling asleep. The call was unexpected, the ensuing exchange short.

"I now want defect. I must now. Understand?" It was Frank Musil. He had been sent by Miroslav Maly, a former client of Winter's. The two players met in West Germany, where Musil was training with Czechoslovakia's national team and Maly was playing professionally. When Musil shared his intentions to defect, Maly passed along Winter's information. And just like that, Ritch Winter was booking a next-day flight to Europe.

After obtaining a two-week holiday visa, Musil had spent a few days with a girlfriend in Yugoslavia. "He was on vacation with a girl. I never met her or knew her and still don't," says Winter. "He never was going to see her again at that stage."

Years earlier, Minnesota North Stars general manager Lou Nanne had tried to convince the defenseman to defect at the 1983 World Championship in Munich. But Musil was not yet ready. The closest Nanne had previously come to helping players defect was a meeting years earlier in which he hosted four Soviet players at his home. "They drank all my vodka and they didn't stay," he remembers.

Without telling his family or even the woman traveling with him, Musil phoned Winter from a Yugoslav resort. The young agent immediately called Nanne. "He said Frantisek was vacationing and that he was ready to come," remembers Nanne. "So I flew over the next day into Trieste [Italy] and I rented a car. I had told him that I would meet him in Zagreb the following day at the consulate."

Nanne had initially toyed with the idea of simply throwing Musil in the trunk of his car and running through the border. But after speaking with an agent at the local consulate, Nanne realized all he needed was a visa. For that, he put in a call to Senator David Durenberger, a Minnesota senator he had met socially.

Unbeknownst to Nanne, Musil and Winter were first stopping in Belgrade for a stirring encounter with the Office of the United Nations High Commissioner for Refugees (UNHCR). "They reminded us to keep our story very quiet because the last athlete who they had seen come through there had never been seen from or heard from again," says Winter. "Did he get caught and whisked back . . . ? They didn't know. It was at that point that I started thinking, 'What am I doing here?' And this young man looked pretty scared; I had to try to figure this out."

As if their encounter with the UNHCR wasn't jarring enough, Winter's rented Yugo broke down on the way to meet Nanne in Zagreb. After popping the hood and blindly fumbling with the engine a little, both men pushed the car about a mile and a half to a dealership and replaced it. Despite the delays, Musil and Winter managed to meet Nanne in Zagreb the next day.

All three men flew to London, where Musil was held for a few hours in an airport holding area until his visa officially cleared. Just a few years older than his newest client, Winter was shaken by the experience. "You know that once they defect they're not going back. It just seemed like such a somber experience. Goodbye. Goodbye forever," says Winter. "I would listen to him speak to his mom on the phone and realize that Frank at that moment had no guarantee that he would see his family again. That was pretty hard to imagine."

Eventually, Nanne, Winter, and Musil flew to New York on a Concorde flight out of England. The pilot even made a special announcement acknowledging Musil's saga, and bottles of champagne were popped mid-flight. It was the send-off Klima had never enjoyed on the run in West Germany.

Later that evening, after a transfer flight from New York to Minneapolis, Musil, Winter, and Nanne held a press conference. "I didn't want to lose my parents," Musil told the media. "I don't want to forget my country or my parents, but I want to play in the NHL."

• • •

Shortly after arriving in America with just two shirts, a pair of slacks, and a toothbrush, Musil visited Petr Klima in Detroit. It was at Klima's house that Musil witnessed firsthand the awesome disparity between Eastern and Western lifestyles. During his stay with Klima, he saw the swimming pool, the sports cars, the three dogs Petr and Irina had adopted. The two even took Klima's new Porsche for a joyride around a nearby racetrack.

The trip set a pleasant tone for Musil's new life in America. He quickly fell in love with American football as well as American culture, even spending one off-season working at a car dealership. Just four months after his defection, Musil's girlfriend Andrea Holikova, one of the world's top-ranked tennis players and the daughter of Czechoslovakian hockey legend Jaroslav Holik, also defected, joining Frank in Minnesota. Following her escape, Andrea's father was demoted from head coach to assistant at the Dukla Jihlava club in Czechoslovakia. But Frank and Andrea were together, and things were starting to seem more pleasant for Czechoslovakians in the NHL.

Energized by the reunion, Klima was most excited about the upcoming Red Wings season. There was a new coach, new players, and a drastically different team mentality. With an improved grasp on English, Petr had even become chummy with some of his teammates. Communicating with his new coach, on the other hand, proved difficult. Demers's communication with Klima was hampered by the bilingual coach's thick French Canadian accent.

"I couldn't understand any of it," Klima says of Demers's English.

That communication breakdown wasn't a glaring problem for Demers, who in his first act as head coach named 20-year-old Steve Yzerman the youngest captain in team history. The move inspired the young Red Wings, particularly Klima, who opened the season with 10 goals in 10 games. Fifty-five games into the 1986–87 season, the Wings were in first place for the first time in over 20 years.

In the midst of Detroit's first play-off run in decades, Klima and Demers's personal relationship saw its ups and downs. But Klima reentered Demers's good graces in an important March contest against the Boston Bruins.

Having already scored two goals in the game, Klima carried the puck alongside Yzerman on a two-on-one overtime rush. With just eight seconds left in extra time, Klima snapped an ice-level shot inside the right post past Bruins goaltender Bill Ranford. The goal iced his first NHL hat trick and a huge win for the Wings. Boston coach Terry O'Reilly later described Klima as Detroit's "ultimate sniper."

Although the Wings played near-flawless hockey on the ice, they started to demonstrate troubling behaviors off it. Along with teammates Probert and Joey Kocur, Klima was developing a reputation. Amid the Wings' revival, word spread that the antics of Klima and his two on-ice bodyguards were becoming a potential problem.

"I don't think he drank on his own. He never really reached his full potential because of his off-ice habits," Lites says of Klima. "He ran with Probert and Kocur. He was drinking, but players drinking wasn't unique to Petr. Lots of guys had those issues."

Demers wasn't quite so blasé about the postgame partying. The son of an alcoholic, Demers spotted troubling tendencies in his Czech star. "That was very difficult for me. When you start winning with a bunch of kids, you start playing father and you start playing doctor," says Demers. "They were just troubled kids. We knew we were always in a time bomb with a couple of those guys."

• • •

Finishing just one point behind the St. Louis Blues for the Norris Division crown, the Wings barely missed out on their first winning season in 14 years. More importantly, the Red Wings were in the 1987 Stanley Cup Play-offs and about to enjoy a run that would shock everyone.

After an opening-round sweep of the Chicago Blackhawks, the Wings beat the Toronto Maple Leafs 3–0 in a decisive seventh game to advance to their first conference final in a generation.

With just four more wins, Jacques Demers's troops would advance
to the Stanley Cup Final. Unfortunately, those four wins would
have to come against Wayne Gretzky and the Edmonton Oilers,
a powerhouse fueled by the world's greatest player.

The Oilers eliminated Detroit in five games before winning
their third Cup in four years, but the Wings' surprising play-off
run had been a learning experience for an up-and-coming team.
It had been a mostly forgettable experience for Petr Klima, however, who scored just one goal in 13 play-off games.

Following his unimpressive play-off showing, Klima
rebounded by scoring a career-high 37 goals the next season.
That landmark 1987–88 campaign, which saw the Wings win
their first division title in more than two decades, was a turning
point for the franchise and its Czech star.

Of course, the winning season hadn't been without its troubles. Rumblings about Klima and Probert's late-night activities
persisted. Particularly with Probert, who over the previous two
years had sought treatment for alcoholism four times. The burly
winger was even arrested in Windsor, Ontario, after crashing
his car into a utility pole while driving drunk. In the midst
of this breakout season, Probert also began taking Antabuse, a
commercial drug that treats addicts by causing a violent reaction to alcohol.

Petr Svoboda and Frank Musil were now adapting well to
Western life, but Klima was bumping heads with his coach. In
January 1988, Demers benched his star winger for a road game
in New York, citing his "selfish play." And it wasn't just Klima's
style on the ice that frustrated Demers. In the midst of a breakout season, Klima had adopted some of the showy flair that
had made him a target in Czechoslovakia. He started wearing
a diamond-studded earring and blond streaks in his long hair,

and even bought a tanning bed for his home. "I don't care what people think," Klima told a reporter. "If I like it, I do it."

Klima had reason to be confident. He was having the best season of his career and planning his wedding with Irina. He even delayed the big day to try to obtain visas for his parents, who eventually came to Detroit in 1990 after the Cold War ended. Once the play-offs started, both coach and player agreed to halt the arguments and instead focus on improving on the previous year's result.

A disappointing 6–2 game one loss in the opening round against the Leafs inspired some panic in the suddenly hockey-mad city of Detroit. But it didn't last. Playing on a line with Probert, Klima quelled any concerns with three goals in a 6–3 game two victory. It was the first Red Wings play-off hat trick in 23 years. With three goals and five assists over the next four games against Toronto, Klima posted a resounding series win and made everyone forget about his postseason stumbling from a year before.

That superstar scoring pace continued through a convincing five-game series win against St. Louis. Another Klima hat trick in game two against the Blues led the way toward an inevitable conference-final rematch against the defending champion Oilers. That fateful series would change everything.

With team captain Steve Yzerman sidelined with a season-ending knee injury, any momentum Detroit had cultivated in the first two series didn't last. While going to his backhand to take a shot in the first period of game one in Edmonton, Klima took a slash from Oilers' defenseman Charlie Huddy. The resulting broken thumb cost Detroit the game and one of their marquee players. And with that, a historic Red Wings season was suddenly on the brink.

After the Wings, now without Yzerman and Klima, lost game two, Probert's goal and assist in a 5–2 game three win renewed hope in Detroit. But Edmonton won game four in overtime, effectively taking the wind out of the Wings' play-off sails. A series-clinching 8–4 loss in Edmonton was a tough end to an impressive season, but it was players' actions before the game that would generate some of the biggest headlines.

● ● ●

The evening before game five in Edmonton, arguably the biggest Red Wings game in decades, assistant coach Colin Campbell enlisted front-office colleague Neil Smith to help him find some players who had missed their team curfew. That search eventually led them to Goose Loonies, a popular Edmonton nightspot. It was there they found a group of players partying at 2 a.m., three hours past curfew. The group allegedly included Probert and Klima.

"Colin Campbell's job was to follow them on curfew. Probert had alcohol issues and Klima had a track record of running wild. So Colin and I went out to try to find them," remembers Neil Smith. "I waited outside and Colin went in and found not only Klima and Probert, but four or five others."

"Neil Smith and Colin Campbell came in and they were looking for Probert. In a hockey town like Edmonton, the word was out that Probert was on the streets and going crazy," says Darren Eliot, the Red Wings' third goaltender who was also found at Goose Loonies that night. "I just happen to see Probert and walk over to him and say, 'You probably should get back to the hotel and get out of here.'"

After hearing about the late night, Coach Demers fumed through the next day's practice, pulling aside each of the players found after curfew. "He read us the riot act about somebody being so drunk he didn't recognize him," says Eliot.

Publicly, the team and its coaching staff tried to downplay the incident. But when Detroit sportswriter Mitch Albom got wind of the story, it quickly took on a life of its own. Enraged by the events, Demers was unable to hide his displeasure around the press.

"It took us two years to build some respect with these players and this team. I'm not about to lose it because a few idiots on this team want to push me," Demers told reporters after the game five loss. "It's absolutely inexcusable. I honestly believe we could have won that game and come back for game six in Detroit. If only it weren't for six idiots."

The "six idiots" included Joe Kocur, John Chabot, and Darren Veitch, who was the only player benched for game five. Demers was particularly disappointed in Probert, whose 21 play-off points that year set a new team record. "Bob Probert has been made a hero in Detroit. Well, when he takes the ice next time, I hope they don't give him a standing ovation because he doesn't deserve it one bit," Demers told Associated Press. "How about the others? They're all guilty. Six idiots had to ruin the season by doing something like this."

• • •

In interviews after the Goose Loonies incident, Bob Probert denied being out past curfew. Demers publicly called him a liar. More than 20 years later, Klima denies being at the bar. "I was in that big story in Edmonton and I wasn't even there," says Klima. "I was not in the bar with the players and I did not come back to the hotel that night because I was not staying in the same hotel."

Both Eliot and Smith attest to seeing Klima and Probert at Goose Loonies that night. "He wasn't the only one there. There is no doubt about that," Smith says in Klima's defense.

In the days following that night in Edmonton, Demers signed a contract extension with the team, and all players involved were fined. While Demers lauded Probert and Klima for their efforts during the season, which included an All-Star Game appearance for Probert, his fury over his two stars persisted. "I've had more problems with these two people than I've had with any others in 16 years of coaching," Demers told the press when asked about Probert and Klima. "It's simply unacceptable."

By the time training camp started in September 1988, both players were still in Demers's doghouse. They didn't help matters when Klima showed up late to a practice and Probert missed a team flight to Chicago. In response, Demers immediately announced that both players had been fined $500 and would be starting the 1988–89 season with the Wings' minor league team in the Adirondacks. That the Wings started the exhibition season with three consecutive losses didn't help.

The prickly situation with both players was quickly exacerbated. According to published reports, both players skipped practice before missing their flight to Glens Falls, New York, to report to their minor league team. Klima and Probert were immediately suspended indefinitely without pay.

Looking back on this troubled time in his career, Klima admits that the reputation he cultivated wasn't undeserved. "I did some stupid things. All my problems with the team were off-ice problems. That's part of hockey. You have players who are troublemakers," he says. "A normal player just had a bad game. If I had a bad game [people thought] it was because I was probably out last night. I couldn't defend myself."

Klima's fragile bond with fans was forever broken when, two weeks after being suspended, he was arrested at 2 a.m. in a Detroit suburb after an evening out at a nightclub. Police found Klima after he allegedly backed someone else's vehicle into a car before storming off and later trying to change places with the passenger. It was his second alcohol-related arrest in 17 months.

For Jacques Demers, this latest incident spelled the end of Klima's career in Detroit. "The value of Petr Klima as a player is totally gone," he told a radio station after the arrest. "I can't understand what's going on with certain people on the team, particularly Klima. It's difficult for me to see a young man destroying himself like that. This is just beyond me."

With Probert in rehab at the Betty Ford Center and Klima in the minors, the Wings stumbled to begin their 1988–89 season. As a result, Petr Klima went from being one of Detroit's most-loved athletes to one of its most vilified, all in less than a year. As the fans turned against the troubled star, a popular local soft drink commercial featuring Klima was swiftly pulled from the airwaves. And though the Wings reinstated Klima shortly there-after, they effectively washed their hands of him. They looked to trade him, but no team was willing to take on the winger's sizable baggage.

Klima entered a not-guilty plea in his drunk-driving case and publicly expressed contrition over his recent troubles, vowing to change his ways. The charges weren't serious, but the violation of the parole imposed on Klima from his first alcohol-related arrest was an issue. Klima had barely avoided a 29-day jail sentence resulting from the first arrest and might not be so lucky this time.

Klima returned to the big-league team in November, and the Wings' bad reputation quickly reemerged. Two weeks after

Klima's return, a Boston woman accused his teammate and friend Joe Kocur of assault.

Shortly after the Kocur accusations, a judge ordered Klima to spend an afternoon in prison and undergo counseling. His driver's license suspended for six months, Klima was allowed to leave treatment only for practices and games. The counseling also included spending 10 days at the Children's Hospital of Michigan working with children left paralyzed by drunk-driving accidents.

After starting the season riding a bus with a losing minor league hockey team, Klima eventually expressed remorse in a meeting with Demers and General Manager Jim Devellano. The team accepted his apology. Fans and media weren't quite so forgiving.

Although that turbulent season saw Klima score a respectable 25 goals, he missed a number of games with a back injury and never quite won his way back into the hearts of fans. The Wings won their second consecutive division title but bowed out in the first round of the play-offs. Despite Klima's six points in six play-off games, his time in Detroit was over.

A few weeks after the 1988–89 season, Klima was again arrested for drunk driving. While much of the Red Wings organization was wiping their hands of Klima, Jacques Demers of all people rushed to his defense. "For the first time, he admitted he had a problem," Demers told reporters in the months following this third arrest. "And for the first time, I sensed sincerity."

After opening up the next season with a 35-day jail sentence and a 45-day stay at an alcohol rehabilitation facility, Klima was traded to the Edmonton Oilers, where he finally made it to the Stanley Cup Final. After being benched for long stretches of game one against Boston, Klima scored the biggest goal of his career, a historic game-winning triple-overtime marker. Back in Detroit,

1990 saw the Wings miss the play-offs and coach Jacques Demers subsequently fired.

The next season, Klima followed up his only Stanley Cup win with his finest NHL campaign, scoring a career-high 40 goals with the Oilers. He would enjoy several more years in the NHL, including a short-lived return to Detroit. After unofficially retiring from the NHL, Klima returned to his home country, now known as the Czech Republic, to play with Litvinov, the club he had starred with as a teenager.

Almost a decade after retiring from the NHL, Petr and Irina returned to their home in Detroit with their twin sons Kelly and Kevin, who today both play local hockey. Embraced once again by the city he came to as a refugee, Petr Klima has come to terms with his past. "The bad things will always follow me, even follow my kids. I'm ashamed of my drinking and driving," he says. "We had players who partied a lot more than me. They didn't get pulled over."

Even Demers, who publicly chastised Klima, has gained empathy over the years for one of the most talented players he ever coached. "He could have had a better career," laments Demers, who links Klima's behavior to his difficult defection. "This is a kid who had to leave his home—that's got to affect you."

For the Red Wings, the experience with Klima taught them how to handle the Russian players who would later come to Detroit. That difference in how the Wings handled Russian stars, including Sergei Fedorov, isn't lost on Klima. "Sergei's got two drunk driving [incidents] and nobody knows about it," he says. "As soon as I got off the plane here [in Detroit], everybody went home and I had nowhere to go. I don't think my problems were because of that. I decided to go behind the wheel when I'd been drinking all night. I cannot point any fingers. It was me."

Now enjoying a life off the ice, Klima has been candid about his past troubles. He isn't quite as comfortable, however, discussing the details of his and Irina's defection. "We hardly talk about it," Klima admits. "If we have somebody over who wants to hear the story, we just avoid it."

He may not talk about it much, but Petr Klima will always remember vividly that summer in 1985 when his life changed forever. "My son plays with number 85," he says. "Eighty-five will always be the number."

4

The Juniors

Everybody said, "Wow, that must have taken a lot of balls." But I was worried more about what our parents would say.

By 1986, with a number of standout players playing in the National Hockey League, the roster for Czechoslovakia's national team had several noticeable holes. From the defection of the Stastny brothers to the escape of two of Czechoslovakia's best young players in Klima and Svoboda, not to mention Musil's impending defection, the core of a nation's hockey program had been chased westward. With their scavenged roster, the Czechoslovakian national team had turned from a powerhouse that had won three golds, four silvers, and a bronze at the previous eight World Championships into an also-ran.

Just one year after being crowned world champion and mere months after Petr Klima's defection, the Czechoslovakian team stumbled out of the gate at the 1986 World Championship. In their first game as defending champions, they lost 2–1 to lowly

Poland, a consistent tournament whipping boy that would not win another game at the 1986 Worlds. In their next game, Czechoslovakia fell 4–3 to West Germany, another team they had beaten countless times on the international stage. With a 3–2 loss to the Swedes in their third game, the defending champions were effectively out of the tournament. After losing to or tying every European team, Czechoslovakia finished fifth, missing out on the medal round and absorbing their poorest finish since 1962, when Czechoslovakia boycotted the tournament and did not even compete. Prior to that, their worst performance had been in 1953, when the team forfeited all their games by leaving early following the death of Czechoslovakian president Klement Gottwald, who succumbed to heart disease just five days after attending the funeral of Joseph Stalin. Before 1986, a Czechoslovakian team hadn't played an entire World Championship tournament and placed lower than fourth since 1937. That the disastrous performance took place in Moscow was one final indignity for the Czechoslovakian squad.

The combination of young players defecting and older players being sold by the Czechoslovakian government had hurt the national team, inspiring the country's sporting authority to cast its lot with its junior team. After finishing second to Canada at the 1985 World Under-20 tournament, expectations remained high for Czechoslovakia at the 1986 World Juniors in Hamilton, Ontario, which they opened with a difficult 5–2 loss to the Americans. That loss would cost the young Czechoslovakians dearly by tournament's end, when they finished fourth, placing just behind the Americans and missing out on a medal at the tournament for the first time in five years.

The performance from the Czechoslovakian juniors was below expectations, but there had been a saving grace in center

Michal Pivonka, the only non-Canadian/non-Soviet named to the tournament All-Star team. With 10 points in seven tournament games, Pivonka followed up his nine-goal performance from the previous year's under-20 tournament to establish himself as one of the world's best young playmakers. But while the national sports apparatus was grooming him to lead the Czechoslovakian national team toward another golden age, Pivonka was entertaining very different ideas.

The son of a track-and-field coach, Pivonka first established himself as a competitive javelin thrower, but his on-ice skills quickly had him on the Czechoslovakian hockey fast track. Dressing alongside Petr Svoboda as a 16-year-old with the Czechoslovakian national team, it had been made plain that Pivonka would one day lead his nation in its foremost on-ice battles. But as with other Czechoslovakian players, the opportunities hockey afforded Pivonka also opened his eyes to a world beyond the Iron Curtain. Those differences between Communist and capitalist cultures were most apparent when Pivonka attended a hockey tournament in North Korea as a teenager. "We landed and there was no lights, it was dark. That was a wake-up call, going to Korea," says Pivonka. "Looking at these people, they all wear uniforms, they all eat dog meat. It was definitely a culture shock. Then two months later you go into West Germany and you go, 'Something is wrong with this.'

"You go through the tournaments outside the Czech Republic, West Germany, then Sweden and Switzerland. Right there, your eyes kind of open and you go, 'Why is it so different here than it is at home?'" remembers Pivonka. "It was just the life that you saw there. More lights in the streets. You would see just a different culture, not that we had time to do much. But for little kids, the little money that you brought over could buy you things you don't have. There were also some scouts out there, I guess."

Sure enough, the scouts were out there, and they certainly noticed Pivonka. Even before he was a 19-year-old playing on the Czechoslovakian national team, he was such a hot commodity that the Washington Capitals were willing to overlook the inherent risks in drafting him. In previous years, NHL teams had waited until the draft's later rounds before selecting Eastern Bloc players. But with a variety of Czechoslovakian defectors now playing in the NHL, Pivonka's path toward the NHL appeared to be widening. With that in mind, the Capitals used their third-round pick, the 59th overall selection in the 1984 draft, to draft Pivonka. Only the Detroit Red Wings used a higher pick on a Czechoslovakian that year when they used the 49th pick to draft Milan Chalupa, who by that time was four weeks away from his 31st birthday and no longer considered a priority for the Czechoslovakian national team.

In his quest to track down Pivonka and sign him to an NHL contract before bringing him to Washington, Capitals general manager David Poile wouldn't be working in the dark. As a member of the Atlanta Flames' front office, he had witnessed the unsuccessful bid to woo Vaclav Nedomansky. A decade after Nedomansky's defection, Poile enlisted the help of Jiri Crha, a former Czechoslovakian national team goaltender who defected to the Maple Leafs in 1980 before returning to Europe and becoming an agent. Before fleeing the Iron Bloc, Crha had played for Czech League team Tesla Pardubice, where club officials told him that he would have to wait until he was 36 to go to the NHL—a lengthy wait he wasn't willing to make. After taking on Pivonka as a client, Crha helped Poile in his efforts to bring the young star to Washington. For Pivonka, it was a boyhood hero who helped him realize that defection, though dangerous, was possible. "Vaclav Nedomansky was kind of my idol growing up back at home, and then he left," says Pivonka. "It was the first time I had heard of someone leaving illegally."

After receiving a few phone calls from Crha alerting him of the situation with the Capitals, Pivonka finally met with his agent in West Germany a few months after he was drafted. It was there that Pivonka relayed the disappointing news to Crha that he would be starting his military service, making him untouchable to the Caps for the next two years. "With defecting from the army, everybody was scared, and obviously it was wrong. Your family would get punished and you would be punished. Doing it from the army was a lot worse," says Pivonka. "Plus I didn't think I would be ready [to defect] at 18."

Throughout his service with the military and on the Czechoslovakian national team, Pivonka maintained contact with the Capitals, making sure they were ready should an opportunity for defection arise. By now, Capitals director of player personnel Jack Button was keeping up most of the correspondences with Pivonka and Crha, even tearing a five-dollar bill in half and keeping one half while giving the other to Pivonka so that the two parties could identify one another. "I think they were trying to make sure that someone else wouldn't come along and say, 'Hey, Jack Button sent me, come with me,'" says Pivonka. "They were protecting our relationship to make sure the Communists or agents wouldn't step in and get in the middle of it."

During the 1986 World Junior Championships in Hamilton, almost two full years after he was drafted by the Capitals and just weeks before his 20th birthday, Pivonka secretly met with Crha, Poile, and Button to outline his eventual defection. It was there that the group negotiated the prized recruit's first NHL contract. It was a far cry from Pivonka's first meeting with Button, which took place in 1984 in a hunting lodge in northern Sweden. Since being drafted, Pivonka had imposed only one rule: at no point were they to meet in Czechoslovakia. Instead, the two parties arranged secret meetings in eight countries over two years.

By the time of the doomed 1986 World Championship in April, Pivonka was having semiregular conversations with team-mate Frank Musil about their respective defection plans, making sure to keep their discussions as quiet as possible. "Some of these guys [with the team], I don't know if they were Communist spies, but they were with the regime and they had no problem saying, 'Hey, these guys are talking about that,'" says Pivonka. "Maybe not the players, but the officials that we had with us the whole time. But you were used to it. You knew that one person on the bus or two people on the plane were there for that reason."

Growing more and more comfortable with the idea of defect-ing, Pivonka began regularly discussing with Crha the prospect of going to the U.S. capital. As the contents of these conversa-tions were relayed by Crha back to Poile, something resembling a plan began to take shape. Six months after the World Juniors in Hamilton, almost exactly two years after being drafted by the Capitals and with his tour in the army completed, Pivonka received the phone call that would change his life.

"If you're ready, we are ready," Crha told Pivonka over the phone. "Jack is here and David is here and we've got some papers ready for you. You have 24 hours to make up your mind."

"And that was it," Pivonka says of the brief conversation.

• • •

At around seven o'clock the morning after Crha's call, Pivonka boarded a bus with his girlfriend, Renata Nekvindova. They met up with another couple before arriving in a resort town in Yugoslavia not far from where Frank Musil had defected just a week earlier. With help from a travel agency, Pivonka and Nekvindova had received a two-week government-issued travel visa. Like Musil, the two would be escorted clandestinely into Italy, where they would meet Crha, Poile, Button, and Pivonka's $1-million contract.

Their parents knew nothing of their plans, a fact that weighed heavily on both Michal and Renata as they made the trip toward Terst, the Yugoslavian resort town that lay near the northern border with Italy. "The only thing we worried about really was the families back at home. My girlfriend back then, her family had no clue whatsoever," says Pivonka. "When you look back, it's a little bit selfish on our part. What if your parents got sent to prison or your sister got kicked out from her school?"

Not long after arriving in Terst, Michal and Renata met briefly with Poile and Button in the men's hotel room. After Poile and Button checked out of the resort to make their way to the eventual rendezvous point in Italy, the young couple took one bag containing some clothes and went to meet a shadowy figure on the outskirts of the resort. He was a Czechoslovakian expat hired by Crha to help usher the young couple through a wooded area that turned from Yugoslavia into Italy. Neither Michal nor Renata had met the man before, and neither has seen him since. "They hired some gentleman from Toronto. I don't recall his name. I was told he was pretty well off. He just did it for the adrenaline rush, for the excitement of the chance of being caught trying to cross the border," says Pivonka. "He was the one who actually walked us through the woods."

At the time, young Michal and Renata were not able to comprehend the incredible risks they took in the woods that afternoon. Renata had barely even gone on vacation before. It's only later, after discussing that night with Poile and Button, whom they

met across the border in Trieste, Italy, that Pivonka truly understood the danger in what he had done. "You were in Yugoslavia
and a couple of hundred yards later you were in Italy. If you get
caught in that zone, I guess they [border guards] could shoot at
you. But for whatever reason, everybody was out for lunch, the
guards. Jack and David, we met them on a dirt road over there,"
says Pivonka. "Whoever the guy was, I don't recall his name, he
jumped behind us and pushed us and I was like, 'All right, we'll
walk.' Everybody said, 'Wow, that must have taken a lot of balls.'
But I was worried more about what our parents would say."

After checking into an Italian hotel with Poile and Button,
Michal and Renata finally got around to the business of inform-
ing their parents that they weren't coming back. The phone
calls did not go well. Pivonka's father had suspected that his son
might defect, but his mother and Renata's parents were all side-
swiped by the unexpected news.

"What are you doing in Italy? You went on one of those daily
trips?" Pivonka's mother asked.

"No, we didn't," Pivonka replied.

"My girlfriend's parents were obviously not happy," recalls
Pivonka. "They blamed my parents and they blamed me for
stealing their daughter. I think the initial surprise was, 'I may
never see my daughter again.'"

For the next 10 days, Poile and Button sent the young couple
on trips around Italy. A few days at a beach resort, a couple of
days seeing the sights in Rome. Meanwhile, the Capitals worked
to secure Michal and Renata's clearance to come to America. But
these trips weren't purely for vacation's sake. Keeping Michal and
Renata moving at all times was of the utmost importance. While
lawyers in Washington worked on their immigration case, the
couple risked capture if they remained stationary. "I had never

done the kind of work we did for Michal because we defected him. It was really a very top-secret, hush-hush project that nobody could know about," says Lynda Zengerle, a D.C. immigration lawyer who worked with the Capitals on Pivonka's case. "We had to arrange a lot of clandestine transport for him. We know that people were looking for him with guns. I'm not sure he even knows, but he was being hunted."

As Pivonka and his girlfriend traveled along the Italian peninsula, unaware that armed guards may be looking for them, Poile and Button remained in constant contact with their Washington lawyers. But a legal hurdle had arisen that would delay the couple's U.S. visa request. Michal and Renata were not married. They could hardly be blamed for that; after all, they were still very young. But that fact did make securing a visa for Renata more difficult. "It's different to have a girlfriend than to have a wife. That added another whole layer of problems," says Zengerle. "In those days there was really no provision for someone who wasn't related to you. So we had to do a lot of fancy footwork to get his girlfriend in. It was a deal breaker if we couldn't get her in."

The paperwork eventually came in and the entire group drove six hours to Rome, where Michal and Renata met with embassy officials, who asked him a series of questions about the consequences of his returning to Czechoslovakia before granting him refugee status. By then, Crha had arrived to assist Pivonka with translation, and the Czechoslovakian government had begun the process of indicting the couple in absentia. As for their parents, they had also begun feeling tensions once word of their children's actions spread through their country. "I understood when I made the decision to cross the border. I'm done. I'm either good enough to play hockey or I'm not. But I'm not going back," says Pivonka, who soon received word that his father was demoted from his coaching job not long after his defection. "My dad was pretty well known. He was a track coach and a lot of his friends turned out not to be such good friends. There were people giving him a hard time because I left. A little jealousy on their part, I'm sure. My dad would never complain."

Shortly after their meeting at the embassy, Poile, Button, Pivonka, and Nekvindova boarded a 747 flight from Rome to New York's Kennedy Airport. From there, they caught a connecting flight to Washington, where Pivonka would have some time to settle before reporting for his first NHL training camp. It was the first time Renata had ever flown on an airplane. For both Michal and Renata, it was their first time in the United States. Upon arriving in Washington, Michal and Renata spent their first few weeks in America living in Poile's house. It was then that the Capitals GM realized how challenging the process of acclimating these young Czechoslovakians would be. "They came with nothing. They came with a duffel bag and a couple of things. They had no clothes or anything," says Poile. "We took them shopping and to set up the doctor and dentist, took them to the grocery store. All the variety, I think they were totally in awe. One night, we had corn. They wouldn't eat the corn because that's what you fed the pigs in Czechoslovakia. They would go in the yard and get mushrooms and fry them up. I said, 'I'm not sure you should eat that.'"

To his credit, David Poile had experience with Czechoslovakian hockey players. After trying to bring Nedomansky to the Flames, one of his first acts as Capitals general manager was bringing over Czechoslovakian star Milan Novy to Washington in 1982. Long considered one of the best players in Czechoslovakia, Novy was already 31 when he legally came to the Capitals as part of a financial transaction between the team and Czechoslovakia's sporting authority. Well past his prime by then, Novy lasted only a single season in D.C. "I think Milan Novy was the start of us getting to Michal. Milan Novy was one of the classiest guys I ever played with, but he never grasped the English language. He was a national hero over there [in Czechoslovakia], but the adjustment was too difficult for him," says Craig Laughlin, a longtime Capitals player. "I thought he had a very difficult time. He would just nod and smile no matter what I said. Obviously, I would trick him and say a whole bunch of bad stuff and he would just say 'ja' and we would be laughing. I just think he was so ingrained in their [Czechoslovakia's] style and culture because he was older."

In all his years dealing with Czechoslovakians, Poile had never dealt with such a young player. Maybe it was the overwhelming responsibility he felt for the young couple. Perhaps he simply didn't know anyone else in Washington who could help. Whatever the reason, David Poile never hesitated to bring Michal and Renata into his Davidsonville, Maryland, home. It was a five-week living arrangement that didn't start smoothly. Just three hours after Michal and Renata arrived, Poile's wife, Elizabeth, fell down some stairs and broke her foot. Days later, while the couple watched the movie *Jaws* on television, a fierce storm caused the power to go out. "We lit candles and played Parcheesi. Suddenly, they started laughing and brought out their Czech version of Parcheesi," says Poile. "They were defecting and possibly leaving for the rest of their lives and they brought Parcheesi."

Not long after the power outage, the Poiles attempted to teach Michal and Renata about Maryland's local culture by treating them to a dinner of fresh crab. It was then that they learned that Michal didn't really like seafood.

"Except for seafood, he doesn't care what he eats," Elizabeth Poile told *Washington Post* reporters shortly after Michal and

Renata's arrival. "I ask what they'd like and they say, 'Anything.' For breakfast one day he had four hot dogs, three boiled eggs, and six pieces of toast."

For Pivonka, the healthy appetite was part of an intense training regimen he had learned playing in Czechoslovakia. By the time he reported for Capitals training camp that fall, his impressive physique didn't go unnoticed by his new teammates. "Michal Pivonka came in and he was this freaking specimen. He could outrun you, he could outjump you, he could outplay you at tennis, he could outskate you. I couldn't believe it," says Laughlin. "I would train like hell and I would never look like Michal Pivonka. He was ripped, and there wasn't an ounce of body fat on him."

A week into training camp, as impressed as his teammates were with Pivonka's physique, the incoming rookie couldn't ·help but in turn notice the overall lack of conditioning in the Capitals' locker room. "I remember seeing some guys and thinking, 'Wow, they are not in very good shape,'" says Pivonka. "[Hall of Fame defenseman] Larry Murphy came in and I remember thinking, 'How can this guy play? He's not in very good shape.' He played 30 minutes a game. By the time November came, he was our best player."

While Pivonka appeared physically indestructible to his teammates, emotionally he was still experiencing some turmoil because of his defection. He continued to be admonished by his home country, whose embassy officials in Washington publicly called the defection "rather deplorable," claiming that "definitely some Czech laws must have been broken." By the fall, Michal and Renata were engaged, but the joyous occasion was hampered somewhat by the stories describing their families' hardships in Czechoslovakia. Renata's father even insisted that she return home.

"No, Dad, you don't get it," she eventually erupted at her father over the phone. "I'm not going back."

Shortly after arriving in D.C., Renata enrolled in school and dedicated herself to learning English, but the Capitals locker room remained an increasingly foreign place for Michal. "You're sitting in a room with 20 guys and you have no idea what's going on," says Pivonka of his first few months with the Caps. "Are they talking about you? Are they talking about the coach, or what?"

Pivonka's story gained particular attention in the sports media, and not just because of the secretive nature of his defection. The same week he arrived in Washington, Czech defector and tennis superstar Martina Navratilova returned to her home country for the first time in almost 12 years to play in the Federation Cup. Having since gained U.S. citizenship, Navratilova famously returned to Prague, saying, "This is my homeland, but the United States is my home. I'm an American now."

As Navratilova's return to the Eastern Bloc made international headlines, the local media in Washington began to swirl around Pivonka's story. John Feinstein of the *Washington Post*, who was covering Navratilova's appearance in the Federation Cup, even tracked down Pivonka's mother, Magdalena, in Kladno. During her conversations with Feinstein, Mrs. Pivonka eventually looked at an open tan suitcase on the floor, one of her final reminders of her son, and turned away in tears. After conducting the interview at the Pivonka's home, Feinstein noticed a small handful of government agents trailing him around town.

The Capitals were thrilled to have their prized recruit finally in Washington, but not everyone in the area shared their enthusiasm. Around the beltway, where most conversations quickly became politicized, Pivonka and the Capitals experienced something of a backlash. William Raspberry of the *Washington Post* described in a column a conversation he had with a Haitian cab driver who asked, "If Pivonka had this well-founded fear of persecution in Czechoslovakia, why was he able to stay out of trouble for the two years he was negotiating with the Washington Capitals?"

Former lawyer Carol Leslie Wolchok, at that time serving as director of the American Civil Liberties Union Political Asylum Project, contributed an op-ed column to the *Post*. In it, she wrote: "Other refugees who have lost relatives to the political turmoil in their homelands have not qualified for refugee status; they have received deportation orders. The government tells us this is so because we have 'strict standards' or that they are merely 'economic migrants.' But does anyone really believe that a hockey player with a million-dollar contract is a bona fide refugee if they are not?" Meanwhile, a *New Republic* opinion column referred to Pivonka's case as a "charade" and stated: "The notion that this young jock meets anyone's definition of a political refugee is absurd."

Still unable to speak or read English, Pivonka was mostly unaware of this abrupt, if marginal, media backlash. After all, he had his first NHL season to focus on. That focus became apparent when, less than a minute into his third exhibition game, Pivonka scored his first goal as a Capital, leading the team to a 5–4 win over New Jersey. In Washington's first regular season win, a wild 7–6 overtime affair against the Rangers, Pivonka registered a goal and an assist.

"Michal Pivonka is going to be a hell of a player," Capitals coach Bryan Murray told the media after the overtime win. "So far at least, the physical play hasn't been a problem for him."

As it was for most Eastern European players, the increasingly physical play in the NHL was the true test of their skills.

Europeans generally had a reputation for relying more on their finesse and the larger international ice surfaces. For a player with Pivonka's talents, most opposing teams' game plans revolved around knocking him down early and often. The perception that Communists were stealing NHL jobs North Americans were entitled to only further motivated opposing teams to put Pivonka on the ground. But Pivonka was up to the task. "In the Spectrum in Philadelphia, they [the Flyers] had a lot of donkeys at the time. We were quite the rivals. They had some tough players. Guys that would really take liberties," Laughlin recalls of an early-season game. "And they targeted the European players to get them off their game. I just remember a very physical game there in which Michal was one of our best players. The one guy that wasn't going to wilt and wasn't going to succumb was Michal Pivonka. It didn't affect him at all."

If Pivonka adapted well to the physical play, he was also able to handle the verbal attacks he occasionally absorbed. Even as his English improved and Pivonka could finally understand what opposing players and fans said to him, it didn't affect his play. "You would hear it all the time. They called us Russians. I think Americans then didn't know much about geography," says Pivonka. "So any Commies were just Russians. Any trash talk you heard was turned that way. It was fine with me. I didn't like the Commies either."

● ● ●

Later that first month of the 1986–87 NHL season, Pivonka scored twice in a 5–2 win over Vancouver, continuing a hot start that helped the Czechoslovakian center win over D.C.-area sports fans. Off the ice, a Capitals roster populated by several veteran players, including Mike Gartner and Rod Langway, helped Pivonka adapt to his new life. "I wanted to get to know Michal Pivonka, because he was an intriguing guy. He wanted to make his mark here in Washington, and that's probably why we had a bond," says Laughlin. "And he was a tremendous kid. He didn't come in and act overbearing. I'm not sure 'laid-back' is the right word, but he was very respectful of what the players had accomplished. To me, we were looking to him as a missing piece of the puzzle."

But after a hot start in which Pivonka tallied seven goals and eight assists in his first 15 games, his game went conspicuously cold. After notching only three goals between November 1 and December 22, Pivonka was moved from center to left wing in an effort to take some pressure off the young star. "I am not tired," Pivonka told reporters in his still-improving English. "But the last 10 or 12 games, everything was down mentally."

The loss of certain Caps players contributed at least partially to Pivonka's slump. Bob Carpenter and Gaetan Duchesne, two veteran players who had initially helped Michal transition both on and off the ice, were out with long-term injuries. Veteran Swedish defenseman Bengt Gustafsson, who was initially relied on to help with Pivonka's arrival in D.C., decided to return to Sweden before the young Czechoslovakian arrived.

By February, Pivonka rediscovered his scoring touch, which immediately led to a modest winning streak for the Capitals. Keeping in touch with former teammate Frank Musil, who was experiencing his own transition with the Minnesota North Stars, Pivonka was finally becoming acclimated to his new life. Even Renata was finding her stride, spending her time learning English and taking tennis lessons. Still, David Poile remained modest when asked about Pivonka's transition. "He has to adjust to the travel, the number of games, the type of hockey, the play-offs, the winning, the losing, the mental aspects," Poile told reporters in March 1987, by which time Pivonka had 17 goals and 25 assists in his first NHL season. "Off the ice, it involves the meaning of the money he makes, the lifestyle he and Renata choose to live. I think we're going to have a two- to three-year period of adjustment."

Poile wasn't entirely wrong. By the 1989–90 season, around the end of that two- to three-year period the Capitals GM had described, Pivonka's time in Washington had been an up-and-down affair. His mother, Magdalena, finally came to visit him in D.C. and his command of the English language had improved drastically. But his performance on the ice had been very inconsistent. After scoring an impressive 18 goals and 43 points in his first season in Washington, Pivonka saw his numbers decrease across the board in his second NHL campaign. He rebounded from that difficult season with a stellar play-off performance, notching 13 points in 14 games for a Capitals team that came within one win of advancing to the Wales Conference Final. But by Pivonka's third season, his performance degraded to such a degree that, after scoring just five goals in his first 47 games, he was assigned to the Capitals' minor league team, the Baltimore Skipjacks of the American Hockey League.

Entering his fourth season, arguably the most pivotal of his NHL career, Pivonka was confronted by a road trip that would bring back a number of difficult memories from his time in Czechoslovakia.

Even though it had been more than three years since Michal and Renata defected and the Iron Curtain had mostly lifted over the course of the previous summer, the Capitals scheduled a road trip that struck fear deep in Pivonka's heart. In

September 1989, the Capitals packed their bags for a series of preseason exhibition games to be staged in the Soviet Union. Five of the Capitals' 29 rostered players had previous experience playing international hockey in the country, and before departing for their trip abroad, they mostly expressed qualms with small, nagging aspects of Russian culture. "The problem with the food is that it's overcooked and dried out," defenseman Chris Felix told Robert Fachet of the *Washington Post* in the days before the trip. "Everything is very bland. They don't use spices. We took a lot of our own stuff, like ketchup, peanut butter and jam."

To be sure, the Capitals did their due diligence before packing the team's bags. Upon hearing that there was no pasta in Russia, the team's vice president of marketing ordered thousands of pounds of pasta and hundreds of jars of sauce for the trip. If the Capitals were going to lose their games in the Soviet Union, it wouldn't be due to a lack of pregame carbohydrates. But there was one player on the Capitals roster who was frightened about much more than his next meal.

Even though he had been in Washington for some time and much of his family had by now been allowed to visit him, the thought of going to the Soviet Union terrified Michal Pivonka. There was no way for him to know that the Soviet Union would no longer exist within the next several months, but Michal still wasn't interested in going on the trip. "I thought, 'I'm not going there, are you crazy?' It was before the end of Communism. They gave us a little assurance that no one was going to do anything to me. But believe me, I had a few nightmares about the plane landing in Prague because of bad weather and going to jail right there," says Pivonka. "I was still in that time being sentenced [for desertion]. I wasn't sure about going on the trip, and the

Caps were not either. But a few days later they said, 'Everything is taken care of.'"

After opening the trip with two wins in the Swedish cities of Karlstad and Gavle, the only real inconvenience was felt by newly arrived winger Alan May, whose sticks were lost in transit. After a whirlwind 8–7 win against Spartak Moscow to start the Russian leg of their trip, the Capitals were thrashed 7–2 two days later by Dynamo Moscow. For the most part, Pivonka had remained unfazed throughout the trip. Then came the match against Dynamo Riga, a Latvian club led by Arturs Irbe, a superstar goaltender who two years later would quit the national team to protest the killing of four Latvians by Soviet troops.

Late in the game against Riga, Pivonka committed a pivotal on-ice gaffe. Just over 12 minutes into the third period of the scoreless game, Pivonka lost the puck near center ice, sending Riga center Harijs Vitolins into the Capitals' zone alongside teammate Niklas Varjanov. Moments later, the puck was in the Capitals' net and Washington was losing 1–0. The Capitals put Pivonka's mind at ease when they tied the game on a Dave Christian goal just seven seconds later. And after Tim Bergland gave the Capitals a 2–1 overtime win over the leaders of the Soviet Elite League, the team hoped that they could compete against the Soviet League's vaunted club teams.

After closing out the tour with a 5–4 win over SKA Leningrad, Pivonka had confronted a number of lingering fears as the Capitals posted an impressive 5–1 record against some of the world's best non-NHL teams. By February, the Communist Party had disbanded in Czechoslovakia, and the Velvet Revolution had effectively ended the Cold War, allowing Michal and Renata to plan their first trip to their home country since defecting over three years earlier. "I cannot wait," Renata told David Sell of the *Washington Post* before their trip. "I'm glad it happened this way, without blood. Sometimes, it doesn't go as quietly. Michal is excited, but he doesn't show it."

The end of the Cold War and the closure it provided in the Pivonka household appeared to invigorate Michal's play. That 1989–90 season was easily Pivonka's best with career highs of 25 goals and 64 points, but the campaign still mirrored his erratic play in Washington. After a difficult start to the season follow-ing their sojourn in Europe, the Capitals fired head coach Bryan Murray and, in an interesting bit of casting, replaced him with his younger brother, Terry.

With Terry Murray behind the bench, Pivonka enjoyed a rebirth. In the new coach's system, which allowed a faster and more fluid attack, Pivonka scored 10 goals in a 17-game span and for the first time truly looked like the star player the Capitals hoped they were getting when he first arrived. Despite only five goals from Pivonka in the last two months of the regular sea-son, the Capitals managed to make the play-offs and, even with a losing record in the regular season, advance all the way to the conference final before being swept by the Boston Bruins. Although the team enjoyed a historic postseason run, Pivonka's late-season slump continued into the 1990 play-offs, where he registered just two assists in 11 play-off games. While he did miss four play-off games due to a bout with kidney stones, Pivonka's play truly drew his coach's ire in the opening game against Boston. His kidney stones by now safely removed, Pivonka and his late-game giveaway led directly to Boston's winning goal. After the loss, Murray sounded off to the press. "He's got to bring up his game several notches—real soon," he said of Pivonka after the disappointing 5–3 loss. "He's got to play a lot better. He's got to be more creative offensively and stronger defensively without

Czechoslovakian goaltender Bohumil Modry in his iconic *Life Magazine* portrait. The star keeper was sentenced to 15 years in prison by the Czechoslovakian government. After working in the uranium mines for several years, Modry was eventually released and died in 1963 at age 46.

The Stastny brothers, early Czechoslovakian émigrés to the NHL: Marian (top), Peter (bottom left), and Anton (bottom right) as members of the Quebec Nordiques. In their first NHL season together in 1981–82, the brothers combined scored 200 points, with Peter's 139 leading the way.

(Miles Nadal / Hockey Hall of Fame)

Peter Stastny celebrates winning the Calder Trophy as the League's top rookie. At age 23, Stastny's 109 points made him the first rookie in NHL history to reach the 100-point mark.

(Paul Bereswill / Hockey Hall of Fame)

The Stastny brothers look on from the bench during a home game at Le Colisée in Quebec City. The brothers became a sensation in Quebec, leading the Nordiques to a then-franchise-record 42 wins in the 1983–84 season.

(Portnoy / Hockey Hall of Fame)

Vaclav Nedomansky, a former Czechoslovakian All-Star, skates for the Detroit Red Wings, where he enjoyed his last productive NHL years before retiring in 1983 at age 39.

(Paul Bereswill / Hockey Hall of Fame)

The iconic number 11, Igor Larionov, makes a pass with the Soviet national team. During his time playing internationally for the Soviet Union, Larionov won two Olympic gold medals and four World Championship titles.

Legendary Soviet defenseman Slava Kozlov suits up for his CSKA club during the team's tour of NHL cities in 1989. Noticeably absent from his jersey is the captain's "K," which was taken from him during a standoff with team officials.

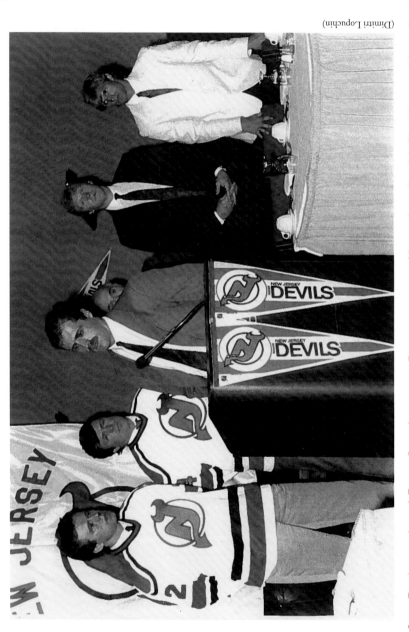

(Dimitri Lopuchin)

New Jersey Devils strength coach Dimitri Lopuchin, acting as Russian interpreter, addresses the media while Slava Fetisov and Sergei Starikov are introduced as new members of the team. To the right behind Lopuchin are Devils coach Jim Schoenfeld and team captain Kirk Muller.

The Devils' newest players, Slava Fetisov and Sergei Starikov, pose along with Fetisov's wife, Lada, at the home of Dimitri Lopuchin. In the top photo, Starikov becomes fascinated by a tape measure, according to Lopuchin.

In front of New Jersey's Meadowlands, Slava Fetisov and Sergei Starikov take a break from their first photo shoot with the Devils to play with Dimitri Lopuchin's young son.

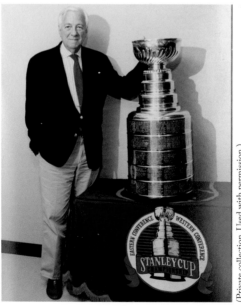

New Jersey Devils' owner John Whitehead poses with the Stanley Cup, which the team first won in 1995. Whitehead moved the team to New Jersey in 1982 after buying the team along with Brendan Byrne and John McMullen.

PETR NEDVED

(Harry Conrad)

PETR NEDVED

(Harry Conrad)

17-year-old Czechoslovakian phenom Petr Nedved skates with the Western Hockey League's Seattle Thunderbirds.

PETR NEDVED

In his first and only season in Canadian junior hockey, Nedved scored 145 points in 71 games and led the T-Birds to a stunning turnaround.

Petr Nedved skates with his first NHL team, the Vancouver Canucks. After dominating the WHL, Nedved experienced growing pains with the Canucks before enjoying a 38-goal breakout season in 1992-93.

(Paul Bereswill / Hockey Hall of Fame)

Petr Klima (second from right) covers his mouth as the Edmonton Oilers begin celebrating their Stanley Cup win in 1990, a dream come true for the former Czechoslovakian star. In the 1990 final against Boston, Klima scored arguably the most important goal of his career when he notched a triple-overtime winner in Game 1.

(O-Pee-Chee / Hockey Hall of Fame)

David Volek, formerly of the Czechoslovakian national team, suits up for the New York Islanders, whom he officially joined in 1988 at age 22. In his first season with the Isles, Volek scored a career-high 25 goals.

(Paul Bereswill / Hockey Hall of Fame)

Alex Mogilny suits up for the Soviet national team during the World Junior Championships. Mogilny emerged as a star at the World Juniors, recording 35 points in 20 games at three separate tournaments.

(Hockey Hall of Fame)

Young Sergei Fedorov practices with the Detroit Red Wings shortly after coming to the United States from the Soviet Union. Fedorov proved to be an instant star in Detroit, notching 79 points in 77 games as a rookie.

(Rick Stewart / Getty)

Slava Fetisov and Igor Larionov carry the Stanley Cup together around the ice at Joe Louis Arena in Detroit. After winning their first Cup, the Soviet stars Fetisov and Larionov were immediately handed the Cup by Wings captain Steve Yzerman.

Slava Fetisov, Igor Larionov, and Slava Kozlov lift the Stanley Cup in Moscow's Red Square after winning the Stanley Cup in 1997. It was the first time the historic Cup had ever been brought to Russia.

The Detroit Red Wings, including Slava Fetisov (bottom left) and Igor Larionov (right) celebrate their second consecutive Stanley Cup with injured teammate Vladimir Konstantinov, who was hurt in a serious car accident the previous summer.

Russia's Green Five of (from left to right) Vladimir Krutov, Slava Fetisov, Igor Larionov, Alexei Kasatonov, and Sergei Makarov don their old CCCP jerseys for a charity hockey exhibition in Moscow's Red Square in 2006. The Russian five-man unit dominated international hockey for almost a decade before disbanding.

the puck. When you have the puck on your stick, then you should clear it in that situation."

In a frustrating up-and-down season, Pivonka had managed to harness his game and break out as a legitimate NHL quantity. But he had also tasted the most bitter disappointment of his NHL career and was subjected to harsh criticism for his inconsistent play. The recent arrival of an old friend made the whole process more bearable.

• • •

In a Czechoslovakian national junior program that boasted stars like Svoboda, Klima, Pivonka, and Musil, slick-skating David Volek was an emerging focal point. Volek was one of the stars of the 1986 junior team that finished fourth in Hamilton, but it wasn't just his skills and personality that brought the team together. His father, Pavel, was a junior coach who was respected by several of his players. In fact, it was the elder Volek who alerted Pivonka that he had been drafted by the Capitals in 1984. Unbeknownst to most people behind the Iron Curtain, the younger Volek had also caught the eye of an NHL team that year.

"I was drafted by the Islanders in 1984 in the latest round. I didn't know I was drafted by them until [almost] three years later," says Volek. "My father had colleagues in the hockey government. Somebody gave my father something with my name on it [along with] which round, which position I was drafted. I was drafted in 1984 and we found out in 1986."

While it's possible that Czechoslovakian bureaucrats didn't want to deal with the negative perception of a national team coach's son being drafted, Volek had also been buried deep within the 1984 draft. Unsure if the skilled left winger would ever come to the NHL, especially with his father a part of the state sporting infrastructure, the New York Islanders waited until the 10th round of the draft, selecting David Volek with the 208th overall pick. He may not have known it for some time, but Volek was now the property of an NHL dynasty, a team that had lost in the 1984 Stanley Cup Final after winning four consecutive championships.

By the time Volek was informed that he was the property of the Islanders, most of his closest friends on the Czechoslovakian national team had already defected. In fact, most people were not even aware that Volek and his girlfriend, Alice, had actually been vacationing with Michal and Renata Pivonka the week they left Terst to go meet David Poile in Italy. "After five, six, seven days, Michal said he had to meet somebody. He came back to the condominium we were sharing and he said he got the offer, and I guess in two days he was counting the money. Then he said he was leaving," says Volek, who soon after began contemplating his own defection. "I didn't have any information from the Islanders. I didn't have any proposals. It was just Michal. For me, it was a very big uncertainty."

With a number of his closest friends playing in the National Hockey League and his father climbing the rungs of Czechoslovakia's coaching ladder, Volek began garnering more attention from the Islanders. The mechanisms of defection really began to move in 1987 when Volek met a man named Charlie Balogh at a tournament in Germany. A shadowy, if recognizable, figure with many connections inside the global hockey scene, Balogh plainly laid out his intentions for Volek. Through his contacts with the Islanders, he could bring David Volek to North America.

It was an intriguing offer that didn't quite pass muster with the young winger. "Charlie Balogh, strange man. Really strange man, and he didn't impress me. I didn't like him much. Just that first feeling when you meet someone, it wasn't very good," says Volek. "He told us he could help us with the contract and help us with the first steps. I didn't believe him. Somebody who knew him said, 'Don't trust this guy.' I don't know how he got the information, but not too many Czech or Slovakian players trusted him. He had a bad reputation around the NHL."

By the time Volek was playing for the national team at the 1987 Canada Cup, things had changed drastically in a short period. After being passed over for a prominent coaching position with the national team, Volek's father was granted permission by the Czechoslovakian government to leave the country to coach club teams in Germany and Switzerland. His friends and immediate family no longer around, Volek moved in with his grandparents. It was shortly thereafter, following a Canada Cup game in Montreal, that the young winger ran into a familiar face.

Thanks to his relationship with Serge Savard, Petr Svoboda managed to get in touch with Islanders general manager Bill Torrey, the architect of the Long Island dynasty. Around the same time, Svoboda, who was a longtime admirer of David's father from their time together on the national team, managed to track down his friend after a Canada Cup semifinal game in which the Islanders' prospect scored twice in a 5–3 loss to Canada. "We talked about his defection and the atmosphere in NHL games. We were talking more about his life after defection," remembers David Volek. "It was new information, which I didn't know. So that helped with my confidence to defect."

It was late one evening during the tournament that Torrey received a phone call at his room in the Sheraton hotel. It was

Svoboda, who was with David Volek and looking to set up a meeting between the two parties. Torrey and Volek had managed to run into each other in the street earlier that week and, during their brief attempt at a conversation, Volek had referred Torrey to Svoboda, his friend and former teammate. Now Torrey was finally getting the call he hoped might bring him his Czech prospect.

Given the agents following the Czechoslovakian national team, Svoboda would have to find the right time to spirit the 21-year-old Volek away. He would also have to find a dark, neutral location where this clandestine meeting wouldn't arouse too much suspicion. The best place Svoboda could find was a popular downtown strip club named Chez Paree. "It was a popular place, especially in the eighties," Svoboda laughs. "And still now."

The meeting would eventually move to the Sheraton, where both sides were relieved to be meeting face-to-face. Volek was awestruck by the presence of a true NHL legend, while Torrey was excited to be finally meeting the player who could potentially lead the next Islanders dynasty. "Was I nervous? I was kind of happy or excited," says Volek. "It was a nice feeling that he [Torrey] would have a public relationship; it was him in person."

"I could tell right away David wasn't sure about the whole thing," Torrey told a reporter for the *St. Louis Post-Dispatch* in 1988. "He said he wanted to defect, but he brought up his girlfriend, who was back home, and the more he talked the more I knew that it just wasn't right; he was ambivalent. Plus, I had no idea if I could get him into the U.S. legally through Canada. I just didn't know."

His confidence bolstered by the meeting and a respectable four-point performance at the Canada Cup, Volek would come back to Czechoslovakia and enjoy one of the best years of his young career. Despite a disappointing fourth-place finish at the Canada Cup in which Czechoslovakia absorbed humiliating back-to-back 4–0 losses to the Soviets and Swedes, Volek's confidence on the ice was at an all-time high. With 47 points in 42 games, Volek proceeded to lead his club team, Sparta Praha, to the Czech League title. But after a shocking sixth-place finish at the 1988 Olympics in Calgary, a tournament rampant with speculation about players defecting, the heat would be turned up on Volek.

Volek had initially planned to defect at the Calgary Olympics, but his girlfriend, Alice, had been left behind in Czechoslovakia with a swimming injury, foiling the plot. In the months following the disappointing finish at the Olympics, Volek began attracting government attention in a way he wasn't previously familiar with. He was then blindsided by his club team alerting him to his having tested positive for a banned substance. Dumbfounded by the news, Volek insisted on donating a second sample to the national doping program, as was the norm per international doping regulations. But his request for a second sample was denied and, just like that, Volek's hockey career, whether it was to play out in Czechoslovakia or the United States, appeared to be over.

"They were ready to suspend me for six months. I know I didn't take it, but they found steroids. Me and a few teammates, we went for vacation to the mountains, and when we came back I got the information that I was positive from drug testing for steroids. I didn't find the person who was behind this whole, I would say, this crime," says Volek. "I had to go before the jury at the hockey federation. I was saying it's a joke, it's impossible. I knew they had to take a second sample if the first is positive. They said the one sample was good enough and they don't need the sample B. There was something against our family. My father and me."

With the prospect of a six-month suspension putting a serious roadblock in his plan to go to the Islanders, Volek decided there was no time like the present to make his way west. Fortunately for him, he had several immediate family members living in Western Europe. The first one he called was his father, who at that point was coaching a club in Landshut, a town about 350 miles southwest of Berlin. The discussion was brief and simple: Volek would be coming to visit with his girlfriend and from there would find a way to get to the United States. But persuading Alice, who wasn't exactly an anonymous figure in Czechoslovakia, wouldn't be easy. A swimming champion in her native country, she was, like Volek, a prized Czechoslovakian athlete whose father was a prominent figure in Czechoslovakian sports. "My family, they agreed. But my wife, [at] that time girlfriend, she wasn't very happy," says Volek. "She was going to university, so she wasn't 100 percent sure."

Despite Alice's apprehensions, Volek was in a car coming to pick her up for the trip to Germany within a few days of the call to his father. From Prague, David would pick up Alice in her hometown of Plzen, a mere 50 miles from the German border. "She was crying at the border," says Volek. "She was crying, from leaving the family."

While spending time in Landshut with his father, Volek was able to get in touch with Bill Torrey through two of the players on papa Volek's team: Miro Maly and Jiri Poner. Both had previously defected to the NHL and could relate to Volek's intentions to leave the Eastern Bloc. Maly had also been instrumental in helping Frank Musil get in touch with Ritch Winter in his quest to come to Minnesota.

After hearing from their prized Czechoslovakian recruit, the Islanders sent a representative to Landshut, where David was keeping in shape by training with his father's team. With Balogh sitting in on these meetings and Poner acting as a translator, the Islanders went over the details of their contract with Volek. But after reviewing the Islanders' offer, Volek found that his plan to come to Long Island might not be as simple as he had initially thought. "I decided under those circumstances I am not going to sign the contract," says Volek. "So they said, 'Then we are not going to help you with the U.S. visa or the trip to the United States.' So Charlie Balogh left and no other word from the Islanders. That was it."

The contract negotiations halted, and David Volek's plans for defection took a considerable hit. Volek's visa to visit his father allowed him to leave the country for two weeks only. Those constraints didn't offer a lot of time to engage in bare-knuckle contract negotiations. Were Volek to return to Czechoslovakia, there would be no way to prove that he had planned to defect, but he would still be subject to a six-month suspension. With a serious problem to contend with, Volek approached Maly about someone in North America who could help with negotiations. Maly could think of only one person.

• • •

Two years after blindly meeting Frank Musil in Yugoslavia and bringing him to Minnesota, high-profile agent Ritch Winter received another surprising phone call that would compel him to board an overnight flight to Europe.

"Miro here," Maly alerted Winter over the phone from Landshut. "I have David Volek, who is ready to defect."

By now, Winter was far more familiar with the ins and outs of spiriting hockey players into North America, especially with the

Communist infrastructure on its last legs in Eastern Europe. "My girlfriend just left for vacation, so it's good timing," he replied over the phone to Maly. "I can probably come over today."

Sure enough, Winter was in Landshut the next day. Between his experience with Musil and dealings with numerous other European players who had come to the NHL, Winter now had a far more concrete plan in Landshut than he had had with Musil in Yugoslavia. "Fortunately, Volek was out, so I was much more relaxed about it. At that point, once he's in a Western country, I just needed permission from the airlines to get him over here," says Winter. "I learned a little from the Musil situation. It all worked out, just like a lot of things in life. You just keep on plugging away and deal with whatever obstacles you encounter."

For Winter, the primary obstacle would be persuading airline employees to allow David and Alice on a plane without visas. Already considered one of hockey's alpha negotiators, Winter managed to board the plane to Edmonton, where his offices were located, with both David and Alice. "That's what I do for a living, I negotiate. I made some calls to the airline, explained the situation," says Winter. "Once I was able to assure them of what the circumstances were, I received a letter from Canadian Airlines and that letter was from a senior enough person that anyone who saw it did what they said. Then I got him into Edmonton and by that time the Edmonton officials at Canada Customs and Immigration had seen me bring Frank Musil and it became a running joke. After David Volek, almost every second flight I went on, they said, 'Hey, anything in the suitcase today?'"

After arriving in Edmonton, Winter placed a call to Torrey, alerting him that Volek was in Canada and ready to iron out the details of his contract, this time with one of the NHL's foremost power brokers at his disposal. Almost immediately, Torrey boarded a plane bound for Edmonton. Once there, he parked himself in a hotel room, looking to arrange a meeting with Volek and Winter. It wasn't long before Torrey received an unexpected knock at his door, especially surprising considering nobody knew he was in the city. When Torrey opened the door, he was shocked to see David Volek, a grin on his face and an Islanders T-shirt strapped to his chest.

Once the contract was done and David and Alice were settled in Long Island, things went surprisingly smoothly. They would soon become Mr. and Mrs. Volek and start a family. Czechoslovakian state-controlled media published some negative articles about the couple and their abandoning of their country. But for the most part, the transition was alright. The young couple met other Czech and Slovak families on Long Island, and David quickly got back in touch with old friends, including Svoboda, Pivonka, and Musil.

To be sure, there were difficult moments, especially for Alice, who couldn't drive and wasn't nearly as occupied as David on Long Island. The first time she walked into a grocery store, she saw the sprawling aisles of food and walked out, assuming she needed a government permit to shop there. The first time she stayed home alone, she accidentally set off the burglar alarm and was unable to communicate with the police who arrived shortly thereafter. But things would get easier. David and Alice would learn the local customs and sample seafood and barbecue for the first time. Eventually, they could even laugh about their cultural reeducation, as was well demonstrated in a *Newsday* article written by Pat Calabria: "Invited to Christmas dinner at the home of teammate Pat LaFontaine's in-laws, David bumped against LaFontaine at the buffet table and said, 'Sorry, —head.' When all the guests gasped, David said, 'Is not good word?'"

When the Velvet Revolution stripped the Communist Party of its control over Eastern Europe just a couple of years after his defection, Volek was able to return home. He would even become a part of Islanders history when, in 1993, he scored the series-winning overtime goal against the two-time defending Stanley Cup champion Pittsburgh Penguins. "Pittsburgh fans, they still can't forgive me," says Volek. "I had a feeling that the Islanders fans, they like me. They like me as a person and as a hockey player, I think. Good fans."

In an interesting twist of fate, Volek moved back to Prague in 1995 to play one final season with Sparta Praha. Around the same time David Volek was beginning a new career in a very new Eastern Europe, Michal Pivonka was encountering a tumultuous time with the only NHL team he had ever known.

• • •

While David Volek enjoyed his finest season in the 1991–92 NHL campaign, his agent, Ritch Winter, was hearing from an old European acquaintance, Miro Maly, that Pivonka and one of his teammates were having trouble with their contract. As he had previously done with Musil and Volek, Maly asked Winter to take Pivonka on as a client. By now, Pivonka was a burgeoning star in the National Hockey League and his teammate was a fellow countryman on the brink of superstardom.

Just as Michal Pivonka was finding his legs in the NHL, Slovakian Peter Bondra was starring for HC Kosice in the Czechoslovakian Elite League. From the moment he joined the team as a 19-year-old, Bondra was a star, leading Kosice to a league championship in his first season with the club. By the end of his third and final season in Kosice, the Capitals selected him with their eighth pick in the 1990 draft, the 156th overall selection. Now that the Cold War was essentially over, the problems the Capitals had confronted with Pivonka's defection were no longer an issue when they brought Bondra to Washington along with 19-year-old defenseman Jiri Vykoukal during that summer of 1990. But although the Capitals didn't have to clear any political hurdles to bring over Bondra, the flashy winger's contract with Kosice was still legally binding, and Poile and the Capitals had to jump through some hoops with the Czechoslovak Hockey Federation to settle the matter. Once Bondra and his wife arrived in D.C., he was immediately placed under the wing of his countryman, Pivonka. By opening night of the 1990–91 NHL season, 21 Czechoslovakian players were listed on NHL rosters, by far the most in league history.

In their first full season together, Bondra and Pivonka demonstrated unmistakable chemistry on the ice. Off the ice, having another Czechoslovakian on the team helped Pivonka further acclimate himself to American culture. At the very least, it gave him someone new to play golf with. In their second season together, the 1991–92 campaign saw Bondra tally an impressive 28 goals, while Pivonka notched a career-high 57 assists and 80 points, enough to lead the Capitals to 45 wins, their highest total in six years.

Having become unmistakable NHL commodities, Pivonka and Bondra wanted to capitalize on their market value. With Winter now serving as their chief representative, the resulting back-and-forth with Capitals management created a standoff that would bring out some unresolved issues from Pivonka's arrival in America. Much like Vaclav Nedomansky had years earlier with the Red Wings, Michal Pivonka wanted to take advantage of a unique opportunity to ensure the welfare of his family.

"I remember sitting in his townhome. He was very businesslike," recalls Winter. "Michal needed that kind of assurance. He is business-oriented. I put my commitment in writing and he eventually introduced me to Bondra."

As Winter and the Capitals' brass engaged in a tête-à-tête over Pivonka, who by now was arguably the team's best player, stories began to surface around Washington of a potential lawsuit. At this time, both Pivonka and Bondra were still technically under contract. A March 1992 story by *Washington Times'* David Elfin claimed that Winter had sent the Capitals a letter. In it, he allegedly asserted that his clients' only counsel in signing their initial Capitals contract had been their original agent, Jiri Crha. Because Crha was then working for the Capitals, Winter purportedly stated that this dynamic rendered both players' contracts "legally unenforceable." According to Elfin's story, Winter also maintained that both players had signed their contracts under duress and without proper English translation. Word soon surfaced that Winter was ready to pursue action in federal district court to have his clients declared free agents. Before declining comment in the story, Poile told Elfin that Winter's letter "so verbally distorts the history of what has occurred that it can only be described as pure fantasy."

While he proudly remains a career Capital, Pivonka looks back with some skepticism on his initial NHL contract. He was aware of the contract issues encountered by countrymen Nedomansky and Volek and wanted to avoid similar problems. "I asked a couple of years later, how is it possible that the agent is representing the player and the Capitals at the same time? That's illegal," says Pivonka. "It was a little bit strange, because Jiri was hired, I would think, by the Caps."

The contract squabble was resolved by August 1992 without any legal recourse, but similar problems resurfaced three years later following a lockout-shortened 1994–95 season, in which Bondra led the NHL with 34 goals. In another contract holdout with Capitals management, both Pivonka and Bondra attended the team's training camp before starting the regular season with the Detroit Vipers of the International Hockey League. Until Winter could come to some sort of agreement with Washington, the two European stars would be keeping their blades fresh in the IHL. Pivonka and Bondra would play only seven games with the Vipers before returning to the Caps after a 39-day holdout. But it was a familiar story that would play out again with another Czechoslovakian defector.

To their credit, Pivonka and Bondra earned their new contracts. After starting the 1995–96 season with the Vipers, Bondra scored three goals in his first game back with the Capitals, a 7–4 loss to Los Angeles. By the end of the season, Pivonka established a new personal best with 81 points, while his former protégé Bondra set the league afire with 52 goals, fourth best in the NHL.

Although Crha's involvement in Pivonka's contract negotiations eventually caused friction between the organization and its star player, Michal looks back graciously on his involvement with his former agent. "He [Crha] was the one who got me out. If I left on the table some money, I wouldn't know then anyway. If he was okay with it, then that's fine," says Pivonka. "Ritch Winter was a pretty aggressive agent, finding loopholes about the legality of the contract that we signed. I think it was more publicity for negotiations on behalf of our agent. It's a business and they're doing their best for you, but human nature does crazy things to people."

Now raising his family in Florida, Pivonka has maintained ties with the Capitals. At the 2011 NHL Winter Classic in Pittsburgh, he even suited up with a Capitals old-timers team to play against a similar team representing the Pittsburgh Penguins. He doesn't reflect often on the events that brought him and Renata to America. More than 25 years later, Pivonka is only occasionally asked about his adventure. And it's then that he's surprised by how little he truly contemplated the consequences of his action when he defected. "You run into people and get into how long have you been here and how did you get here. Then you get to the story about defecting," says Pivonka. "The decision was part of taking a chance, not knowing what was going to happen. It's impressive to most people. Looking back, I don't know if I would do it [again]. But at [age] 19 and 20, we made the decision."

5

The Russians Are Coming

It was me against the system. And I beat the system.

They were, without much argument from even the keenest hockey minds, the best in the world. Not the best team, although they were arguably that as well. But the best five-man unit, a group that demonstrated such finesse and synchronicity that for roughly a decade they simply could not be beat. That reign began with one of the most humbling defeats in their nation's history.

Known as the Green Five for the practice jerseys they wore, center Igor Larionov, wingers Sergei Makarov and Vladimir Krutov, and defensemen Viacheslav Fetisov and Alexei Kasatonov had been groomed by the Soviet hockey machine and turned into an on-ice force the likes of which had scarcely been seen. Of the five, only the then 19-year-old Larionov was left off the 1980 Olympic team that lost to the Americans in what quickly became known as the "Miracle on Ice." At the time of the Lake

Placid Games, Fetisov and Makarov were 21, Kasatonov was 20, and Krutov was 19. "That was a very difficult time, especially for coach. I was young, [so] not so much for me," says Kasatonov of the 1980 Olympics. "For the guys from previous teams, it was a very, very tough time. It was almost tragic for us. The U.S. team was mostly students."

The coach to whom Kasatonov refers is Viktor Tikhonov. Having taken over the national team as well as the powerhouse CSKA club team (the official club of the Soviet Army), heaps of expectations had been placed on the former head coach of Riga, of the Elite League. And in his first Olympic Games as the national team head coach, he had come home on the losing end of one of the most indelible sporting moments in American history. He had won the previous two World Championships, his first two major tournaments as the Soviet national coach, but the loss at Lake Placid, coupled with the tragic death of Soviet star Valeri Kharlamov in a 1981 car crash, marked the end of an era. The Green Five Tikhonov had slowly groomed to take over the national program had already tasted defeat on the grandest platform and were now ready to take center stage.

"Tikhonov started to change players. Started to change leaders. He started to build a new team after this," says Kasatonov of his coach's rebuilding efforts after 1980. "We became a younger team between Slava [Fetisov], Larionov, Krutov. We stepped up and we started to build [the] team for 1984."

The first major test for this new group came at the 1981 Canada Cup, a prominent tournament that provided an opportunity to defeat a team of Canadian All-Stars on their home ice. Led by legendary goaltender Vladislav Tretiak, as well as two goals from Larionov and one from Krutov, this new Soviet team cruised into the tournament final, where they demolished the Canadians 8–1 at the Montreal Forum. Tretiak was named the tournament's most valuable player, and the 21-year-old Kasatonov led the team in scoring, with Makarov, Krutov, and Fetisov close behind. The new wave of young Soviet talent had officially arrived. By the time Tretiak surprisingly retired at age 32 after a gold-medal performance at the 1984 Sarajevo Olympics, the national program was effectively handed over to this group of five young stars.

Through the 1980s, this group of five would become as dominating a unit as any that had ever played the game. Over the course of the decade, they won Olympic gold in 1984 and 1988 and captured six golds, one silver, and one bronze in the eight World Championships staged between 1981 and 1990. Through it all, they played hockey in its purest and most elegant form—a perfect mix of long fluid strides coupled with pinpoint accurate passes and shots. Even the most anti-Soviet crowd couldn't help but admire the way this group played their flawless, balletic game. Between the countless international victories and the 1981 Canada Cup, the world was put on notice that these five players could take on any level of competition.

"It was really magnificent. They were so dominant. Not only that, they played a great type of hockey. They were just magnificent, [that's] the only word I can use," says Igor Kuperman, a longtime Soviet sports journalist who also acted as assistant general manager for Russia's 2002 Olympic hockey team. "They never played below their potential. Any time they played for Central Red Army [CSKA] or the national team, I really had the feeling that they were going to score on that particular shift, every time. For me, I was more surprised when they did not score, rather than score. It was like that."

The dominating group's superior athletes complemented one another perfectly, but there was one player who enjoyed a particularly meteoric rise from prized hockey recruit to one of his country's most beloved figures. Discovered by Soviet scouts in Moscow, Slava Fetisov almost immediately became a key building block for Soviet hockey. By the time Fetisov was 15, his Soviet teams were already being flown to tournaments around the world. The bourgeoning Soviet star and his bantam teammates came to Canada in 1974 to face off against some of Canada's best 14- and 15-year-old players. Even at Fetisov's young age, his otherworldly game was in plain sight.

"He was a superstar. He was skilled. He could skate, he had power. He had everything a hockey player needs," says Alexander Tyjnych, the goaltender on that bantam team and a longtime friend and teammate of Fetisov's. "He played offensively, he played defensively, he blocked shots, he pushed everybody."

The first Soviet team to come to Canada since the fabled 1972 Summit Series, the young players finished with a record of four wins, one loss, and one tie, their only loss coming against a Toronto Marlies team made up of older players. That game took place at the hallowed Maple Leaf Gardens in front of a crowd of 15,000 people, by far the largest crowd any of these young boys had ever seen. The team stayed in Western hotels and was escorted to NHL arenas by a police motorcade. And on top of the complimentary hockey equipment they received from their Canadian hosts, the group encountered plenty of other Western creature comforts on their trip. By the time the boys went shopping for various souvenirs, the trip had made quite an impression.

"I was 15 years old and it was my first time flying in my life. Flying 14 hours from Moscow to Montreal. For us, it was shocking. We were dressed very different from Canadian guys. It was the first time we saw jeans. I remember platform shoes. We also found gum. This is what we did first, go to stores and buy gum. I remember Wrigley," says Tyjnych. "We stayed in downtown Montreal in a nice hotel. Two hours before the game, there was already 10,000 people waiting."

By the time the Green Five had galvanized the nation and was starring for the Central Red Army and national teams, Senior Lieutenant Fetisov and his four Red Army comrades had grown into national icons afforded a standard of living that not every Russian was used to. At the helm was Tikhonov, who had inherited the overwhelming training regimen imposed by the godfather of Soviet hockey, Anatoli Tarasov. Known for his dictatorial style, Tikhonov had his teams train all day, every day, for 11 months out of the year. The site of their training was usually a barrack-style compound where family members were not permitted. It was his program, and its results certainly couldn't be argued with.

"Tikhonov was like Tarasov. He also used the totalitarian approach. It was dictatorial, but the system did produce results. This was the justification. Apparently, it is connected with general social psychology of that time in this country," says Lev Zarokhovich, a member of the 1980 Moscow Olympics organizing committee and former international secretary for Soviet sport. "His motivational techniques centered around the patriotic mind-set. That was it."

While they did have some differences, there was one other commonality that Tarasov and Tikhonov shared. They were not keen on the idea of their players, especially their best players, playing for anyone other than their Soviet teams. In the 1970s and early '80s, Zarokhovich was approached by some NHL owners about the possibility of acquiring premium Soviet players, including Boris Mikhailov, Vladimir Petrov, and Valeri Kharlamov. At every turn, any NHL inquiry into bringing over Soviet talent was rebuffed.

From Tarasov to Tikhonov, the Soviet hockey program instilled such intense levels of discipline that the Soviet hockey player had become something of a stereotype—a cyborg-like soldier who patrolled the ice with the utmost efficiency, incapable of any sort of demonstrative emotion. The image, as it was perceived by the rest of the world, was probably best described by *Sports Illustrated*'s Andre Laguerre in his report from the 1956 Winter Olympics:

> For two weeks I had watched that Soviet hockey bench, as the squad, smooth as a well-oiled, high-speed machine, glided from victory to victory. As they huddled in their blankets, their faces, which often looked cruel to Western eyes, rarely betrayed a flicker of elation. Others could casually give colleagues a friendly smack on the rump in recognition of good play, shout encouragement from the bench or bang the boards with their sticks when a goal came along. Even when, one night from last, they had crushed the U.S. 4–0, the Russian players barely permitted themselves a half smile. But when the final victory was theirs, they went crazy.
>
> They kissed each other, they kissed their coaches, they jumped and sang. One player had blood trickling from a cut in his head, and a colleague playfully stretched out a hand and smeared the blood over the other's face.
>
> That demonstration . . . testified to release from a discipline, rigidly imposed from the start of the competition, unlike anything Western athletes had known.

There we had, in a psychological nutshell, what we are up against in competing with the Soviet Union.

While the Cold War ran quite hot in the early 1980s, one Soviet player made the unprecedented move of coming west. His name was Victor Nechaev and he wasn't a player on the level of Fetisov or Larionov. To hear most Russian hockey experts tell it, he wasn't even close. But he did make history shortly after being drafted by Los Angeles in the seventh round of the 1982 NHL draft. At the time of the draft, the Siberian winger wasn't much of a budding prospect. He was actually 27 years old and had next to no experience with the Soviet Union's vaunted national team. But he did want to play in the NHL.

Nechaev was able to eventually take that step, becoming one of the first Soviet players to play in the NHL when he married Cheryl Haigler, a Boston woman he met while she was visiting Leningrad. "She invited me to take coffee and ice cream. A hockey player, I had certain privileges. I took her to places ordinary tourists could not go. We decided to be married. I could tell no one, only my parents and a few close friends," Nechaev told the *Globe and Mail*'s Allen Abel shortly after his arrival in the United States. "But to defect, everybody was very afraid, for themselves, for their relatives. It was a mental attitude of the Russian people. It was very different, compared to the Czechoslovakians. We talked about coming here, about never going home, but not at the airport. Not when there was anyone around."

The marriage allowed Nechaev to acquire the necessary paperwork to come to the United States, although by every account the Soviet sporting officials weren't exactly devastated to see him leave in the summer of 1982. "Nechaev is a very different story. I know him very well. He got married. He wanted to go to America just as a person. He never played for the national team," says Kuperman. "He had a great junior career, but that was it. He played three games for L.A. and scored one goal. He was the first one, but he was cut from a couple of teams in Russia, so he had nowhere to play. So he went there and played one year."

Although it lacked much fanfare, Nechaev's arrival in Los Angeles set something of a precedent when it came to Soviet players coming to North America, a concept considered impossible just a few years earlier. At the very least, Nechaev's arrival set in motion a swift acceptance in NHL circles of drafting Soviet players and hoping that they might eventually come over. It might take a month, it might take 10 years, but NHL teams no longer feared seizing legal entitlement to some of the world's best players. The year after Nechaev arrived in Los Angeles, NHL teams took kindly to selecting Soviet talent at the 1983 NHL Draft. The same year that Lou Nanne took a flyer on Frank Musil and Jim Lites selected Petr Klima, a number of Soviet players long considered untouchable to NHL executives were taken in the draft. The most conspicuous draftee was Tretiak, who was selected by the Montreal Canadiens in the draft's seventh round, 138th overall. Seven selections later, at the beginning of the eighth round, the New Jersey Devils selected Slava Fetisov, whose rights were forfeited by the Canadiens after they selected him in the 12th round of the 1978 draft.

Not to be outdone, the Devils would take two other Soviet players in the 1983 draft. In the 10th round, they selected forward Alexander Chernykh, who by that time was almost 27 years old and had accomplished relatively little compared with other Soviet players. In the draft's 12th and final round, the Devils selected Fetisov's defensive partner and close friend, Alexei Kasatonov. Six picks later, the Calgary Flames got Sergei Makarov.

These selections made a mostly superficial mark on the hockey world, but they were signs that things might be changing in the Soviet Union. After 26 years as general secretary of the Communist Party, Leonid Brezhnev passed away in November 1982, the loss of his intense cult of personality leaving a power vacuum within the Soviet government. Despite some recent political changes in the Soviet Union, there was no indication of when or even if Soviet hockey stars would be allowed to play in the NHL.

By 1984, when Petr Svoboda became the highest-drafted Eastern Bloc player in history, the bold idea of taking Soviets continued to gain traction. The Capitals picked Mikhail Tatarinov in the 11th round of a draft that saw a record 12 Czechoslovakian players taken, including David Volek in the 10th round by the Islanders. Then, almost overnight, one of the most celebrated hockey players in history decided never to play again. At the age of 32, Tretiak announced that he would no longer play hockey in the Soviet Union, a move some believe was made out of Tretiak's frustrations over wanting to play in the NHL. "Tretiak retired in '84, he was only 32 years old—that's nothing. He tried really hard [to persuade] the government to let him go play for the Canadiens," says Kuperman. "They didn't let him go. He told me and I heard from other sources."

With Tretiak's abrupt retirement, perhaps over his inability to come to Montreal, Soviet sporting officials found themselves at an interesting crossroads. In just a few decades, the country had recovered from a debilitating war to become one of the world's top producers of athletic talent, but that incredible sporting history was about to encounter an interesting new chapter.

• • •

Statistics estimate that between 10 percent and 20 percent of the collective population of the Soviet Union, Poland, and Yugoslavia had been lost during World War II. The Soviet Union had seen particularly horrific losses, with at least 25 million people dead, 6 million buildings destroyed, and much of the nation's farming and industry obliterated.

But one institution left standing—barely—after the war was sport. From the first days of the Soviet Union and the Soviet Communist Party, sport had been an absolute imperative. World-class athletes would not just rally the people but also demonstrate the might of the Soviet system in an international arena. As a result, sports were completely ingrained within Soviet society. Teams in the Soviet Union weren't separated simply by region but by industry. The powerhouse CSKA team, for example, was the official team of the Soviet Army. All the Dynamo teams represented the KGB, whereas Spartak clubs historically represented the unified trade union, which included state trade, light industry, civil aviation, education, culture, and health services. VVS Moscow, which was run for a short time by Joseph Stalin's son Vasily, represented the Soviet air force; Lokomotiv represented the ministry of transportation and Russian railways; and Krylya, also known as Soviet Wings, represented the Soviet aircraft industries. There was also Khimik for the chemical industries, Traktor for the tractor factories, and Torpedo for the automobile plants.

Because they were part of the massive Soviet bureaucracy, these sports leagues were subject to considerable political wrangling: some forceful letters from a powerful union or political leader could bring about controversial changes in the sporting world. That was particularly true of the Soviet soccer leagues, where the last-place team in the Class A division was usually

relegated to the second-tier Class B. Thanks to some active lobbying from certain groups, this rule could be overlooked, most
notably in 1977, when Dynamo Briansk finished last in Class
A but was "forgiven" and allowed to remain in the division for
another year.

After World War II, it didn't take long for the Soviet Union
to find an optimum opportunity for their athletes to help
recapture the nation's pride. As World War II ally England also
struggled in the war's aftermath, the Dynamo soccer club was
invited to play the English Premier League's top soccer teams.
"The first big event that convinces Stalin of the possibility of
sports comes in 1945, just after victory in Europe. This Dynamo
soccer team tours Great Britain, they do very well and everyone goes crazy. The stadiums are filled to overflowing. They
beat Arsenal, they tie Chelsea, they beat some weak team from
Cardiff, then they tie Glasgow Rangers. They had played pro-
fessionals before, but this was the height of the game," says
Professor Robert Edelman, a professor of Russian history at
the University of California, San Diego, and the author of several books and articles about Soviet sports. "Unfortunately, in
England, the war had so discombobulated things that the teams
were only beginning to get reorganized. They tie Chelsea in the
first match and they play brilliantly; they're carried off the field
by the fans. And the lightbulb goes on. All of a sudden, they're
broadcasting the games live back home."

Within two decades of that triumphant soccer tour of
England, the Soviet hockey program had established itself as an
absolute dominator. After being an also-ran for most of the early
days of international ice hockey, Anatoli Tarasov turned the
Soviet Union into the preeminent hockey power on the planet,
dominating tournament after tournament through the 1960s

and '70s before handing the reins over to Tikhonov. And through that time, the constant had always been Tarasov's, and later Tikhonov's, myopic dedication to training and conditioning.

"There was a study done, probably early 1970s. At that time, the average Soviet player, between training and games year-round, I believe [logged] 1,000 to 1,200 hours a year. I think the Czechs were about 800 hours. I think the Scandinavian teams about 600. North American elite players trained about 300 hours. That's training and playing," says Lou Vairo, the longtime American national team coach who, through his lifelong friendship with Tarasov, gained insight into Soviet training methods.

"Why do you do so much [training]?" Vairo once asked Tarasov.

"The Canadians had a big head start on us and the only way we had to catch up to them is if we work three to four times harder," Tarasov replied. "What's wrong with an eight-hour workday? Everyone in the Soviet Union works eight hours a day. Why shouldn't our hockey players?"

By 1980, the Soviet Union had poured so many resources into the development of their athletes that the country boasted 600 Olympic reserve schools and allegedly tried out 90 million Soviet athletes in various local and regional contests. For the elite Soviet hockey players, life didn't have all the perks of NHL employment, but the best Soviet players were entitled to benefits most citizens weren't privy to. Things like nicer apartments and cars, as well as generous benefits for World Championship and Olympic victories. Throw in the Soviet ideals ingrained in athletes and perhaps there wasn't as much incentive for hockey players to defect as one might think. Star winger Alexandr Yakushev expressed that Soviet contentment when asked about defection by *Sports Illustrated*'s Mark Mulvoy in 1976. "I've thought about it. The money, I mean, not leaving my country," Yakushev said. "I read about all those [NHL] salaries, but I don't understand them. Why does someone need that much money, anyway?"

That dedication of Russian athletes to Soviet ideals was one of the major things setting them apart from other Eastern European athletes. As more and more citizens of numerous Eastern European countries contemplated defection, Soviets seemed more inclined to operate within the parameters of the Soviet system. A shared revulsion across the Iron Bloc for a Russian nation portrayed as the evil empire magnified that deep division between the Soviet Union and other communist countries.

When the Green Five emerged, smaller communist countries had already been acting out against the Soviets in the sports arena for decades. In a culture where demonstrations and protests were systematically crushed, catcalls at sporting events were one of the few safe ways to voice a dissenting political opinion. The spectators at a 1954 chess tournament in Romania were among the first to defiantly lash out at Soviet competitors. A TASS correspondent in Bucharest reported "even outside the venue where the tournament was being held, the applause heard from the auditorium let everyone know who was winning: feeble applause meant wins for Soviet players whereas noisy applause signaled wins for everyone else."

By the time Czechoslovakia-Russia had turned into one of the world's bloodiest sports rivalries, all the prevailing factors had come together. Some Soviet people still had clandestine plans for defection, but Czechoslovakia's democratic traditions and the demonization of all things Soviets had formed two wildly different outlooks on the world. "Czechoslovakia was this place with a real democratric tradition, even before World War II. They did not have massive anti-semitism in Czechoslovakia. It was kind of a different place," says Edelman. "There was a case in 1967 in Slovakia when a bunch of fans ran on to the field and started beating up this Soviet club team. Basically a lot of people in the world didn't like Russia that much."

But as the Soviet Union became more progressive in the 1980s and Soviet players became more exposed to Western culture, an unprecedented back-and-forth began between players and management. It centered primarily on one of the country's most recognizable athletes, Slava Fetisov.

• • •

"I was honest to the game. I tried my best wherever I was playing. I had great teammates, great coaches, unbelievable fans, and I'll never forget this," Slava Fetisov says when reflecting on his Hall of Fame career. "I was so happy to represent my country in all international competition. To play for the Red Army Club and the Soviet national club, it was [the] happiest [time] in my life."

By the time he was the captain of the Soviet national team in the 1980s, leading them to multiple World Championships, Fetisov was garnering attention beyond the borders of his massive homeland. The New Jersey Devils, who had drafted Fetisov and his longtime defense partner Alexei Kasatonov in 1983, were now taking larger steps in their quest to bring both players to America. Over time, as the team struggled to find a marketable identity within the National Hockey League, the quest to bring over the Russians became even more vital. But it was apparent early on that simply drafting players wouldn't bring them any closer to American soil. "It was like being drafted by a team that played on the moon," Kuperman says of the Devils selecting Fetisov.

The Devils' ultimate plan started the year before Fetisov and Kasatonov were drafted, when John Whitehead, an investment banker then serving as a senior partner at Goldman Sachs, received a call from the recently elected governor of New Jersey, Thomas Kean.

"I need a hockey team. You're an investment banker. How do I go about getting a hockey team that we can move to New Jersey?" the governor asked Whitehead. "We have this arena and we have a basketball team, but it can't break even unless we have a hockey team that plays on alternate nights."

Whitehead's first phone call after that conversation was to John McMullen, a longtime friend he had first met in the Boy Scouts, who had just recently sold his ownership stake in baseball's Houston Astros. The two made a short list of teams they could relocate to New Jersey and quickly took notice of the Colorado Rockies, a bankrupt team legally controlled by two of its biggest lenders: the Ford Motor Credit Company and the General Motors Credit Company. With both the connections and funds needed to acquire the team, Whitehead and McMullen soon gave Governor Kean his hockey team, which was named the Devils through a regional fan contest. From there, the immediate task was to find the right players to elevate this moribund franchise to the next level.

McMullen was no stranger to how the right players could galvanize fan interest. As owner of the Astros, he had signed Texas product Nolan Ryan in 1980 to at that time one of the richest contracts in sports history, instantly giving his franchise a much-needed shot in the arm. The hope had been that, by potentially adding a star of Fetisov's stature and international appeal, the Devils could have a similarly instant impact on local fans. But from the very beginning, negotiations with Soviet hockey officials stalled and the quest to bring Fetisov and/or Kasatonov to New Jersey hit an impasse.

For the Devils, hope truly sprang in 1985, when President Ronald Reagan appointed Whitehead to be his deputy secretary of state. In one of his first acts on the job, Whitehead placed a call to the Soviet ambassador, Yuri Dubinin, to discuss the case of Fetisov. "We in the state department were looking for cultural exchanges that we could make with the Soviets; sending American athletes to Russia and cultural people like musicians and athletes. Of course, the Russians had the best hockey players in the world," remembers Whitehead. "I talked to Dubinin about arranging an exchange where, if they were to allow those two Russian hockey players to play for just one year in the United States, we would reciprocate by persuading one of our leading athletes in some sport, maybe baseball or basketball or football, to go."

Dubinin's response to Whitehead's proposal was simple.

"Mr. Whitehead, you are charging me with a very, very difficult job. As you know, all Russians are equal in our socialist society. Nobody is more important than anybody else," Dubinin said. "But when it comes to who has the best apartment, we have two tall apartment buildings. They are considered the choicest apartment buildings in all of Moscow. On the top level of one apartment, the best apartment is used by our top army general. And the top floor of the other apartment is used by our top hockey player, whom your team has drafted."

To his credit, Dubinin did get in touch with Fetisov and made some efforts to further the Devils' cause. But Tikhonov and the Soviet government only pushed back harder whenever the topic of the Soviet Union's most famous athlete going to America was broached. In one last-gasp effort to bring the Russians over and improve their team, McMullen and Whitehead cast their lot with a respected figure in college hockey who they hoped might be able to gain some traction in these proceedings.

Before being hired to be the Devils' president at the conclusion of the 1986–87 season, Lou Lamoriello had cultivated a reputation as a keen hockey mind. After starting out as a Rhode Island math teacher, he had built the Providence College Friars into a respected college program and played a large role in the formation of Hockey East, college hockey's first prominent conference. After he became the Hockey East Association's first commissioner in 1983, the conference named its championship trophy in Lamoriello's honor shortly after he resigned to go run the Devils in 1987. He would need to harness all of that hockey knowledge to fix the Devils, who had just finished dead last in their division. Considering the team had yet to make the playoffs in the five years since it moved to New Jersey, Lamoriello knew what his first major task as team president would be.

"I think that the priority of the position is always to try to make the team as best you can. When you have on the reserve list a couple of players like Fetisov and Kasatonov, you have to do everything you possibly can to get them to be on the team. That was the thought process the day I took the job," says Lamoriello, who saw the upcoming 1988 Olympics in Calgary as an opportunity to further negotiate with the Soviets. "It was going to be a process because this is something that had never happened. I never [thought] it was going to be easy but I never [thought] it was going to be difficult. I just saw it as a step-by-step process, the next step . . . after Calgary was to go to the Soviet Union."

When the Soviets captured yet another Olympic gold in Calgary, Fetisov was feted as a national hero. He had captained a Soviet team that had steamrolled the competition in Calgary, and he and three of his Green Five comrades had placed among the top six tournament scorers, a list headed by Vladimir Krutov's 15 points in eight games. With the tournament completed and Fetisov's place in Russian history enshrined, Lamoriello soon made contact with officials within the Soviet government and began the process of finally bringing Fetisov to New Jersey. Lamoriello's second visit to Moscow coincided with Fetisov being awarded a trophy considered one of the Soviet Union's most prestigious civilian honors. As soon as the ceremony was completed, Lamoriello got down to the business of finally bringing Fetisov to the Devils.

"He was coming back from the ceremony and we were meeting. It was just me on my own. I remember clearly going up the stairs, up three floors and going in this room and seeing these generals there. Then Fetisov came in. At that time, I had actually brought a contract over with me. I felt that everything was going to go along. This was all set, that he was going to be able to come," says Lamoriello. "[That's when] Fetisov was told in my presence that he wouldn't be able to go. We made eye contact and I knew . . . that he was surprised and disappointed. I couldn't communicate with him, but I had a feeling that before the night was over, I would see him."

Lamoriello and Fetisov did continue to communicate, but the main stumbling block appeared to be money. The Soviet infrastructure was starting to fall on hard times, and their sporting agencies asked the New Jersey Devils to pay a sizable transfer fee for Fetisov. Lamoriello refused and Fetisov was also not enthusiastic about being reduced to an international financial transaction. He instead wanted to come to the United States legally, without defecting or greasing palms. "I wanted to [make a] statement," says Fetisov. "I was the first Soviet citizen who got a work visa to the United States. I want to be clear, it was the official way, not defection from the country."

But trying to do things the honorable way actually made things increasingly difficult for Lamoriello. In trying to keep in constant contact with both Fetisov and Soviet officials, Lamoriello enlisted the help of Dimitri Lopuchin, the Devils' strength coach, who as the son of Russian immigrants could speak fluent Russian. "I remember all the time trying to call over there late at night. Lamoriello was giving me messages to give to him. Fetisov was giving me messages to give to Lamoriello. It was all really clandestine," says Lopuchin, who served as a constant go-between connecting Lamoriello and Fetisov. "It was such a pain in the ass trying to get contact back then. It's a seven-to eight-hour difference, so I'm trying to call at two or three in the morning. I'm trying to get ahold of an international operator and I couldn't always get through, so you would be calling and calling. Finally, it would get through and they would take your number and then have to call you back. I wouldn't get through to him until it was five or six in the morning our time."

Before long, the constant back-and-forth had caused a real strain on all parties involved. Various issues further exacerbated the tense situation, until Lamoriello finally lost patience and decided to make one last effort to see if Fetisov would simply defect and end the circuitous negotiations. He found an opportunity when the Soviet team was training in West Germany. Upon hearing about the team's training west of the Berlin Wall, Lamoriello immediately called Marshall Johnston, the Devils' director of player personnel and one of the few people still remaining from the club's failed stay in Colorado.

Calling Johnston was a calculated move by Lamoriello. Johnston's first trip to Moscow in 1963 as a player on the

Canadian national team had always stayed with him. "When we got off the plane, I remember this vividly, because it was two in the morning and the tarmac was all lit up and every 50 feet there would be a Russian soldier with a machine gun. So you walked off the plane and you were probably there two hours at least while they went through your luggage," Johnston says. "I got stopped years later, probably in the eighties. Somebody had given me a cassette of the book *The Spy Who Came in from the Cold*. It was in my carry-on bag and they took that."

Johnston had been on the road and was caught off guard by Lamoriello's call. Time being of the essence, Johnston had to have his passport shipped to him in Minneapolis, where he contacted an old Slovakian colleague whom he had met in Germany. The next day, they were in a secret meeting with Slava Fetisov and Igor Larionov, who served as Fetisov's interpreter.

"It was kind of a clandestine deal. Fetisov came over to where we were, and he had Larionov with him. I was under the impression that he was going to defect. We had made some arrangements in case this was about to happen," says Johnston. "As it turned out, he wasn't going to defect. He had a wife back in Russia, he wanted to do this legally if possible, and the right way. He was going to [earn a] visa to get out of the country."

Lamoriello was frustrated by this failed attempt to persuade Fetisov to defect, but the exchange had gained him insight into the honorable man he was dealing with. "You saw at that time the character. He said, 'I've got to go through this process. I hope you're willing to go through it with me because it's not going to be easy. But it will open the door for all the young kids behind me,'" recalls Lamoriello. "That night in that room was the beginning of our commitment to get this done."

Difficult as it was to bring Fetisov to the United States, a number of colliding political factors gave the perception that this deal might happen sooner rather than later. At the beginning of the 1980s, the war in Afghanistan had resulted in a serious heating of the Cold War, compelling former U.S. ambassador to the Soviet Union George F. Kennan to exclaim, "Never since World War II has there been so far-reaching a militarization of thought and discourse in the capital."

But Brezhnev's death and the ascension of Mikhail Gorbachev in 1985 to the position of general secretary of the Soviet Communist Party sparked a new wave of political liberalism in the Soviet Union. Leading a country that had been increasingly exposed to Western life and culture, Gorbachev and his foreign minister, Eduard Shevardnadze, spread a variety of new ideas through the Kremlin. Both men were committed to ending an arms race with the United States that had been accelerating for years, a demilitarization that by 1988 had led to a reduction of Soviet forces throughout Eastern Europe. From there, a series of democratic revolutions began to take place throughout the region, including Czechoslovakia.

Through the 1980s, the world, and sports in particular, had also begun adopting more capitalistic ideals. The watershed sporting moment had been the 1980 Summer Olympics, which were boycotted by the Soviet Union. The first privately organized and financed Olympics, the Los Angeles Games, introduced the idea of generating profit through international amateur sport. Similarly, in the Soviet Union, the policy known as perestroika began introducing wide-ranging market and political reforms.

"In the Soviet Union with perestroika, they are looking at the West and thinking, 'Some of these models make more sense than what we've been doing, especially in popular sports, like hockey and soccer.' The players are very interested in testing their skills. Some of them obviously want to make some money," says Professor Robert Edelman. "Then, in 1988, the soccer team comes in second in the European championships to Holland. All of a sudden a lot of these players are hot commodities, and the [Soviet government is] actually agreeing to let them go. [Then] the Soviets win in [Olympic] basketball in 1988 and the players don't have to defect, they don't have to put their families in danger. It's all kind of normal."

As the Soviet Union began to let their athletes play abroad and with the market value of Soviet talent never higher, a number of Russian hockey players began toying with the idea of playing in the NHL. Domestic conditions in Russia had deteriorated drastically as perestroika got into full swing, and its athletes saw an opportunity to leave. "This was a very bad time in Russia. There was a crisis in Russia. We had no milk, no meat, no bread. Then the Soviet Union collapsed," says Alexander Tyjnych. "I know it was a difficult time for my friends. Lots of my friends lost their jobs. Russia became like a new system, new market. It was tough to find a job. The factories were not doing anything."

And while Soviet athletes in many other sports were finally getting an opportunity to leave the Eastern Bloc, hockey players, and Fetisov in particular, were hitting a diplomatic wall. They still had to contend with Viktor Tikhonov, who by that time had established himself as one of the world's best, toughest, and most powerful coaches in any sport. "Tikhonov came to [the] Red Army Club. He was totally different. He was all hockey. He think, he eat, he sleep 24 hours only hockey. Any players who did not believe in Tikhonov or were against Tikhonov, he take them away," says Tyjnych. "No question, he had all power. You can't even argue with him, talk with him or not agree. If Tikhonov don't like it, you have no choice. You stay in Russian dormitory 30 kilometres from Moscow. We sleep here, we eat here. It was a lot of workouts and not a lot of days off."

With Lamoriello in constant contact with Fetisov, and Tikhonov reticent to let go of the five-man unit he had personally groomed into superstars, a difficult conflict was forming deep within the Soviet locker room. And even though Fetisov was attempting to leave the Eastern Bloc in the most legal and honorable way possible, his intentions to go to the West made him a target.

"So now Fetisov is being looked at a little bit as a rebel," Lamoriello remembers of the standoff. "Which was not the case at all. He only wanted what was promised."

• • •

The Green Five by now established as arguably the greatest five-man attack in hockey history, dissension eventually grew in the Soviet locker room, much of it targeted at Tikhonov and his tactics. That defiance began in the mid-1980s with Alexander Tyjnych, who had served as a backup for eight years behind Vladislav Tretiak. The legendary goaltender's unexpected retirement finally thrust Tyjnych to the forefront of the dominant Soviet hockey program. In one of his first games as the number one goaltender, Tyjnych led the national team onto the ice in 1984 against an overmatched German team. His team down 2–1 after one period, Tikhonov tore into his locker room, paying particular attention to his recently crowned starting goaltender.

"Tretiak quits and you already think you are number one," Tikhonov exclaimed at his goaltender.

By his own admission, Tyjnych snapped back at his coach. "I yelled at him," says Tyjnych. "I lose my emotions and he lose emotions. I was so angry and so sad. Then Fetisov broke it up between us, and the other goalie finished the game."

This kind of unbridled rebelliousness against any Soviet coach, especially Tikhonov, was unheard of before then. To be fair, the Soviets would win the tournament, and when Tyjnych was named the tourney's best goaltender, Tikhonov was one of the first people to embrace and congratulate him. It was a tactic Tikhonov had used countless times before: motivating his players with a father's scolding in defeat, embracing them with a father's love in victory. But despite the happy ending for Tyjnych, he strongly suspected that his time as the Soviet Union's top goaltender was over. "Tikhonov came to me and hugged me and said, 'Relax. Forget about what happened here.' But I see his eyes. They show me that you [are] done. This was a difficult time for me," says Tyjnych. "He started looking for other goalies. If I was in Canada or in a different country, I could go to another team. But here I stay in Red Army and I have no choice to move to another team because Tikhonov made the decision for everything."

For most of the hockey world, Tikhonov was the embodiment of the entire Soviet system. Fair or not, the coach and the government became difficult to distinguish from one another. But in his increased efforts to come to New Jersey, Slava Fetisov tried to separate the two. "You should understand, it's not about Tikhonov," says Fetisov. "It was me against the system. And I beat the system."

Perhaps no coach dealt with more pressure in the 1980s than Tikhonov. Following the silver-medal Olympic performance in 1980, there had been rampant speculation that he would lose his job were the team to repeat that disappointing performance in Sarajevo in 1984. Even after the Soviets won gold in 1984 and Tikhonov's Green Five was firmly established as the best unit in hockey, the pressure from the Kremlin continued. When Soviet

Wings coach Igor Dmitriev was hired to be Tikhonov's assistant in 1987, it raised further speculation that one of the world's best coaches was on his way out.

Ultimately, the Soviets had established such an incredible standard of excellence that even the most inconsequential loss in international competition could lead to calls for Tikhonov's head. By 1985, a year in which the Soviets lost the World Junior Championship, Izvestia tournament, and World Championship consecutively, word was that Tikhonov's days behind the bench were numbered. This period was also particularly tough on the Soviet captain, Slava Fetisov, who was slowed through most of the 1984–85 international season with a broken ankle. But the physical injury was nothing compared with what transpired in the summer of 1985, when Fetisov survived a car accident that took the life of his younger brother, Anatoly, who was only 18 at the time.

As all these difficulties swirled around the Soviet national team, coach and players alike felt incredible strain in playing up to this lofty standard heading into the 1987 World Championship in Vienna. In the opening round, the Soviets won all seven games by a combined score of 48–12. But in the medal round, ties to Canada and Sweden gave Sweden the gold medal based on goal differential, thanks mostly to the Swedes' final game, a 9–0 drubbing of the fourth-place Canadians. Krutov, Makarov, and Larionov finished first, second, and third respectively in tournament scoring, and Fetisov established himself as possibly the world's best defenseman. But despite one of the most dominating performances in recent hockey history, the Soviets settled for silver.

By that summer's Canada Cup, media speculation was rampant that all five members of the Green Five would soon be playing in the NHL. Even the team captain, Fetisov, didn't shy away from questions about these rumors. "I am aware I could earn a great deal of money in the NHL. And yes, there have been offers. I won't say where from," Fetisov told reporters. "But hockey players grow up with a strong love of the motherland. It is part of us. There is a bond that none of us would ever break. To go away, with no chance of returning—that is impossible to imagine."

Despite his loyalty to the Soviet Union, Fetisov had no problem expressing his frustrations with its national hockey program. "Playing for both the Army club in Moscow and also the national selection has been a difficult life and I am beginning to feel tired. Here I am, only 29, and this could be my last season of international hockey," he continued telling Canada Cup reporters. "For example, we began training on dry land at the end of June. I was on the ice with Army July 10, and with the national side July 25. Now there is the Canada Cup and after that, our normal season except that the Olympic tournament is coming, too. The pace is always hectic, and I can now understand what Vladislav Tretiak meant when he said he was worn out and couldn't continue."

Unbeknownst to the media, Fetisov had enlisted the help of one of the Soviet Union's most high-profile competitors in his quest to join the Devils. In a country replete with world-class athletes and world-changing thinkers, there may not have been a more respected combination of the two than chess grandmaster Garry Kasparov. Born in Baku in the Soviet region now known as Azerbaijan, Kasparov was the son of an Armenian mother and Jewish father who at 22 became the youngest-ever undisputed chess world champion in 1985. He would retain that title for the next eight years, becoming a Soviet icon. Known for his own rebellious streak, especially when it came to the Soviet government, the chess champion soon befriended the hockey champion and assisted him in his mission to play in the NHL.

"He [Kasparov] was the instrumental person in trying to get this accomplished. He was a friend of Slava's, and Garry really at that time had more power than anybody outside the country," says Lamoriello. "Garry was very helpful. I was trying to communicate with him daily. In fact, we hired someone in the office whose job was just to dial Russia every minute. You couldn't get through lines at that time. When he trained for his chess match, he actually did physical training, which was very interesting. He was instrumental in helping me get to the right channels and helping Slava."

In the summer of 1987, rumors persisted that the Green Five were roughly a year away from playing in the NHL. Larionov and Krutov were drafted by the Vancouver Canucks in 1986, making the group's NHL arrival increasingly plausible. During that summer's Canada Cup tournament, Soviet coaches and players alike were swarmed by North American reporters, all asking the same questions about these five champions coming to the NHL. Tikhonov dismissed the rumors as nothing more than media speculation, but the talk simply wouldn't go away.

Through it all, Fetisov's "will he or won't he" saga remained a fixation in the hockey world. Talk of his skills degrading coupled with the death of his brother had put increased pressure on the Soviet Union's most high-profile athlete. The silver medal at the 1987 World Championship and a disappointing loss to Canada at that summer's Izvestia tournament abruptly led to a different tone from Fetisov. Now being hounded by the international press about coming to New Jersey, he speculated that perhaps he and his longtime defensive partner, Alexei Kasatonov, should be separated, as should the entire Green Five. Perhaps most alarming, he was questioning his coach publicly. "I think if I were him, I would do some things differently and this is my own opinion," Fetisov told Lawrence Martin of the *Globe and Mail* in January 1988, just one month before the Winter Olympics in Calgary. "I've been working with him for 11 years. He is distinguished by the extent of his devotion to hockey. He gives himself fully to it. The fact he is always in search of solutions causes sympathy for him."

Surprising as these comments from the Soviet captain may have been, they were further inflamed by a simple, bold statement made to reporters shortly before the Olympics: "I'd love to play in the NHL."

Those words by Fetisov gained greater credence on the eve of the Olympiad, when players union head Alan Eagleson told reporters that there was "no question Soviet players will be made available this fall."

The deal between Lamoriello and the Soviets, as it was related to the media by a number of hockey insiders, was that Fetisov and Kasatonov might be allowed to join the Devils if they could bring back Olympic gold from Calgary. As expected, the Soviet team kept up their end of the bargain, going undefeated in their five round-robin matches, outscoring the competition 32–10, and proceeding to win four out of five medal-round games by a combined score of 25–7. In leading the Soviets to their second consecutive Olympic gold, the Green Five boasted the tournament's top three scorers in Krutov, Larionov, and Fetisov. But despite the emphatic Olympic win and joyous celebrations, Tikhonov made it clear to Fetisov that he would not be leaving the national team. The reasons given for this sudden change of heart vary. Many believe Tikhonov simply didn't want to part ways with his best player, though Russian insiders claim

Lamoriello reneged on a deal to provide financial compensation to Soviet officials. "Tikhonov agreed thinking that the club [New Jersey Devils] will issue some reimbursements for those players, but Lamoriello chose a different approach," says Zarokhovich. "Therefore Tikhonov changed his mind."

There had been other indications during the Calgary Olympics of an abrupt shift in the Soviet locker room. After spending the previous months openly expressing themselves to international media, Soviet hockey players, and the Green Five in particular, were unexpectedly muted during the Calgary Olympics. The scene may have been best captured by David Casstevens of the *Dallas Morning News:*

Viktor Tikhonov looked straight ahead as he shoved his way toward the bus. His face was set. His flat gaze had all the warmth of a Leningrad winter.

The coach of the Soviet hockey team wasn't talking. Perhaps under orders, neither were his players.

Vladimir Krutov didn't acknowledge his name. Larionov. Fetisov. Kasatonov. Kozhevnikov. Say. Yoo hoo. No response. Are these guys deaf?

"Excuse me . . ."

Sergei Makarov shook his head. "Interview after," he said. Makarov walked on, never breaking stride.

In a dominating performance in Calgary, the Soviets clinched gold with an emphatic 7–1 win over the Swedes. As team captain, Fetisov had started the rout early, opening the scoring just 26 seconds into the game when he overpowered forward Michael Hjalm and snapped a shot by goaltender Peter Lindmark, who was eventually pulled from the game after allowing four goals on 11 first-period shots. By every appearance, the Green Five had done everything there was to do in the international arena. In a postgame scrum with reporters, Tikhonov, speaking of the "main joy" of winning Olympic gold, shed some light on what his team had gone through in the previous years.

"Everything has been measured by first place, and second place is a failure," Tikhonov told reporters. "For any team, any coach, I think that's an incredible burden. Yet throughout the whole last year we very deliberately and carefully sought to improve the play of our national team. I think the Olympics will change the opinions of many about the strength of the Soviet team."

Following the Olympics, the NHL and Soviet sports authorities finalized the parameters of a deal that would allow Soviet players to come to the National Hockey League. Amid false reports by the Soviet news agency, TASS, that Tikhonov had resigned, the agreement had been built primarily around the NHL's plan to stage exhibition games in the Soviet Union, the same exhibition tour that terrified Michal Pivonka when he heard the Washington Capitals would be involved. But there was a catch: the Soviet government would allow only about 10 of their players to come to the NHL, and they would choose which players. The expectation had been that the Soviet government would release this list during the Calgary Olympics, but delays quickly arose.

While the NHL waited for this list to finally make its way from the Kremlin, word began to spread around the league of the impending influx of Soviet talent. Not everyone was thrilled with the idea. Philadelphia GM Bob Clarke told reporters, "I don't think the U.S. Immigration Department wants a bunch of Russian soldiers walking the streets." In an interview with Herb Gould of the *Chicago Sun-Times*, Minnesota GM Lou Nanne expressed his dissatisfaction. "I'm not enthralled by it. For me, this goes deeper than the Swedes and the Finns coming. It's an ideological thing," he said. "I don't like the idea of them taking away jobs. It would be different if they wanted to get out of that system."

With spirited debate now waging in the hockey world about these players and continued questions as to which players would even be allowed to come to the NHL, the Red Army team entered as tumultuous a time as it had ever seen in its storied history. In April, there were reports of Krutov deciding he had had enough of Tikhonov's ironclad system. In a story published in the *Globe and Mail* on April 9, 1988, Lawrence Martin claimed the winger had complained to Tikhonov about his unflinching approach to the team, before storming off to a bar near their training facility in Arkhangelskoye, about 50 miles west of Moscow. According to Martin, Krutov walked into the bar and found a teammate, who had defiantly leaped the training camp's fence earlier that evening. Despite the teammate's pleas, Krutov then found a stranger to drive him to Moscow, where he spent time with his family. Krutov allegedly told the stranger during the drive, "I want to lead a normal life."

After spending the evening with his family in Moscow, Krutov rejoined his team the following day for their flight to Voskresensk. From Martin's description, the Soviet hockey team appeared to be coming apart at the seams:

Krutov came back, but his overnight departure underlines the tension at the top level of Soviet hockey after the country's victory at the Calgary Olympics. The team's peerless starting five, together throughout most of this decade, are headed toward an inevitable crackup. A watershed is approaching in terms of the leading players and, some will argue, in the running of the system itself.

War-generation hockey people are feeling the pressure of modern-day glasnost thinkers. Tikhonov clings to power and to the old style, but the players are more inclined to Mikhail Gorbachev's new deal—more freedoms, more open expression and democratic reform.

Despite eventually being told by Soviet authorities that their list of NHL-eligible players would be ready by June 1, 1988, in time for the draft, the NHL received no such list and accused the Soviets of shenanigans. "I've learned to expect nothing from the Russians and I am never disappointed," Eagleson told reporters.

Even with the delays and tensions, that year's draft saw a record 11 Soviet players selected by NHL teams. By December, Fetisov was in North America, but not under the conditions he had initially hoped for. As part of the exchange negotiated between the NHL and Soviet hockey, two Soviet clubs, including Central Red Army, made a trip to North America to play a series of exhibition games against NHL teams. In the months leading up to the series, Russian officials had claimed publicly that Fetisov no longer wanted to play for the New Jersey Devils, a claim that both Fetisov and Lamoriello steadfastly denied. "I have absolutely done everything desired of me to go to New Jersey," Fetisov told TASS, the Soviet news agency, in the weeks leading up to the NHL tour. "I can't understand why it hasn't happened."

Reportedly injured, Igor Larionov was rumored to have been left behind in the Soviet Union. Although he joined CSKA for the series of games billed as the Super Series, there was speculation that he would be left off the team as retribution for an article he had written for a Soviet magazine criticizing Tikhonov and the entire Soviet hockey mainframe.

• • •

It had all actually started with the standoff between Tikhonov and his captain. Earlier that year, fed up with Fetisov publicly expressing his issues with his coach as well as his wishes to play in New Jersey, Tikhonov stripped his star player of his captaincy in a move that shook the entire locker room. Then, shortly after having his captain's "K" taken away from him, Fetisov was kicked off the national and Red Army teams, prohibited from so much as practicing with his longtime teammates. In one final indignity, there was word that one of Russia's greatest athletes would be exiled to Siberia, where he would be sequestered away from the team he had led on the ice in countless victories. "He took the captaincy from him and he was not allowed to practice with the team. He can't even talk to the players. It was a big issue," says Tyjnych, who had previously had his own issues with Tikhonov and the Soviet sport institution. "If he went to Siberia, he would probably teach some young soldiers to be athletes. Maybe do push-ups and sit-ups, he could be coach."

For months, the world's greatest hockey team played without its leader, the rudder that had steered them through so many fierce on-ice battles. Before long, the remaining members of the Green Five approached Tikhonov, demanding that Fetisov return to the team. Not wanting to cause too much of a stir among his star players, Tikhonov relented. But a fire had been lit under one Green Five member in particular.

If anyone in the Green Five could relate to Fetisov's predicament, it was Igor Larionov. A brash, confident player who had learned English at a young age, Larionov had secretly been banned from traveling with the team outside the Soviet Union just two years earlier. That the 1986 World Championship took place in Moscow had made the decision easier, but the experience planted a seed in the young Larionov. "Basically he played for the national team when they played in Moscow, but he was prohibited to go abroad for that year," says Kuperman, the former sportswriter and Olympic Team assistant GM. "After this, they let him go. But KGB didn't let him go on foreign trips for the whole season."

The suspension was more than likely retribution for a series of interviews Larionov had done with members of the Canadian sports media. When he saw his good friend, beloved teammate, and captain's livelihood threatened two years later, Larionov responded with a blistering public display. Having had enough of Tikhonov's strong-arm tactics, Larionov wrote an open letter to the Soviet national magazine *Ogonyuk*. Published in October 1988, the letter hinted that some hockey players had taken artificial stimulants. But Larionov's most damning passages were reserved specifically for Tikhonov. He referred to his coach as a "hockey monarch" who had used a culture of fear to control his players. He also made reference to an incident that had taken place shortly before his suspension two years earlier.

According to Larionov's letter, he had been reprimanded by army intelligence over his Canadian interviews as well as a "provocative" visit a Canadian woman had paid to his parents around this time: "The woman was attending a youth congress in the U.S.S.R. in 1985. She spent half an hour with my parents who, in the tradition of Russian hospitality, invited her to have a cup of tea," Larionov explained in the letter. "But I was forced to give an account of myself on the grounds that Soviet army officers have to keep their distance from foreigners."

Within weeks of the letter's publication, Fetisov was back on the Red Army team, while Larionov was unexpectedly absent. But still, a message had been sent by Fetisov's teammates supporting his rights and acknowledging the respect he had earned. For Tikhonov and much of the old Soviet guard, the writing was on the wall. "Tikhonov can't kick off everybody [from the team]. Fetisov had problems, Larionov had problems, I had my issues, Makarov has his issues, Krutov has his issues. Everybody became 30 years old and started thinking about themselves. It wasn't a team anymore," says Tyjnych. "Everyone had an opportunity to go away. For the first time in our lives, we were thinking, 'I can be free. I can go where I want to go. Not what Tikhonov wants or what the army wants.'"

But there was one notable exception to this sudden Green Five uprising. While most of these star players had at least marginally expressed their wishes to pursue new hockey opportunities, Alexei Kasatonov stuck by his longtime coach. That fact wasn't overlooked by Fetisov when he returned to the team, whose members began referring to Kasatonov as "Victor's son" in condemning his siding with Tikhonov. Without warning, two of the world's best defensemen, whose partnership had forged an incredibly close friendship, were no longer speaking to each other. "What can I say about a coach who makes me two-time Olympic champion?" Kasatonov says when asked about the rift. "My position is that there was change in my country and some people understand, some not understand so much what is going on. My position was, five guys leaving the team is very tough. Tikhonov fight for team, you know? Guys tried to think more about NHL, I understand too. I was between these two positions."

• • •

By the time the Red Army club touched down in North America to play a series against NHL teams, the strain of recent events and the rumours about Larionov's absence were hurting the club. The strain was magnified when the team realized their hockey pants had been left back in Moscow, forcing them to borrow pants for their upcoming games. There was still all kinds of speculation about whether or not Fetisov actually wanted to play for the Devils, a discussion that boiled over by the time the team arrived on Long Island on December 28 to play the Islanders. Asked about Fetisov's wishes after an intense hour-long practice, Tikhonov angrily asserted that he had offered Fetisov every opportunity to come to New Jersey. After being told that Tikhonov had signed a permission slip allowing for Fetisov's release, the media horde quickly stormed across the locker room to Fetisov's stall, where they asked him about Tikhonov's claims.

"Who did he sign it with, you?" Fetisov replied bluntly through an interpreter, maintaining that Tikhonov was the only person keeping him from coming to New Jersey. "He's all talk and no action. He keeps telling me that he's going to do something then he doesn't do it. I haven't seen it with my own eyes."

As a palpable tension commandeered the entire room, Larionov added his bit to the conversation. "The matter should be resolved as soon as possible," he told the press scrum. "I think that it's a vital ingredient of our quality of life to have sports exchanges like this. It's time."

When asked if he would like to follow Fetisov to the NHL, Larionov simply said, "Why not?"

When the team arrived at the Meadowlands a few days later to play the Devils, it was the culmination of years of efforts to bring Fetisov to New Jersey. If nothing else, it was the first time that Fetisov, Kasatonov, Lamoriello, John Whitehead, Yuri

Dubinin, and the entire Devils team were under the same roof. After beginning their exhibition tour with two wins and a tie, the Fetisov-captained Central Red Army team descended on New Jersey for one of the most anticipated games in Devils history. These may have both been world-class teams, but the massive talent disparity was apparent almost from the moment the players hit the ice. With a goal from Kasatonov in the first period and Fetisov in the second period, the Soviets rolled to a convincing 5–0 win over the Devils. Throughout the game, Tikhonov was routinely blasted by the New Jersey crowd, while Fetisov was showered with applause, which culminated in an arena-rocking roar when he scored. Devils brass hoped it was a sign of things to come for their team.

The moment the final siren sounded on the exhibition, the Central Red Army locker room was besieged by international press as well as Devils' executives. Not surprisingly, the lion's share of the attention centered on Fetisov, who by now had been waiting for months to come to New Jersey and had effectively severed his friendship with Kasatonov. Despite the tribulations he had experienced in the previous year, Fetisov was not shy in sharing his thoughts about the game in what could potentially be his future home arena. "I really liked the fan reception here," he said through an interpreter. "In Moscow, they don't cheer me quite as loud."

By now Lamoriello and the Devils had exhausted all avenues in their pursuit of Fetisov. The team president had made countless trips to Moscow, where he had spent time with Fetisov as well as Soviet officials. With glasnost and perestroika now in full swing, Lamoriello could at least enjoy certain Western creature comforts that had never previously been available in Russia. He even had an opportunity to sample Russia's interpretation of his

Italian heritage, dining at the Soviet Union's first Italian restaurant, which was dubiously named Lasagna.

After the game at the Meadowlands, with the entire Red Army team cleaning out their lockers, Lamoriello and his strength coach and interpreter, Lopuchin, entered the room. "I'll never forget walking into their locker room. The smell could have dropped an elephant. They didn't wash their gear. The level of hygiene, it blew me away," says Lopuchin, who had escorted Fetisov and Larionov around the team's facilities earlier that day. "We took Larionov and Fetisov over to show them the practice facility. Then we went to dinner with them, someplace in New Jersey. A guy, they said he was an attorney or some sort of legal representative, he just came along for the ride."

But Lamoriello wasn't simply content to woo Fetisov. He now had unfettered access to the Red Army team during their trip to New Jersey and so confronted Tikhonov head on. "I even spent time with Tikhonov when they came and played here. I went to the hotel, this was after they said he couldn't go," says Lamoriello. "He said, 'Yes, no problem.' But I knew I was being yessed."

Frustrating as these aimless exchanges could be, Lamoriello knew that Fetisov was dealing with much worse. "They tried to degrade him. They tried to slander [him] and I'm sure some other things that I don't feel too comfortable talking about," says Lamoriello, who identifies Tikhonov as the main hurdle in these negotiations. "To me it was Tikhonov. I don't think there was any question in my mind. It didn't have anything to do with the government."

In all the meetings and exchanges that took place during the Red Army team's visit to the Meadowlands, some assurances were made that Fetisov would soon come to New Jersey.

But all in all, very little had changed. Following a conversation with Lamoriello and Whitehead, Dubinin sent a message to the Kremlin pleading for Fetisov's release from the national program. There were even rumors that a team appearance on *Late Night with David Letterman* was canceled by Tikhonov. Through it all, there was no indication that Dubinin's request would do any good, but there were signs of hope. Once the postgame media barrage ended, Fetisov was able to share a moment with New Jersey's 21-year-old captain, Kirk Muller, in an adjoining hallway. "I told him I hope we see him in our uniform soon," Muller later revealed.

A week later, Central Red Army sustained its first loss in their NHL tour, a 6–5 overtime defeat in Buffalo. Immediately after the heated matchup, after weeks of answering questions about his status with the Devils, Fetisov admitted he was contemplating quitting the Red Army team. "It really doesn't depend on whether I'm allowed to play in the NHL or not. I just feel like I'm tired of playing with the Red Army team. I don't know. Maybe I'll wake up tomorrow and say, 'That's it,'" he told the media horde. "I've been with Tikhonov 12 years now. I feel I have nothing more to learn from the man. For a long time I really had faith in Tikhonov and our relationship was good. But I've seen a different side of Tikhonov. It's an ugly side I don't want to talk about."

Three days later, with the team preparing for its return to Moscow, Fetisov officially announced through an interpreter his intentions to leave Central Red Army before embarking on a two-month vacation. Larionov also announced his intentions to leave and instead play for Khimik Voskresensk, a Soviet club team near his hometown. Even Kasatonov was sounding off, announcing his intentions to request permission to also play for the Devils. Almost two years after the Soviets' much-anticipated "eligibility list" had first failed to materialize, every indication was that the legendary Green Five was now no more. "We are made to live like ice robots," Fetisov said in a story printed in the *Moscow Daily Youth*. "We are people with joy, cares, disappointments and concerns of our own. I'm tough but I can't take it anymore. I can't deal with a dictatorial regime."

Three months later, after what seemed like an eternity of waiting, history was finally made and the Soviet Union allowed one of its citizens to legally play for a National Hockey League club. But that citizen wasn't Slava Fetisov, nor was it any of his Green Five comrades. Fetisov had always hoped to be the first, but the devolution of his relationship with Tikhonov eventually compelled the Soviet program to select forward Sergei Priakin to be that player. While Priakin was reporting to the Calgary Flames, Fetisov was rumored to be toiling at a government desk job after leaving the Red Army team.

Fetisov returned to Central Red Army in April for a series of games against Swedish Elite League teams as the national team began preparing for the upcoming World Championship. But, in a controversial move by Tikhonov, Fetisov was left off the roster for the upcoming worlds. At the time, Fetisov had been out of hockey for three months. After the NHL tour, his only time on the ice was spent playing with a local factory team. Then, in a stunning show of solidarity, Larionov, Kasatonov, Makarov, and Krutov all appeared together on a Soviet television program vowing to boycott the 1989 World Championship if Fetisov was not included on the squad. Shortly thereafter, the national team decided in a players vote to restore Fetisov's captaincy.

Despite all the turmoil surrounding the celebrated squad, the Soviets ran roughshod through the 1989 World Championship in Sweden. In perhaps the most dominating performance of their legendary international career, the Green Five led a Soviet squad that won all 10 of its games by a combined score of 47–16. After completing the tournament with a resounding 5–1 victory over the host and defending world champion Swedes, Fetisov, Larionov, Kasatonov, Makarov, and Krutov cemented their place in sports history. Three weeks later they would be gone.

• • •

On May 25, 1989, as part of a military reduction program imposed by progressive Soviet leader Mikhail Gorbachev, the Soviet Ice Hockey Federation announced that Fetisov, Makarov, and Larionov were officially relieved of their military duty and were no longer members of the Central Red Army team. As their military duties primarily involved playing hockey, the announcement really meant that the three international stars were now free to pursue their respective hockey careers outside the Soviet Union. A new government agency, Sovintersport, had even been established with the expressed purpose of selling athletes to the West. Not surprisingly, Lamoriello expressed immediate skepticism about the announcement. "When Fetisov is on our blue line, then we'll get excited," he told reporters.

With these players now free to come to the NHL, doubts about their abilities began to surface. All three were in their 30s, and the performance of Sergei Priakin with the Flames had been lackluster at best. In two games with Calgary, Priakin had not just failed to register a point, he hadn't even registered a shot on goal. On the surface, NHL executives in Calgary, New Jersey, and Vancouver were thrilled at the prospect of including these star Russians on their rosters. But there were still doubts among players as to whether the Soviet stars could withstand the rigors of the lengthy NHL season. "He [Fetisov] did have some wear and tear, no doubt, because he played so much hockey in international competition, but we knew he could be pretty good," says Ken Daneyko, a Devils defenseman who faced the Green Five in both the 5–0 drubbing at the Meadowlands as well as the 1989 World Championship. "He was ranked the best defenseman in the world at one time, so anytime you can get a player of that caliber you know he's going to be pretty good."

After countless failed negotiations over financial compensation, Fetisov, Makarov, and Larionov immediately stood their ground once their NHL eligibility became official. After hiring an American agent, the three collectively announced that they would not be sending any of their NHL salaries back to the Soviet government, as had been the hope of Soviet officials. But the Soviet hockey federation did make money, with some NHL teams reportedly paying as much as $700,000 for the rights to certain players. The Devils, however, refused to partake in these types of negotiations, instead choosing to make a sizable donation to the favorite charity of Soviet first lady Raisa Gorbachev.

"Fetisov made a decision about the way he wanted things handled. He felt very strongly that he wanted to give part of his money to a children's fund and part to support minor league hockey in the Soviet Union," Lamoriello told reporters after Soviet officials expressed their anger over the Devils' arrangement. "It's not that he's trying to get away with anything. This is just the way he felt best. And he's one of our players and I have to respect and honor his wishes."

Later that summer, Lamoriello made the move official, announcing that Fetisov would indeed be coming to New Jersey for the 1989–90 NHL season. He would even be accompanied by his former Soviet defensive partner, just not the one the Devils had anticipated. Instead of his longtime partner, Kasatonov, Fetisov was instead accompanied to New Jersey by Sergei Starikov, a stout Soviet defender who didn't have nearly Kasatonov's skill set but was an immovable object in his own defensive zone.

"Starikov. Great guy, love him. Great person, but he was obviously the lesser name. It was more to bring a couple of them over to give Fetisov a little bit of support," says Daneyko. "He was a great guy and he played alright, but he wasn't obviously the marquee name. That was Slava."

With one final week-long sojourn to Moscow, Lou Lamoriello was able to iron out the details of both players' Devils contracts, as well as the paperwork that would facilitate their legal arrival in the United States. More than six years after first drafting the Soviet captain, Lamoriello had finally, and legally, brought Slava Fetisov to the National Hockey League.

Just weeks after Fetisov and Starikov's visas were issued, the Soviet government granted Krutov the right to go with Igor Larionov to Vancouver. It was an abrupt change of course for the Soviet government, which had previously told Alexei Kasatonov that he would not be granted his full release until his 30th birthday. But Krutov was barely 29 when he was granted his release, compelling Kasatonov to request permission for his own transfer to the National Hockey League. After being regarded in his home country as a career military man and Tikhonov loyalist, Kasatonov was now the last member of the Green Five left behind the Iron Curtain.

By the time NHL training camps started, four of the Green Five stars were in NHL cities and a few other Soviet players had found their way onto NHL rosters. The Quebec Nordiques signed Sergei Mylnikov, Alexander Tyjnych's replacement with the Central Red Army, and the Minnesota North Stars acquired

Helmut Balderis, a 37-year-old forward who had been coaching in Japan and hadn't played hockey in four years. Even Tyjnych joined the Edmonton Oilers' minor league team in Cape Breton, Nova Scotia. While Kasatonov remained in the Soviet Union, newcomers like Fetisov and Starikov were about to undergo a major culture shock.

"I had to take them around, get them kind of cultured here. We took them to all the bureaus for immigration. We had to go to Toronto to get them set up so they could cross the border to play in Canada. I had to teach them the driver's manual, help them get their licenses, explain to them how to use credit cards," says Dimitri Lopuchin, who was tasked with introducing the pair to America. "It really was a blur. I had a toddler son at home and we were scrambling to do that. It was crazy. Everyday we're looking for a house for them and then when the wives came, that was a whole other adventure."

From there, the first real culture shock took place when Lopuchin took Mr. and Mrs. Fetisov to a local grocery store. In Russia, where supplies of certain goods were sparse, Fetisov had grown accustomed to snapping up massive quantities of groceries for fear they wouldn't be available the next day. Lopuchin says Fetisov spent close to $600 on groceries his first time at an American grocery store. Larionov and Krutov shared similar experiences. "The fruit, the steaks, everything," Larionov told John Powers of the *Boston Globe* after his arrival in North America. "My daughter likes buttermilk. In the Soviet Union, if you did not buy it by nine or ten o'clock in the morning, it was finished."

But grocery shopping and credit cards were the least of these players' worries once they hit the ice for their respective NHL teams. Shortly after the arrival of the Soviet players, a backlash started to percolate among NHL players. Even Wayne Gretzky, the game's greatest player, expressed some reservations about the arrangement the league had with the Soviet government. "I don't think it makes much sense that we're paying their federation $700,000 a player," the Great One told reporters. "Nobody knocked on my door and paid $700,000 to my mother for me to play hockey."

Although his training wasn't nearly as rigorous as with the Soviet national team, Fetisov was not used to the hectic travel schedule an NHL season mandated. In his first exhibition game at New York's Madison Square Garden, Fetisov was booed mercilessly. "Like a lot of places," he explained to reporters.

Accused of stealing NHL jobs that Canadian and American players were entitled to, the new Soviets were immediately targeted by opposing teams. In some cases, that resentment wasn't confined to the visiting locker room. "Slava had a couple of guys on the team who openly hated him, at least didn't like him," says Igor Kuperman. "But in the end he showed what kind of person and what kind of athlete he is."

Fetisov's first real on-ice test would take place that first month of the season in a game against the Toronto Maple Leafs at Maple Leaf Gardens. In that game, Leafs winger Wendel Clark, easily one of the toughest players in hockey, singled out Fetisov and floored him with a borderline hit. Later that game, after the eruption of an all-out brawl that included a fight between Devils goaltender Sean Burke and his Toronto counterpart Mark LaForest, Fetisov and Clark sparred in one of the early season's bloodiest games. In the end, New Jersey came away with a 5–4 win to set a franchise record with their fourth straight road win. More importantly, Fetisov demonstrated his toughness on the NHL stage.

"Slava was prideful, even though that [fighting] wasn't as much a part of his game. As far as the fighting, he stood up for himself," says Daneyko. "Other players got involved to help him but he had to go through it himself. He wasn't going to take a backseat to anybody. That's what stood out."

The incident with Clark set the tone for Fetisov's first NHL season, which was indeed a rough-and-tumble affair. After appearing in the 1987 conference final in Lamoriello's first season in New Jersey, the Devils missed the play-offs completely the season before Fetisov arrived. With the prized defenseman now on their red line for the 1989–90 campaign, the Devils showed marked improvement, but Fetisov's transition continued to be difficult. That Starikov was sent down to the Devils' farm team in Utica after just a handful of NHL games didn't help. Barely a month into this first season in New Jersey, Devils coach Jim Schoenfeld benched Fetisov, whose mobility was hampered by a left-knee injury. The benching, coupled with a poor start by the Devils, soon inspired Lamoriello to fire Schoenfeld. After waiting years for this opportunity, Slava Fetisov found his first NHL season off to a rough start. But there had been some moments of levity, like when Fetisov was stuck with a monstrous bill after a team meal at a nice restaurant. As part of a rookie hazing ritual, Fetisov would have to buy dinner, along with the team's other first-year players, for the entire team. Of course, at the time, the 31-year-old "rookie" was more than 10 years older than some of his "veteran" teammates.

If there was one Soviet player who was acclimating incredibly well to the NHL, it was Makarov. With Priakin around to share his own experiences on a Calgary team that was the defending Stanley Cup champion, Makarov inherited an enviable position, even if he was occasionally criticized for playing selfishly. Meanwhile, in the Pacific Northwest, the Vancouver Canucks saw their two new Soviets adapt to the game with varying degrees of success. After collecting 12 points in his first 17 games with Vancouver, Larionov appeared to be picking things up rather quickly. Krutov did not.

"Larionov adapted very fast. It was new for these guys. They had never had bank accounts, had never written a check," says Jack McIlhargey, a Canucks assistant coach who spent the previous summer exchanging hockey techniques with Anatoly Tarasov as part of an international hockey exchange. "Krutov had problems, he did not adapt. He struggled over here with the lifestyle. I remember we rented him a house over in North Vancouver; nice house, brand new house. His wife didn't want to live in it. Too big. They just wanted a little apartment. That's all they lived in over there."

• • •

With a working comprehension of English and all kinds of international experience, Larionov took to Vancouver naturally. The team had barely lost to eventual Cup winners Calgary in the first round of the previous year's play-offs and, with two members of the fabled KLM (Krutov-Larionov-Makarov) line now on their roster, the Canucks were enjoying a resurgence among the Vancouver faithful. "We sold season tickets like hot cakes. As a matter of fact, we used to have people who sold season tickets and they got paid commissions for all the season tickets that were sold. When we heard about the Russians coming, we thought, 'Oh boy, this is going to change the game,'" says Glen Ringdal, who was hired as the Canucks' vice president of communications and marketing in the months before Larionov and Krutov's arrival. "So we changed the way we paid people who sold season tickets, because if we hadn't, each one of the four guys that were selling season tickets would have made more than [team president] Pat Quinn if they never got out of their pajamas."

As Vancouverites clamored to see their globalized Canucks, Krutov experienced problems almost immediately upon arriving. After being assured that his wife and children would quickly join him in Vancouver, the stalled Soviet bureaucracy left Krutov alone in a strange land much longer than he had anticipated. Even more problematic, Krutov arrived at Canucks training camp noticeably out of shape. By the season's 31st game, Krutov was scratched from the lineup by Canucks coach Bob McCammon. "One of the tough things with Krutov and his wife was teaching them about money. Pat [Quinn] gave them a checkbook. They were overdrawn and said, 'No, that can't be, we still have checks,'" says Ringdal. "I remember one time they were walking through the airport on a road trip and all of a sudden Krutov disappeared. Where did they find him? Standing at a hot dog stand eating hot dogs."

While Krutov was chided in North America for his conditioning, Larionov made waves back in Russia with his book *The Front Line Rebels*, which was published in Finland shortly after his arrival in Vancouver. In the book, Larionov made the stunning allegation that Soviet players and laboratory workers had fooled drug testers at the 1986 World Championship by submitting clean urine samples that were hidden behind toilet stalls. The statement was clarified by Larionov's assertion that each of the Green Five had refused any performance-enhancing injections.

Makarov was quickly starring on a powerhouse Calgary club as Larionov and Krutov experienced varying degrees of success on a losing Vancouver squad. As for Fetisov, things changed dramatically around Christmastime. After months of lobbying his government, Alexei Kasatonov, who had inherited the national-team captaincy when Fetisov departed, turned 30 and was finally granted his release from the Red Army club. Almost a decade after they first started patrolling the red line together as one of the world's greatest defensive pairings, Kasatonov and Fetisov would finally be reunited in New Jersey. But it wasn't a reunification either player was looking forward to. Kasatonov hadn't yet been forgiven for his siding with Tikhonov during the most tumultuous time of Fetisov's career. "No, I would not be happy," Fetisov told reporters when asked about Kasatonov's impending arrival. "He sold out. We five were close. Four stayed together. He went alone."

In a cruel twist of fate, Alexei Kasatonov arrived in the NHL to find that the only teammate with whom he could communicate had absolutely no interest in exchanging pleasantries. "They didn't talk at all. But when they got on the ice, they played and focused on the game," remembers Daneyko. "We kind of stayed out of it. They were both good players. They were professional enough when it came to game time to put that aside and play hard."

His feud with Kasatonov renewed in New Jersey, Fetisov quickly harnessed the kind of aggression Wendel Clark had brought out of him earlier in the season. Just days after Kasatonov's arrival, in a home game against the Pittsburgh Penguins, Fetisov baited Pens' superstar Mario Lemieux so mercilessly that the All-Star center lost his cool and went after the Soviet. The infraction got Lemieux ejected from the game, which the Devils won 6–3 against a Pittsburgh team that was powerless without its captain.

The animosity between these former best friends was magnified later that season with the arrival of another foreign star in New Jersey. After a decade in Quebec City, Peter Stastny was

sent to the Devils at the March trade deadline. Suddenly, the
hockey star who still vividly remembered Soviet tanks rolling
into Bratislava during the Prague Spring was forced to coexist
with a walking, talking symbol of Soviet dominance. Just like
that, one of his most-hated rivals was now his teammate. That
season also saw Stastny take a young Czech player under his
wing when the Devils called up a young winger named Zdeno
Ciger, who admitted that, growing up in Czechoslovakia, he had
never heard of the Stastnys because of government censorship.

Fetisov wouldn't reconcile with Kasatonov in New Jersey,
but he would set aside any differences with Stastny as the Devils
came together as a team. It actually turned out that Stastny had
already abandoned any contempt for Soviet hockey players when
goaltender Mylnikov joined him in Quebec. "You can't hate the
person. You do not like the politics of his country, but the human
being is warm and modest, and he will help this team," Stastny
told *Sports Illustrated*'s Jay Greenberg in 1989, expressing his
excitement over the arrival of Soviet players in the NHL. "I had
my doubts this would ever happen. This is so nice. I really believe
this and other things that we hear are happening over there tell
us that we are heading into a nice, peaceful period in the history
of mankind."

While the relationship between Stastny and Fetisov was amica-
ble, that between Fetisov and Kasatonov was not. During practices,
the two lifelong teammates stayed as far apart as possible from one
another. In the locker room, they avoided each other entirely.

Despite the locker-room animosity, and possibly because of
it, the Devils finished the 1989–90 season second in the Patrick
Division. As Fetisov's performance improved with every game,
New Jersey rolled on its way to a 10-win improvement over the
previous season. In the 6–4 win over the Rangers that clinched

the Devils' second-place finish, Fetisov notched a goal and four assists in his best game of the season, breaking a team record for points in a game by a rookie and tying the team mark for points in a game by a defenseman. Even Kasatonov had kind words to say of Fetisov's performance. "He is playing as well as he did in the World Championship," Kasatonov told reporters. "And you know it's difficult for me to say anything about him."

Although the game against the Rangers had been a high point for Fetisov and the Devils, the truth is that Kasatonov's arrival had sparked both the team and the player, culminating in a March 1990 record of 11–4–0, the best March in Devils' history. Fetisov may have had some trouble adapting to the NHL right away, but Kasatonov's on-ice transition seemed effortless as he posted six goals and 15 assists in just 39 games while compiling a plus-15 rating; his plus-23 the next season would set a new Devils' record for defensemen. The 1989–90 Devils, led by the improving play of their Russian backstops, would go on to set a new team mark for points with 83. Perhaps most importantly after losing more than $16 million in the Devils' first seven seasons in New Jersey, John McMullen and John Whitehead finally broke even in the 1989–90 campaign.

But despite the Devils posting a league-best 10–4–1 record in their final 15 games, their success wouldn't continue in the playoffs, where they were upset in the first round by the Washington Capitals. The Capitals' upset had been aided in large part by a game plan built around aggressively forechecking the two Russian defensemen. That attacking style was epitomized by Dale Hunter, a Capitals' center who had previously played with the Stastnys in Quebec. Whenever Washington dumped the puck toward Fetisov and Kasatonov in New Jersey's zone, Hunter took long strides into the Devils' defensemen, making sure to raise his elbow ever so slightly as he throttled them into the boards. "They're going after our defensemen," confirmed Devils coach John Cunniff, who replaced previous coach Jim Schoenfeld earlier in the season. "They're going at the Russians."

In their first NHL play-offs, the Green Five contributed very little to their respective teams. While Larionov and Krutov's Canucks didn't even qualify for the postseason, the Flames' first-round loss to Los Angeles saw Makarov removed from the team's top line alongside Joe Nieuwendyk and Gary Roberts. Fetisov and Kasatonov were a combined minus-seven in the six-game series against Washington. It wasn't long before Russian coaches voiced their opinion of the Soviets' play-off performance. "I think they were not so prepared for the NHL," Russian national team assistant coach Igor Dmitriev told Robert Fachet of the *Washington Post*. "You have to understand, they were in training their whole lives. They didn't have to do anything on their own before."

In an interesting turn after the Devils' play-off elimination, both Kasatonov and Fetisov were approached by Tikhonov and the national team to play in the upcoming World Championship. Despite years of animosity, Fetisov accepted the offer to play for his country without hesitation. Of course, the call hadn't come from Tikhonov directly but from assistant coach Dmitriev. Kasatonov, who sustained a cheekbone injury during Washington's merciless forechecking, was forced to stay home. Krutov and Larionov also did not attend, a fact that Viktor Tikhonov didn't hesitate to point out during the tournament. "Krutov had private business and I don't need Larionov on my team because I have enough good centers," the Soviet coach told the press. "Besides, he would rather take a holiday than play with us."

At the 1990 World Championship in Switzerland, a Soviet team that also featured Sergei Makarov overcame an early 3–1 loss to Sweden and 3–3 tie with Canada to go undefeated in the medal round, winning another gold medal for a country that was mere months away from no longer existing.

In four seasons playing together with the Devils, Fetisov and Kasatonov never found the right place or time to resolve their differences. After becoming one of hockey's most legendary defensive duos, it would be more than a decade before they would finally renew their friendship. After going their separate ways, Kasatonov and Fetisov experienced their own crowning NHL achievements away from New Jersey. Kasatonov played in the 1994 All-Star Game as a member of the Anaheim Mighty Ducks, while Makarov enjoyed continued success in his six NHL seasons but never duplicated the success of his first campaign, which he finished by winning the Calder Trophy as the league's top rookie. The controversy surrounding a 32-year-old "rookie" winning the Calder inspired the NHL to impose an age limit on the award. Krutov, on the other hand, returned to Russia after just a single season with Vancouver. "I think for Kruts it was probably a relief," McIlhargey says of Krutov's unceremonious return to Russia.

Each member of the legendary Green Five would be left off the 1992 so-called Unified Team that represented 12 of the 15 former Soviet republics at the 1992 Olympics in Albertville, France. Featuring a noticeably younger roster, the Unified Team would be the last Russian hockey team to win Olympic gold. Nearing the end of his legendary international coaching career, a 62-year-old Tikhonov, his eyes gleaming with tears, approached media after the 1992 gold-medal game and described having "the kind of joy I haven't experienced in a long time."

Despite the 1992 Olympic oversight, Larionov and Fetisov would finish their own storied careers with Detroit, where they would win back-to-back Stanley Cups in 1997 and 1998. In a fitting moment for two of the most epic careers in hockey history, Larionov and Fetisov were simultaneously handed the Cup by Detroit captain Steve Yzerman in 1997. Together, they skated around the ice with the Stanley Cup, punctuating a run of success that may never be matched in any sport.

While Fetisov and Larionov were winning their first Stanley Cup, Alexei Kasatonov was finding that old reputations die hard. After leaving the NHL in 1996, Kasatonov was tasked with helping to build the Russian Olympic hockey team for the upcoming Olympics in Nagano, Japan. But still associated in many Russian hockey circles with the Tikhonov era, Kasatonov had trouble finding players willing to join the national team. Fetisov and Larionov, who both still had a prickly relationship with their former Green Five comrade, passed on the opportunity, as did other established Russian stars like Sergei Zubov, Slava Kozlov, Alex Mogilny, and Nikolai Khabibulin. Despite missing many of their most iconic players, Russia won silver at the 1998 Olympics, losing 1–0 to the Czech Republic in the gold-medal game on a goal scored by Petr Svoboda.

After returning to Russia as a legend, Slava Fetisov was named Russia's minister of sport in 2002. By the time he became president of CSKA, the club was a privatized version of the fabled Central Red Army club. In one of his first tasks as president, Fetisov knew who to turn to when it came time to find a front-office compatriot. "He made me proposal to become vice president of Red Army club in Moscow. He is president, I am vice president. I say yes and we start to spend a lot of time together," says Alexei Kasatonov, who formally reconciled with his old friend at Fetisov's 50th birthday party in 2008. "He is boss, he is brother, he is everything."

As for Fetisov, he prefers not to discuss in any detail his friction with Tikhonov and Kasatonov, instead pointing out that he now considers both men good friends. But he isn't at all shy about reflecting on the awesome undertaking that was coming to New Jersey safely and legally. In his recollection, it was always the Soviet system that was his real enemy. "I wanted to do statement. I was the first Soviet citizen who got a work visa to the United States. I want to be clear, it was the official way, not defection from the country. I was first to fight for the human rights, to get freedom of choice for your life, and I'm very proud I did it," says Fetisov. "I fight for my freedom and democracy and my country. That's why I earned respect from my teammates and my country."

6

The Young Ones

Read the sports page tomorrow and you'll know what this was all about.

The dominant performance by the Soviets at the 1989 World Championship symbolized a crossroads for the Russian hockey program. In the Soviets' declaration of international hockey supremacy, the Green Five's imminent release from the national team happened to coincide with the emergence of a few young prospects considered the future of the national team. Although 20-year-old winger Alexander Mogilny registered only three points in 10 World Championship games, his center and good friend Sergei Fedorov was a shining star in the tournament with nine points in 10 games. With winger Pavel Bure making his mark with the national junior team, the Soviet hockey program appeared to have found the next iteration of the storied KLM line in a group it had started training three years earlier.

In the mid-1980s, as Fetisov and Larionov were beginning to lay their NHL plans bare to Soviet sports authorities, 16-year-old Alex Mogilny and 15-year-old Sergei Fedorov were being thrown into Central Red Army's training regimen. As the future of Soviet hockey, Fedorov and Mogilny also represented the widening grasp of the Soviet scouting network. Whereas the Green Five were all discovered in or around major Soviet urban centers, Fedorov and Mogilny had been found playing in more isolated regions. Fedorov was discovered more than 100 miles outside Moscow, near the Arctic, making him something of an anomaly. Mogilny, on the other hand, may as well have come from another planet. A native of Khabarovsk, a city so far east that it lies a mere 19 miles from the Chinese border, Mogilny had traveled further than practically any player in Central Red Army history. Traveling to Moscow from so far away at such a young age was daunting enough for the two teenagers. By the time they were subjected to the intense training regimen of the Red Army program, the immenseness of their hockey journey was just beginning to dawn on them. "That first week training was the toughest week I ever experienced in my life. I practiced right with the top team," says Fedorov. "Oh my God. The weights, off-ice training. We practically lifted in two and a half hours almost 30 tons of weights. That was just the morning session. Evening session, usually we would run long one-hour runs."

Almost two years later, amid criticisms that the Soviet hockey program was depleted, Viktor Tikhonov introduced the two 18-year-olds, Fedorov and Mogilny, along with 20-year-old winger Yevgeny Davidoff. The young group stormed out of the gate that 1986–87 season, their first with Central Red Army. While Fedorov's 12 points in 29 games were impressive for someone so young, Mogilny immediately found his scoring touch with Russia's most famous hockey club, scoring 15 goals in 28 games. That torrid scoring pace was enough to persuade Tikhonov to include Mogilny on the 1988 Olympic team. Ten days after his 19th birthday, with 5 points in 6 Olympic games, Mogilny became the youngest player in Soviet hockey history to win Olympic gold.

Mogilny was lucky enough to play a supporting role on the famous 1988 Olympic team, but his much-anticipated junior career with Fedorov got off to a considerably bumpier start. Playing in their first World Junior Championship in 1987, Fedorov and Mogilny were counted on to help the Soviet juniors repeat their gold-medal performance from the previous year. Fedorov failed to register a point in his six tournament games; Mogilny, on the other hand, was an immediate team leader, registering five points in six games. But none of that would matter in the tournament finale in Piestany, Czechoslovakia, against the Canadians. Entering the game with a disappointing 2–3–1 record, the Soviets were hoping to play spoiler to Canada, whose 4–1–1 record coming into the game guaranteed them at least a bronze medal in the round-robin tournament.

As play intensified in the third period, a fight broke out between Canada's Theoren Fleury and the Soviet Union's Pavel Kostichkin. Noticing the escalating fracas, Davidoff left his seat on the bench to engage in battle, leading to one of the most violent brawls in international hockey history. With both benches cleared, there wasn't a player on either team who was spared in the violent confrontation. In the aftermath, there was even word that a head butt from Soviet defender Vladimir Konstantinov had broken the nose of Canadian forward Greg Hawgood. The game was never completed and, after an emergency session held by the International Ice Hockey Federation, both teams were suspended from the tournament. As of 2012, it remains the only time in tournament history that neither Canada nor Russia placed in the top three.

The next year in Moscow, both teams returned to the tournament, with Canada narrowly edging out the Soviets for the gold medal. Although they had failed to avenge the 1987 punch-up in Piestany, Fedorov and Mogilny did manage to establish themselves as junior hockey stars. Both finished in the top four in tournament scoring and were named to the tournament All-Star team, with Mogilny's impressive 18 points earning him the tournament scoring title. The next year, this time accompanied by Bure, the Soviet Union's new powerhouse offense led a 7–2 thrashing of the Canadians, propelling the Russians to the 1989 World Junior Championship, their first gold at the tournament in three years. With Bure, Mogilny, and Fedorov all placing among the tournament's top six scorers, Soviet hockey was officially back. But the impending departure of the Green Five would soon open the eyes of the newest Soviet hockey stars, who had been thrown headfirst into the strenuous Tikhonov-led hockey program.

"That was hard living, a hard life. Not many times we spoke about past times, how we were in Soviet Union," says Fedorov. "The less I say about that, the easier it is. That was hard practices, weeks, months, years."

Fedorov learned about certain aspects of Soviet life long before becoming a part of the Soviet hockey program. During Stalin's time as leader of the Soviet government, Fedorov's grandfather allegedly disappeared, reemerging years later without any explanation as to where he had been. "I never spoke to my parents about it," says Fedorov. "Maybe I will someday."

While the Green Five was slowly starting to come apart, Fedorov and Mogilny were establishing themselves as two of the best young hockey players on the planet. By the time they both made the tournament All-Star team at the 1988 World Junior Championship, both were officially on every NHL team's radar. And so, in a 1988 NHL Draft that saw a record 11 Russians selected, Mogilny became the leader of a breakthrough pack when Buffalo selected him with their fifth-round pick, 89th overall—the highest a Russian player had ever been taken in the draft. Almost immediately, speculation swirled around how long it would take the Sabres to bring Mogilny to Buffalo. A number of NHL insiders, including Alan Eagleson, publicly stated that they had little to no faith that Mogilny would don a Sabres jersey anytime in the next decade. The Sabres had other plans.

"I remember watching and seeing how he could skate and handle the puck at top speed and beat guys one-on-one. I had never seen any player do it before. That caught my eye," says Don Luce, a Sabres assistant coach who had just been promoted as the team's head of player development when he first scouted Mogilny at the World Junior Championships. "He wasn't afraid of the physical part of the game. He would hit and take a hit and do things that at that time European players were supposedly not willing to do. I came back and I told the general manager that if we had a chance this coming draft, we should draft Alex. At that time, no one was taking them high because we didn't know if they were coming out or not. And no Russian had ever come out. The talent was so great that it was worth the risk."

The Sabres brass spent the following year looking for ways to bring their young Soviet prospect to Buffalo. But with the Soviet sporting authority spending much of its time battling its most established players over their NHL eligibility, negotiating the release of a youngster like Mogilny was impossible. With the Soviets' victorious 1989 World Junior Championship performance taking place in Anchorage, Alaska, Luce took full advantage of Mogilny competing on U.S. soil. During a down period between games for the Soviet team, Luce managed to track down Mogilny and hand over his business card, doing his best to transcend their language barrier and explain that the Sabres had drafted Mogilny seven months earlier. "I didn't know if he understood me or not. They had played earlier that afternoon. He played okay, but he hadn't scored a goal. So trying to make conversation I said, 'You didn't score a goal today.' He kind of smiled at me. It was funny. He was pretending he didn't speak English but he understood more than he let on," says Luce. "So the next game was against Canada and, as he was leaving, he said, 'I score tomorrow three.' And he did. They beat Canada and he scored three."

After Luce returned from Anchorage, his only real accomplishment may have been inspiring Mogilny's otherworldly performance as the Soviets captured gold at the 1989 World Junior Championship. But although Luce hadn't returned with the star winger, he had managed to plant the idea in Mogilny's head that defection might be his best option for coming to the National Hockey League. Considering the stories circulating about how the Green Five players would have to wait until they were in their 30s before earning the opportunity to play in the NHL, every indication was that the 20-year-old Mogilny would be waiting some time before he earned that same privilege. The young star was also growing exceedingly frustrated with the Soviet system, especially after he was allegedly denied a new Moscow apartment that he had been promised by the government. Mogilny was also growing tired of the intense training imposed on him by the Soviet hockey federation. He got to see his parents only 20 days out of the year, which wasn't much considering the travel involved in getting to Khabarovsk from Moscow. When Mogilny lobbied the government to give his parents an apartment closer to Moscow, he was reportedly greeted with laughter.

Four months after winning World Junior gold in Anchorage and with the Green Five on the verge of earning their right to come to North America, Mogilny and Fedorov accompanied the Soviet national team to the World Championship in Stockholm. They may not have been the focal point of the 1989 national team, but Fedorov and Mogilny helped the Soviets complete one of the most dominating performances in World Championship history. The tournament in Sweden was mostly regarded as the Green Five's final farewell before each player embarked on his NHL career, but it was ultimately remembered for Alex Mogilny's fateful decision to become the first Soviet hockey player in history to defect.

In the months leading up to the 1989 World Championship in Sweden, Mogilny's situation in the Soviet Union had deteriorated drastically. After engaging in a fight in a Soviet Elite League game, he was suspended for 10 days. In the ensuing fallout, the son of a trolley repairman was stripped of his "Master of Sports" order and docked a month's salary. Before long, Mogilny stopped keeping his intentions to defect a secret, telling one Soviet newspaper that he had no interest in serving in the Soviet military.

In the days leading up to the tournament, the Soviets sports offices received a phone call from an American woman asking about the national team. At the time, nobody thought anything of the strange call, but its significance would become more apparent in the coming days. "One American lady telephoned in 1989 when Mogilny defected. I was the only one in the federation office who could speak some English. So she asked where the Russian team was staying," says Lev Zarokhovich. "I told her the name of the hotel and that was it. There were so many phone calls, many people were asking the same question, so I didn't suspect anything."

In all likelihood, the woman on the phone was Teresa Harrington, a 23-year-old University of Alaska Anchorage biology major Mogilny met at the World Junior tournament in Anchorage. It is believed that the two developed a fondness for each other at the meeting, which may have contributed to Mogilny's decision to defect. In one of her few interviews, Harrington spoke with Mark Zwolinski of the *Toronto Star* in the days after Mogilny's defection. "I'm very proud of Alexander. He's a great athlete and he will make it in the U.S.," she told Zwolinski. "It [romance] had absolutely nothing to do with [the defection]. I think he did it for the sport, not so much for me."

But Harrington wasn't the first person to hear about Mogilny's intention to defect in Sweden. That distinction went to Sergei Fedorov, who after three years of moving up the Soviet hockey hierarchy had developed a close bond with Mogilny. The shocking reveal took place in the hotel room the two young hockey stars shared in Stockholm. Fedorov was dumbfounded. "He asked me if I wanted to go with him. But right away I said, 'Absolutely not.' I didn't know what was happening," says Fedorov. "I wasn't sure what would happen to my parents if I go. We would never [be able to] leave Russia for international competition. You don't discuss those things period, if you wanted to stay [on the team]."

Fedorov initially dismissed Mogilny's intentions as a bad joke, but Mogilny's plan shifted into high gear in the 48 hours following their secret conversation. After getting in touch with Sergei Formachev, a Soviet expat living in Sweden who had promised to help him contact the Sabres, Mogilny placed a phone call to Don Luce on May 4, 1989. It was 10 a.m. at the Buffalo Memorial Auditorium, where Luce was working at his desk, when the call came from Sweden. "I was told that Alex wanted to come over and play for us. To be honest, I was a little leery," says Luce. "So I asked to talk to Alex. He may not be able to answer back but I knew he would remember our conversation in Anchorage. I asked him a question about that conversation. Only Alex would know the answer to that question and he answered it, so I knew it was him. We were on a plane by one o'clock that afternoon. We got over there as fast as we could."

Accompanied by Sabres general manager Gerry Meehan, Luce had arranged to meet his young star at Formachev's home in Stockholm. But when they arrived, Luce and Meehan only found Formachev's Swedish wife. As a reward for their gold-medal performance, the Soviet team had been given some time to go shopping, so the mission to find Alex Mogilny took an unexpected turn. "We got a call at the house from Sergei, who was with Alex. He called us and let us know that it was a good time to pick them up," remembers Luce. "They were shopping at a mall. We just drove and picked them up at the mall. He had no luggage."

In any other situation, picking up someone at the mall wouldn't seem terribly difficult. But picking up a world-famous hockey player on the run from the Soviet national team was another story entirely. In an attempt to be as inconspicuous as possible, Meehan and Luce parked their car by a side entrance. By the time Mogilny and Formachev emerged, it was clear that they weren't alone. "They didn't walk out, they ran out. And some people came out behind them. I was the wheel man so we tailed it out of there," says Luce. "It was a side door and not well lit. We had the timing down so at exactly that time they would come out. They came out and jumped in the car and people came after them. I saw them in the mirror as we were driving away."

For the next few days, Mogilny and Formachev were spirited from hotel to hotel around town, and eventually Mogilny phoned his parents, who were shocked by his decision but encouraged him to follow his dream. While Mogilny occasionally spoke to Teresa Harrington on the phone, there were forces within Europe that were also trying to make contact with him. At different times in their navigation around Stockholm, Mogilny was paged at various locations by strangers Luce and Meehan believed to be KGB. The more they moved, the more apparent it became that Russian agents were only a few steps behind. "It was a remarkable strength he had, considering what could happen to him. Supposedly the KGB was after him. It was quite an experience to say the least," says Luce. "He was very upbeat, very determined, not down. A little bit worried, but not as much as you or I would have been in the situation. He was 20 years old. It was amazing how much determination and how much calmness was there."

While Meehan was enlisting the help of the consulate in Stockholm, Sabres assistant coach Craig Ramsay managed to get in touch with his neighbor and good friend Ben Ferro, who also happened to be the director of the Buffalo region for the Immigration and Naturalization Service. The high-profile case was a difficult one for Ferro, especially considering Mogilny's passport had been seized by Soviet authorities, but he wasn't completely unprepared for what would no doubt be a high-profile immigration case. Just six months earlier, he had been interviewed on television by Diane Sawyer about the case of Canadian writer Farley Mowat, who had been denied entry into the United States before boarding a flight from Toronto. "Craig [Ramsay] came over to my home after work and we had a hook up in Stockholm and talked to Gerry Meehan. They did know it was a serious thing because by this time he [Mogilny] had left the team and was being paged at the hotel and they were sure guys in fur coats were running around looking for them," says Ferro. "It was apparent the Soviets were not going to let him go easily. From an immigration standpoint, they had to find a way to get him on a plane. You need certain documents and he didn't have them with him at that point. Usually an embassy or consulate has to provide the airline with a travel document or certification and then they'll board him. Getting that done wasn't easy."

By the time Mogilny failed to meet his Soviet teammates at the Stockholm airport, officials had already acted quickly to learn the details of his defection and figure out his whereabouts. In his hotel room, Soviet officials had found only his bags and some letters and photos from Teresa Harrington, whom he allegedly called shortly before leaving. Coach Viktor Tikhonov immediately made a statement about Mogilny being lured by NHL riches, and Fedorov was quickly interrogated by Soviet authorities. With the Green Five still working on their own road to the NHL, the Soviet state news agency TASS accused the Sabres of "piracy" and claimed the incident might "harm relations between the Soviet Hockey Federation and the NHL."

"After Alexander left, there were some investigators trying to figure out why he left. I basically told them what I know. He said he was leaving and he left. I thought it was a joke, I didn't really believe him until he left," says Fedorov. "I didn't know anything. I just saw him in the room a couple of nights before he left. I didn't choose to tell anybody because I thought I would get in trouble for it."

Once Mogilny explained that he had willingly chosen to defect and faced potential persecution were he to return to the Soviet Union, especially considering he had just evaded his military service, the young defector received the proper paperwork to come to America. After Meehan got in touch with the Immigration and Naturalization Service's assistant commissioner in Washington, Mogilny was cleared to board a plane bound for the United States. "Two or three days later, I had a phone call after all the dust settled from a guy who identified himself as an undersecretary of state who said we had caused a major problem with U.S. government relations," says Ferro. "We gave him [Mogilny] protective custody under a program we had for people who defected at the time—making sure that during this period we had some control over anyone getting access to him. Just monitoring where he was, where he was going to be."

After being interviewed by the FBI at New York's JFK airport, Mogilny finally gained clearance to come to Buffalo, where he was granted parole, a special seven-day immigration stay handed out for humanitarian reasons. As a mob of reporters looked to greet Mogilny at the airport, a scheduled press conference was scrapped, Meehan claiming Mogilny was far too tired from the previous days' adventures to meet the press. The mass of journalists at the airport had grown so large in anticipation of Mogilny's arrival that the Sabres arranged for three cars to meet the group. Meehan took the wheel of one car, attracting much of the press's attention, while Luce secretly drove Mogilny to his home in suburban Buffalo. With his Sabres contract finalized and the Soviet military allegedly seeking the young star's extradition back to the Soviet Union, Mogilny spent the next few months living with Luce and his family. "In May, Alex got up one morning and it was actually snowing. He doesn't know English [very well], but he turned to me and said, 'I thought I left Siberia,'" says Luce. "My wife [Diane] and Alex became very close. Alex's mother said my wife was Alex's second mother. They had a very close relationship, and Diane did a lot of taking him shopping, showing him the ropes, and helping him out whenever she could. It was funny, she always thought if you talked louder he might understand better. He would laugh and smile at that."

Mogilny wasn't privy to most of the details at that time, but the backlash against him had already begun in Russia. Tikhonov told the Russian publication *Sovietsky Sport* that "Mogilny's decision not to return to the motherland together with his team provokes nothing but disgust."

Quoted by the youth newspaper *Komsomolskaya Pravda*, Mogilny's mother Nadezhda said, "I don't have words to express what we have lived through. Our eyes are still wet with tears. We have aged many years. Our son is not right."

To his credit, Mogilny wasn't shy when it came to firing back at his Soviet critics. When reporters asked him about Tikhonov's critiques, Mogilny wasted no time exercising his newfound freedom of expression. "Only his wife and his dog like him. And I do not understand how they do," Mogilny said of Tikhonov to the press. "I didn't want to wait 10 years of my life and destroy my health waiting to be released to play in the NHL. They play for garbage in the Soviet Union. You play for nothing, and what they give you won't buy anything anyway. You cannot get laundry detergent in the stores anymore. And because the people use sugar to make liquor, you cannot find sugar either. And they think things were changing. I did not see the changes."

But there had been one semi-approving voice from behind the Iron Curtain. Just weeks away from making his own move to the NHL, Igor Larionov had expressed neither approval nor consternation, but it was clear that he understood Mogilny's decision. "I don't defend him, but I also don't want to be [critical]. One has his own sense of duty and patriotism," Larionov told a Soviet newspaper. "Mogilny is not much of a military man, but a youngster who was forced to join the army. It's easy for a player of the Red Army and the Soviet national team to become an officer. But it's quite a problem to be discharged."

An army lieutenant at the time of his defection, Mogilny would soon be charged with desertion in his home country, but considering the United States had no extradition agreement with the Soviet Union, the charges weren't much of an issue. By the time Sabres training camp came around near the end of the summer, local media gained more access to the young winger and learned about how his plans to defect had come together. How he took issue with having only one 20-day period a year to visit his remote hometown and see his family and how he had taken to Western culture and even started wearing cowboy boots from time to time.

As he entered his first NHL training camp, the youngest NHL defector in history benefited from something none of the previous Eastern Europeans who came to the NHL enjoyed. Sabres rookie head coach Rick Dudley was one of the few bench bosses in the league who had experienced the other side of the Iron Curtain firsthand as a player. In 1977, when Dudley was playing for the Cincinnati Stingers of the World Hockey Association, his training camp took place in several European countries, including Czechoslovakia. "The special police were there and one of our players, Dennis Abgrall, was arrested for taking a picture. All he did was take a picture of a building, which had an entrance into this special police department, and he got arrested for that and we had to go through some hoops to get him out. It was interesting," says Dudley. "I was mostly vegetarian at the time and that was something that was completely unheard of over there."

On a Sabres team that already featured stars like Pierre Turgeon, Dave Andreychuk, and Phil Housley, there was no shortage of talent in Buffalo. But with a reputation for occasionally being selfish and arrogant, Mogilny made an instant impression on his first NHL coach. "He was a brutally honest guy. I was his head coach and he was telling me how little he was looking forward to training camp. On one side it worried me a little bit, but on the other side his ability to be candid was amazing," says Dudley. "Alex was very interesting. Very bright, incredibly talented. Everything was new to him. All of a sudden he had money and his philosophy was to enjoy what you had. And he did. He bought fancy cars and he did all that, but Alex was a guy that I really liked personally."

"How far did you live from Moscow?" Dudley asked in one of his first conversations with Mogilny.

"Eight hours," the Soviet rookie replied.

"That's a pretty good drive," said Dudley.

"No, that's by plane," said Mogilny.

Living with the Luce family, Mogilny was able to learn English and adapt to Western culture rather quickly. The Luces even managed to keep Mogilny shielded from the prying eyes of the hockey-mad Buffalo press, although the occasional reporter did end up on Don Luce's front lawn from time to time. Perhaps most importantly, Mogilny liked chicken wings, Buffalo's resident comfort food. As for any concerns about Mogilny's attitude, they were immediately resolved when he scored in his first exhibition game in Buffalo. The goal elicited a standing ovation from the Sabres faithful and, with three goals and three assists in his first four NHL exhibition games, Mogilny became a star in his new home practically overnight. Red tape momentarily delayed his asylum process, but by the beginning of the 1989–90 NHL season, he was granted political asylum in the United States and all immigration matters were settled in the case of Alex Mogilny.

After starting his time in western New York with the Luce family, Mogilny took some time to go on trips to New York City and Disney World before moving into a pleasant townhouse next door to teammate and fast friend Christian Ruuttu. Sergei Formachev and his wife soon came to live with him, Sergei immediately becoming Mogilny's interpreter and agent. An intensive six-week language course improved his grasp on English and, with the exception of a single visit from KGB agents, his family in Russia was spared any hard government reprisal. When the season finally started, Mogilny decided to don the number 89, in honor of the year he defected.

It didn't take long for Buffalo to fall in love with Alex Mogilny. Just 20 seconds into his first NHL shift, Mogilny scored, leading the Sabres to a 4–3 win over the Quebec Nordiques. Dudley's immediate reviews of Mogilny after the game couldn't have been more positive. "He's going to be a star in the league," the coach told reporters.

Despite eight other Soviets playing in the National Hockey League, including recent arrivals Fetisov, Larionov, and Makarov, Mogilny remained an anomaly. For one thing, he was a decade younger than his NHL countrymen, who played the game in a less brazen fashion and with a greater sense of subtlety and wisdom. Playing 11 time zones away from his family near Manchuria, Mogilny was unleashed on his NHL opposition. "It's a very difficult thing oftentimes for someone that talented, whether they're from North America or Europe, to understand that there is a parallel between the collective good and the individual good," says Dudley. "He [Mogilny] wanted to be a star. But it was on his terms."

That kind of defiant attitude from a young Soviet could be problematic. Especially in a National Hockey League still coming to terms with the arrival of more and more players from behind the Iron Curtain. Most of these players were ultimately accepted by teammates despite a precedent that saw newly-arrived Russians and Czechoslovakians bear the brunt of some leery players, coaches, and front-office figures.

"Slava had a very, very difficult time. He had to adjust to the game, and the reception he received not only from his teammates but also from other teams and other owners was just a disgrace," Lamoriello remembers of Fetisov's arrival in North America. "A lot of slander in the papers and people saying things. Some things that were done on the ice. He overcame all of that. He's a remarkable man. His character is just impeccable."

That hesitancy to fully accept Europeans wasn't isolated to Czechoslovakians and Russians. By now, the National Hockey League had witnessed players from other countries given a less-than-warm welcome upon their arrival in North America. That frosty reception would remain a part of hockey culture until the late 1990s, by which time foreign players, and Eastern Europeans in particular, were fully integrated into the League.

"The one guy owed more credit than anybody else, and I coached him his last year in Detroit, is [Hall of Fame Swedish defenseman] Borje Salming. That guy paid a huge price," says former Red Wings coach Jacques Demers. "He took everything physically that people threw at him. He was physically manhandled. They took the lumber to him, they hit him and he stood tall. Those people who complain about Europeans better wake up because the National Hockey League is as great as it is today because of the presence of Europeans."

Although Mogilny acclimated remarkably well to Buffalo, there was the occasional hiccup in his development. Shortly before his first road game in Toronto, Mogilny went to the wrong hotel to meet his teammates and missed the team bus. Forced to drive himself the 100 miles to Toronto in his Jeep Laredo, Mogilny was spotted by a friend of Ruuttu's, who led him the rest of the way to the arena. It was Mogilny's first time driving into Canada.

In January, Mogilny's rookie season was complicated by the arrival of the Dynamo Moscow club in Buffalo to play an exhibition game against the Sabres. Months earlier, Soviet officials had threatened to call off the 21-game series between Russian and NHL clubs over Mogilny's defection. So, at the request of NHL president John Ziegler, Meehan and the Sabres eventually agreed to withhold Mogilny from their roster for the exhibition game against Dynamo, which Buffalo won 4–2. "This was kind of a mutual decision to avoid embarrassment to anyone," Ziegler told Joe LaPointe of the *New York Times*. "There were all kinds of problems."

Mogilny had adapted well to his new surroundings and endeared himself to his teammates, but the first cracks in his cool exterior emerged just a few weeks after the Dynamo game. Before boarding a flight to St. Louis to play the Blues, Mogilny suddenly froze, admitting to the Sabres that he suffered from a debilitating fear of flying. Somehow, this phobia had never come up before. The Sabres would lose the road game in St. Louis, but the question of how to resolve the flying situation would prove to be the real dilemma for Buffalo management.

With Mogilny unable to fly, media speculation began to swirl about the star winger leaving the Sabres after just four months with the team. It was later revealed how a "stomach virus" that had caused Mogilny to miss five games earlier in the season was really his fear of flight. A story in the *Buffalo News* claimed Mogilny even went as far as to tell teammates that he was done playing with the Sabres. On some flights leading up to the St. Louis incident, Mogilny rode in the cockpit with the pilots, but this did little to resolve his fears. Rick Dudley had battled his own fear of flying and could relate to Mogilny's problems, but there was nothing he could say to help him. Looking to eliminate any and all rumors of Mogilny's departure, the Sabres took swift action. "We had a driver a couple of times," says Luce. "Back then, American Airlines had a course for people who were afraid of flying. He took this course to alleviate a lot of the fears."

Mogilny was given a medical leave of absence, during which he celebrated his 21st birthday before returning after a couple of weeks. He used the driver to help him get from game to game, then sought out a Russian-speaking psychologist. The story of Mogilny's fear of flying eventually became so widespread that the Sabres began fielding constant calls from experts offering to assist their grounded star. They even received a call from the American Automobile Association, which offered to route all the driving trips for Mogilny, who would go two months without boarding another plane. In one case, he was driven 13 hours from Buffalo to St. Louis for a game. It wasn't the most convenient arrangement, but he was back on the team and making a contribution, with a goal and an assist in his first three games back.

Mogilny overcame his fears to post a modest 43 points in 65 games during his rookie campaign. The next season, Mogilny broke out with 64 points in 62 games, and by his fourth NHL go-round, Mogilny exploded, cementing his superstar status with a remarkable 76-goal 1992–93 season, the fifth highest total in league history. But with that superstardom came some unexpected problems.

In 1994, five years after he assisted in Alex Mogilny's defection, Sergei Formachev began asking for financial compensation. The two countrymen had gone their separate ways years earlier, but according to an investigation conducted by the U.S. Attorneys' office, Formachev followed Mogilny after a Sabres practice in March 1994, meeting him at a Russian restaurant and allegedly threatening to shoot or stab the Sabres star if he wasn't paid $150,000. Mogilny immediately went to the police, where he explained the extortion attempt and stayed home rather than play in the next Sabres game. When questioned by police, Formachev claimed his name was Pavlovsky and handed over a passport that was later proven to be a fake. After being charged with attempted grand larceny, Mogilny's former friend pleaded guilty to visa fraud and was later deported back to Sweden.

In the years following the extortion attempt, Mogilny expressed reticence about discussing his personal life. In a 1995 interview with Iain MacIntyre of the *Vancouver Sun,* Mogilny gave one of his most heartfelt confessions regarding the details of his amazing life in North America. "I don't like talking about my past," he admitted to MacIntyre. "People are always looking for something to get their hands on. It's a cruel world out there and you have to be careful what you say. I don't like talking about my personal life."

Fortunately for Mogilny, while Sergei Formachev was making his way back to Sweden, another Sergei was adapting to

Western life and becoming reacquainted with his old friend
and teammate.

• • •

Sergei Fedorov had refused Alex Mogilny's request in Sweden to
accompany him to Buffalo. But the exchange had made the idea
of defection increasingly viable for the young Soviet centerman.
By the time he was drafted by the Detroit Red Wings in 1989,
Fedorov had begun putting together a concrete plan for defection. But it wouldn't be easy for one of the most high-profile
young athletes in the Soviet Union.

The first real opportunity for Fedorov to make his move took
place six months after the Wings drafted him in the fourth round
of the 1989 NHL Draft, at that point the highest a Soviet player
had ever been taken, besting his friend Alex Mogilny's fifth-
round selection. That same draft also saw the Wings take one
of Fedorov's Soviet teammates, imposing defenseman Vladimir
Konstantinov, in the 11th round. Fresh off a dominating performance at both the 1989 World Championship and World
Juniors, Fedorov would be joining the Central Red Army club
for an exhibition tour of several NHL cities. Four days after Alex
Mogilny sat and watched the Sabres defeat Dynamo Moscow 4–2
on January 3, 1990, Fedorov and the Red Army team descended
on Chicago for a game against the Blackhawks. Shortly after
the 6–4 CSKA win, Red Wings president Jim Lites had Fedorov
whisked away to a room at the Drake hotel, where he engaged
the 21-year-old Fedorov for the first time.

In their room at the Drake, Lites introduced himself to the
young recruit, explaining that he was representing the Detroit
Red Wings, the team that owned Fedorov's NHL rights. This

was all communicated to Fedorov with the help of Michel Ponomarev, a Soviet contact who had tracked down Fedorov on the Wings' behalf. It was there that, equipped with a contract and a briefcase containing $10,000 cash, Lites asked Fedorov to defect immediately. Fedorov refused. "I remember those times very well, I had to sneak out to meet him," says Fedorov. "It was an exciting meeting."

"If you sign, this is yours and we'll give you a car and an apartment. Here's your contract for life," Lites beckoned. "Walk away right now."

"I can't do it," Fedorov replied. "I'm here, I'm committed to playing, and I'm not out of the army yet."

"It was a good thing he didn't leave. Because he would have been a deserter because he still had a military obligation," remembers Lites. "He was a nice kid, and we probably met for two hours. I had photographs of a beautiful Corvette, and of riverfront apartments next to Joe Louis Arena and a note from [Wings captain] Steve Yzerman."

Lites gave Fedorov $1,000 for his trouble. Before returning to his team's hotel, the young Russian star revealed he would make his move that summer. In the months that followed, Fedorov completed his military requirements and, after a ho-hum World Championship performance that saw the Soviets take bronze, began preparing for his defection.

That July, the Soviet national team ventured to the Pacific Northwest for the Goodwill Games, the second iteration of the athletic exhibition founded by media tycoon Ted Turner. The largest gathering of Soviets at an American sporting event in a century, it was supposed to be the final stop for the national team after a series of exhibition games against the U.S. national team. Then, without warning between 11 p.m. and midnight in

Portland, after a 5–3 Soviet win over the Americans, Fedorov disappeared. One of the few public statements on the abrupt disap-
pearance came courtesy of Richard Smith, district director for the
federal Immigration and Naturalization Service in Seattle. "We
are aware he is not with the team," Smith told reporters. USA
Hockey spokesman Mike Schroeder barely clarified the incident,
telling reporters that the Soviets "have no idea where he's at."

The next day, Fedorov surfaced in Detroit with an NHL contract. It was then that the details of Fedorov's defection began
to emerge. Around the fourth of July holiday, Lites received a
call from Ponomarev saying that Fedorov would be looking to
defect the next month while competing at the Goodwill Games.
A month later, Lites received his follow-up call. "Two days from
now he's going to be playing in Portland, Oregon, in an exhibition," Lites was told. "He'll leave that night and come to Detroit
to play for the Red Wings."

Almost immediately, Lites enlisted the help of Nick Polano,
who by now had become his go-to traveling companion for these
very types of missions. The two boarded Mike Ilitch's private jet
and met Ponomarev, who flew into Portland from Montreal. Lites,
Ponomarev, and Polano discovered the Soviet hockey team staying at a small airport hotel and the Wings' brass straight away
booked a room near Fedorov's. Lites and Polano actually attended
what would be Fedorov's last game for the Soviets, leaving halfway
through to go meet Ponomarev back at the hotel. By the time the
Soviet team returned to the hotel, Lites, Polano, and Ponomarev
were all together. Wearing a fancy black suit that contrasted
sharply with his teammates' scruffy postgame attire, Fedorov
walked into the hotel with his team, taking just a moment to
spot Lites. It was then that Fedorov, who had spent time on his
own learning limited English, told Lites that he was ready to go.

"The way we worked it out was Sergei would leave his suit-case on top of the bed when he was leaving his room. His suitcase would be on the top of his bed fully packed. He would then come to Michel's room and put the [room] key under the door. Michel would go up and get his suitcase and put it in the car," says Lites. "Our driver in the car would be outside and he [Fedorov] would just follow me out the door, and we would be on the plane back to Detroit as soon as we could. In two minutes, we were at the airport, on the plane, ready to go. So that's the story."

The car in this case happened to be a limo, which Lites and Polano had reserved. While Lites and Ponomarev waited for Fedorov in the Portland hotel, Nick Polano agonized in the limo, its driver eyeing him curiously.

"He should be coming off that bus and we'll get him out of here," Polano kept assuring the driver, who eventually felt comfortable enough to start asking questions.

"Are you doing something stupid here?" asked the curious driver, who had simply been hired through the limo rental company. "What are you guys doing? Is this a hit on somebody?"

"We're just picking somebody up," a frustrated Polano replied.

Everyone eventually piled into the limousine and, once they arrived at the airport for their flight to Detroit, Jim Lites thanked the nosy driver with a monstrous tip. As everyone exited the car, Lites momentarily poked his head back into the limo to address the driver. "Read the sports page tomorrow and you'll know what this was all about," he said.

With their second high-profile defection in five years, Lites and Polano began to gain something of a reputation around the league for their international exploits. If nothing else, their experience with Petr Klima had taught them a number of lessons that they looked to apply with Fedorov. "That [Klima's defection] was something new that not too many people had ever done. [After that] we knew we could get it done," says Polano. "Mr. Ilitch always said, 'I don't care if it costs us money, we just want to improve this hockey team.' He would do whatever it took to improve that team. He made his pilots and private jets available to us, and that really helped a lot. I was the hockey guy, but Jimmy Lites was a big help, being a lawyer and everything. They were exciting times."

Having learned from some of the problems Petr Klima encountered, the Wings bought Fedorov a condo near Joe Louis Arena and surrounded him with people to help him transition to North American life. Foremost among them was Alex Gertsmark, a longtime Chrysler employee and Red Wings fan who immigrated from what is now Latvia in 1977. Upon hearing the news of Fedorov's defection, Gertsmark called a friend of his who happened to work in the Wings' public relations department. In that short conversation, he was asked to come to Joe Louis Arena at once. "So I went over there, and there was Sergei sitting in the office and they cannot communicate. The coach, [former Capitals bench boss] Bryan Murray, was there. Jim Lites was there. I think [Wings GM] Jim Devellano was there. Somehow we started communicating," says Gertsmark. "That was a little awkward, that meeting. Everybody was sitting there and nobody knew what was happening."

"I really need you to explain to him what's going on," Lites told Gertsmark just moments after he entered the room.

"Whatever I can do," Gertsmark replied.

After helping Fedorov and the Wings negotiate the first NHL contract for the team's newest arrival, Gertsmark was enlisted to help Sergei acclimate to Detroit. First and foremost, that meant going to Saks and adding to the young center's meager wardrobe. From there, he helped Fedorov buy his first car, a Jeep Cherokee, before taking him to the Detroit Auto Show the following month. From that point on, Gertsmark became an important aide in Fedorov's new life. The two spoke several times a week over the phone, and Fedorov was a constant visitor to the Gertsmark household, usually dropping by in the evening to enjoy traditional Russian meals. "He was crazy about Nintendo. He loved the Nintendo. He liked music, he liked MTV," remembers Gertsmark. "He would never want to appear like something surprises him. Mr. Cool, you know? Been there, seen that. He's unbelievably street smart, so he didn't need much coaching from me. Detroit loved him. The minute he took the ice, Joe Louis Arena just exploded."

Fedorov adapted well to life in Detroit. Being young and unencumbered by a wife or girlfriend may have helped, although there was the occasional gaffe that young foreigners could be prone to. A month into his first season in Detroit, the Wings were running through Montreal's Dorval airport when teammate and fellow rookie Per Djoos set off the metal detector while going through Security. Attempting to bring some levity to the situation, Fedorov joked in English that Djoos was carrying a bomb. Almost immediately, Security grabbed Fedorov and Djoos and interrogated them both. Having learned about the seriousness of airport security, Fedorov joined his teammates shortly thereafter for their flight to Vancouver.

Fedorov took to Detroit quite naturally. but it was some time before he got in touch with his family. The circuitous Soviet telephone network required multiple operators, so contacting Fedorov's parents in their remote Russian village was difficult. As a result, it was almost two months before Fedorov spoke with his mother and father, who had never shared a proper goodbye with their son before his defection. "Nothing really happened to them. Only some things were moved around the apartment when they weren't home. I'm sure their phone was tapped," says Fedorov. "They noticed small changes in the apartment, how it looked. They didn't give me details. It was not their favorite thing to talk about. Even now, as they get older. We just don't talk about it."

It would be even longer before he made contact with his old friend and confidant Alex Mogilny. Despite the fact that they were both competing in the National Hockey League, the intense strain of their respective defections had made communication difficult. "You know, I had no contact with Alexander until we met in Buffalo before a game," says Fedorov. "For us, we still didn't want to let anybody know that we were meeting. We kept it under a Cold War atmosphere. [It's] just the way Soviet people think. The less people see or know, the better it is."

With 14 points in his first 14 NHL games, Fedorov immediately made his mark on the league, and after posting 79 points in his rookie season, he was a bona fide NHL star. His smooth transition had also given the Red Wings ample confidence about their abilities to bring other Russians to Detroit and help them acclimate.

Emboldened by Fedorov's arrival, they spent their third-round pick at the 1990 NHL Draft on Soviet winger Slava Kozlov, an incredibly high pick for a Russian, even if the Soviet government was on the verge of collapse. The following year, the Wings' front office could read the tea leaves and, two months before an August coup attempt that would eventually lead to the end of the Soviet Union, the Wings selected two more Russians, defensemen Dmitri Motkov and Igor Malykhin, at the 1991 draft.

When the Wings started looking to bring Vladimir Konstantinov to Detroit, Gertsmark was again enlisted to help.

• • •

Most people within the Soviet Union seemed to understand the pleas from the Green Five to come to the NHL, yet the defections of Mogilny and Fedorov seemed to inspire shock through much of the country. After all, Fetisov and Larionov had served the Soviet national team for over a decade before finally arriving in the NHL. Mogilny and Fedorov, on the other hand, were teenagers when they defected, an act long considered unheard of among Soviet hockey players. Regardless of the public response to these defections, there were signs of a changing tide in Soviet politics. "The reaction of media and public at large was one of disdain but not of sharp condemnation or criticism. Many took it as an egotistic move by the players in question. But Hockey Russia leaders had to live with it," Lev Zarokhovich wrote in a personal e-mail. "A friend who was chef de mission in Fedorov's case was strictly reprimanded and had other problems on return, but nothing really serious ensued. The Soviet state system was falling. The 'old' [i.e., Soviet] sports system was effectively demolished."

Five months after Sergei Fedorov's defection, his former Soviet club, Central Red Army, arrived in Detroit to play the Red Wings as part of what was now becoming an annual tour of NHL arenas. Leading up to the game, Soviet authorities had momentarily threatened to call off the exhibition tour and even sue the Red Wings for what they characterized as a gross violation of Soviet labor law. But with lots of money on the line in the exhibition series, Central Red Army and another Soviet club, Khimik Voskresensk, embarked on their Christmastime tour of the NHL.

The terms of the Soviet tour of the NHL were resolved, but a series of games featuring NHL teams in the Soviet Union months earlier had renewed tensions between the NHL and Soviet officials. In a September 3–2 overtime loss to the Central Red Army squad in Moscow, Montreal Canadiens coach Pat

Burns called his team off the ice for some 10 minutes after Russian fans began pelting the playing surface with coins and vodka bottles following a brawl involving several players. Upon his team's return to Montreal, Canadiens general manager Serge Savard cautioned other NHL teams against playing in the Soviet Union. "Going there didn't do much to prepare us for the regular season. All that travel did nothing for us. It hurt us. The frustration and the accommodations left us mentally tired," Savard told reporters. "I'm trying to think of one good reason for a team to go. I can't."

By the time Central Red Army arrived in Detroit on December 26, 1990, Fedorov was put on full display. His friend Alex Mogilny having been held from a similar exhibition game a year earlier, Fedorov now starred against his former teammates, scoring a goal and notching the winning goal in a shootout exhibition staged before the final period that didn't figure in the final score. Despite the Soviet club humbling the Wings, beating them 5–2, Fedorov had made his mark by excelling under awkward competitive circumstances.

While most of the attention centered on Fedorov's play against his former comrades, behind the scenes, the Wings were looking to bring Soviet defenseman Konstantinov to Detroit. Although not blessed with outstanding height or reach, the burly defenseman, with his low, sloping forehead, piercing blue eyes, and flattened nose, had by then cultivated a reputation as one of the toughest and most imposing rearguards in the world. After emerging from Murmansk, a small port 150 miles north of the Arctic Circle, Konstantinov became famous—and hated—for drawing outside the lines when it came to hockey's rule book. By making sure to lift his elbow or his stick just a little bit higher, he infuriated the opposing team's best players. With his deceptive speed, he could absolutely crush an unsuspecting opponent with a well-timed hit. A signature Konstantinov sneer was sometimes all that was needed to throw the opposition off their game. When the Green Five was finally dismantled, it was Konstantinov who replaced Fetisov on the top Soviet defensive pairing alongside Kasatonov. *Sports Illustrated*'s David Fleming famously called him the Vladinator.

After a practice the day of the game at Joe Louis Arena, Gertsmark got in touch with Konstantinov and arranged for him to escape from the team hotel while his teammates took a mid-afternoon nap. "I remember it was difficult to find parking by the hotel. So I pulled right into the front, gave the doorman 20 bucks, and I said, 'I need to park here for five minutes,'" says Gertsmark. "I went to the lobby and I see Konstantinov come out of the elevator wearing sweatpants. I asked, 'What did you tell your [teammate]?' He said, 'I told him I'm going to get something from the candy machine.' So we jumped in my van and three minutes later we were in the Red Wings office."

Konstantinov was handed a jacket to help him combat the December Detroit chill and Gertsmark delivered the defenseman to Jim Lites's office, where the parties negotiated the particulars of Konstantinov's NHL contract. Konstantinov did not defect that day and by September, with the Communist government no longer ruling Russia, the team had arranged other meetings with Konstantinov. Their most notable meeting occurred outside Turku, Finland, where Konstantinov was forced to sneak out of his team hotel to meet Nick Polano and Jim Lites in the dark woods surrounding the area. Red Wings brass had also come to the tournament to inquire into the availability of another of their prospects, a Swedish defenseman named Nicklas Lidstrom. But this meeting with Konstantinov also introduced a new member of the Wings' family to the world of hockey espionage. Bryan Murray, Michal Pivonka's first NHL coach in Washington, had been hired as head coach of the Wings the previous year and, in his first act of international intrigue, accompanied Lites and Polano to meet Konstantinov in Finland.

"What the hell are we doing here, Nick?" Murray asked Polano as they entered the woods in Finland. "Are you crazy?"

With a wife and child, the 23-year-old Konstantinov required more planning for his arrival in Detroit. Lites eventually pieced together a plan to meet his prized defenseman as well as Russian intermediary Valeri Medveev at the airport in Moscow before bringing him to America. As part of their plan, Medveev and Lites had agreed on a deal in which Lites sent $25,000 cash and a car to Russia. In exchange, two days before Konstantinov was scheduled to arrive in Detroit, Medveev would bribe a military tribunal and have Konstantinov falsely diagnosed with terminal cancer to get him dismissed from his military service. By now, the slow crumbling of the Soviet political infrastructure had made these kinds of bribes more common. Thanks to the covert palm-greasing, the stage was set for Konstantinov's escape. But in a country that was now dealing with a cavernous power vacuum, things wouldn't go as smoothly as expected.

On August 18, 1991, just days before Vladimir Konstantinov was expected to leave the Soviet Union for Detroit, the hard-line members of the Soviet Union's Communist Party staged a coup against Mikhail Gorbachev, the Soviet president. In a matter of hours, the military placed barricades throughout Moscow. Before long, tanks began storming toward the White House, the Russian parliamentary building. It was there that they were confronted by Boris Yeltsin, who months later would become the first president of the new Russian state. In an incredible act of civil resistance, a number of Russian citizens confronted the tanks by forming a human wall around the building. Yeltsin was involved in the human barricade, as was Slava Fetisov, who was spending that summer in Moscow with his family. After Fetisov's on-ice exploits and battles with his government, his participation in staring down these tanks in the failed coup cemented his place in Russian history. Meanwhile, in Detroit, Jim Lites was trying to figure out how to get Vladimir Konstantinov to America.

"There was an attempted coup, so they shut down the airport. I said, 'Well, we've got to get him out because God knows what will happen if the military takes over. The door will close on Konstantinov,'" says Lites. "So he [Medveev] took them by train to Budapest and I got Mr. Ilitch's plane, grabbed an immigration lawyer in Washington, and flew to Budapest . . . to pick up Vladi, his wife, and his kid."

The mission to bring the Vladinator to Detroit had its share of twists and turns, but getting Konstantinov and his family on Mike Ilitch's jet hadn't been too dangerous. If anything, the scariest moment of the entire trip occurred when Polano, who per usual had accompanied Lites overseas, fell asleep on the flight back to America. "I was asleep on the jet. I woke up and opened one eye and glanced over at the cockpit and saw him [Konstantinov] sitting up there," remembers Polano. "I thought, 'Holy cow, what is going on?' I said to the pilot, 'What the heck?' He said, 'He's not doing anything, it's on automatic pilot.' I thought he was flying the plane!"

A few months after Konstantinov came to Detroit, the Soviet Union collapsed, along with its central sports committee, Gossport. Just like that, 25,000 world-class athletes and 1,200 coaches were completely cut off from government resources. There was even speculation that the Soviet Olympic Committee would not have enough money to send its delegation to the 1992 Summer Olympics in Barcelona. Without a central sports federation to train them, Russian athletes immediately started leaving for other countries. Soccer star Andrei Kanchelskis signed with Manchester United, while boxer Konstantin Tszyu fled for Australia.

The medical diagnosis that helped Vladimir Konstantinov leave the Russian military had been forged, but a very real and very scary medical emergency would arise that had the potential to halt the career of another coveted Red Wings' prospect. Shortly after the Konstantinovs arrived in Detroit, Lites and Polano received word that another prized Russian prospect, Slava Kozlov, had been involved in a fatal car accident. The highest Russian draft pick in Wings history, Kozlov had been driving to practice with a teammate when he lost control of the vehicle and slammed into a Moscow bus. The passenger, 17-year-old defenseman Kirile Tarasov, died in the accident and Kozlov was in a Russian hospital bed with various injuries, including a fractured skull, broken cheekbone, and several broken ribs. At the time of the accident, the expectation had been that Kozlov would be allowed to leave for Detroit after the 1992 Olympics, which were staged three months later in Albertville, France. But with a teammate dead and his playing career possibly in jeopardy, there was more at stake than just goals and assists.

Immediately upon hearing of the accident, Polano volunteered to go to Moscow and visit Kozlov. Medveev was able to track down exactly where Kozlov was nursing his severe injuries and arranged for Polano to meet the young winger. For the veteran Wings employee, it was a turning point in a long history with the young Russian star.

Polano had been insistent that the Wings draft Kozlov from the moment he first saw the flashy winger play as a 16-year-old.

Competing in an under-18 tournament in Lake Placid, Kozlov had actually faced off against a Team U.S.A. featuring Polano's son, Mike. "They didn't give us any information on the players. So the scouts didn't know any of these guys," says Polano. "After the last game, they were having a pizza party with the U.S. team and the Russians. I told my son, 'Make sure you get this guy's name for me.'"

Two years later, Polano met with Kozlov at a tournament in Saskatchewan. Hearing that Kozlov liked his car, Polano let the young prospect take the wheel in the hotel parking lot. Peeling through the lot in the rented Toyota 4Runner in sub-zero temperatures was a bonding experience for scout and player. But later that afternoon, when Polano asked Kozlov to defect, Kozlov refused. Not sure how to proceed, the Wings eventually offered Central Red Army $300,000 for Kozlov's rights. They flatly refused the offer.

Polano first learned about the car accident through a phone call from Kozlov's agent, Paul Theofanis. As Polano came to grips with the horrible news, Theofanis made a statement that would prompt the Red Wing executive to immediately book his flight to Moscow.

"Nick," Theofanis told Polano. "The father would like to meet with you."

By the time Polano touched down in Moscow, two team contacts in Russia had not only tracked down the hospital Kozlov was staying in but also bribed the hospital guards to allow Polano to visit. After years of covert meetings in dangerous settings, Polano was caught completely off guard by the scene he was entering. "I wore a black winter coat, black slacks. We walked through the gate, guards there had guns. It scared the hell out of me. I was given instructions not to speak English. As far as they knew I was just another Russian guy," says Polano, who was escorted through the hospital into Kozlov's room. "He seemed to be really happy that I was there. He didn't look very good, he had all his injuries. His father and his sister were there with him."

After the painful meeting with Slava Kozlov, Polano went to a nearby restaurant to have dinner with the young player's father and sister. It was then that Kozlov's father, who had coached Slava with Khimik of the Elite League, told Polano that his son was ready to go. Almost immediately, Polano told Jim Lites to make arrangements to secure Kozlov's visa to come to Detroit.

Kozlov's father didn't simply want his son brought to Detroit to pursue an NHL career. Still shaken up by the car accident, he expressed serious concerns about the quality of the medical care Slava was receiving. The hope was that going to Detroit would not just open a new chapter in Kozlov's hockey career but also give him access to some of the world's finest medical care as he recovered from serious injuries. By the time Jim Lites took the necessary steps to finally bring Slava Kozlov to Detroit, the country formerly known as the Soviet Union had found a very different recourse in combating the Wings.

For years, the Soviets had combated defection with surveillance and intimidation. A constant KGB presence around Soviet hockey teams had become so common that players referred to each of these agents as Vasil Vasilivich, a generic Russian name that was effectively the Soviet equivalent of "John Doe." This time around, when encountering the startling departure of one of their best hockey players, Russian sporting officials didn't resort to intimidation tactics. In the case of Slava Kozlov, they simply sued the Red Wings.

Kozlov was already in Detroit healing and slowly making his way onto the Red Wings' roster when a lawsuit filed by the

Central Red Army team arrived in U.S. federal court. A month after the 19-year-old Kozlov finalized his first contract with the Red Wings in February 1992, the Russian lawsuit began playing out in an American courtroom. In the suit, the Central Red Army club, now known as the Central Sports Club of the Army, claimed that Kozlov was still contractually bound to his Russian team after signing a contract with them the previous year, a contract Kozlov and the Wings claimed was "signed under duress and invalid." By the beginning of Kozlov's second Red Wings training camp in 1992, Chief U.S. District Judge Julian Cook Jr. ruled that Kozlov's Red Wings contract was legally binding.

With the Kozlov conflict resolved and borders between Russia and the United States open, NHL GMs pounced on the opportunity to draft Russian players, who would now have far fewer hurdles in their path to the NHL. In the summer of 1992, in the first NHL Draft held since the dissolving of the Soviet Union, eight Russians were selected in the first 17 picks. They included Alexei Yashin, who was taken second overall by the Ottawa Senators behind Czech defenseman Roman Hamrlik. Five more Russians were taken in the second round.

In the sudden rush of Russian talent to the NHL, word began to spread, primarily through the North American media, that Russian mobsters were targeting this exodus of million-dollar hockey talent. In the summer of 1993, Los Angeles Kings defenseman Alexei Zhitnik was reportedly approached by gangsters while visiting his family in Ukraine. Zhitnik claimed the group attempted to extort money from him, threatening to blow up his car. Alexander Alexeev, a Winnipeg Jets prospect, later claimed mafia thugs beat him up while he was visiting Kiev. As the economy crumbled in Russia along with much of the infrastructure, enterprising criminals appeared to be looking for a new source of revenue. None of the Green Five nor Mogilny or Fedorov were ever believed to be linked to the Russian mafia, a short-lived media fixation that died down rather quickly. "I guess they say there is no fire without smoke. But there is no evidence of it," says Zarokhovich. "I don't think these stories were true. But people look out for sensational news on both sides of the Atlantic."

• • •

After playing alongside Sergei Makarov for two seasons with the San Jose Sharks, Igor Larionov was traded to Detroit in 1995. It was here that he would enjoy a pleasant and long-overdue reunion with Slava Fetisov, who was traded to Detroit by the Devils the previous season. In a way, Fetisov and Larionov coming together with Fedorov, Kozlov, and Konstantinov seemed inevitable. The previous year, in the midst of a 1994–95 NHL season that was delayed greatly by a lockout, many of the former Soviet Union's best players came together for their new country. Much had changed since they left. For one thing, Central Red Army now featured penguins on their jerseys, the result of a recent transaction in which the Pittsburgh Penguins acquired part of the team.

With no NHL hockey being played, a dream team of Russian stars assembled for a tour of Russia that for many of them marked their first return to the mother country since leaving for the NHL. Fetisov, Larionov, Makarov, Krutov, Kasatonov, and Fedorov were all included in the tour, which stopped in Yaroslavl, Nizhny Novgorod, and Magnitogorsk before culminating in a five-game charity tournament in Moscow, where both Tikhonov and Tarasov made appearances. Fedorov in particular expressed nervousness about coming back to Russia, especially considering he was still technically considered a criminal in the country given his defection. But after playing alongside his old linemates Alex Mogilny and Pavel Bure, he and his comrades were all greeted as heroes by the thousands of fans who came out for the first major hockey event in Russia since the fall of Communism. "It was absolutely crazy," Fedorov told reporters in Moscow. "It was a great feeling. The three of us never thought we would play together again."

Seeing the two Red Army legends now on his roster, Wings coach Scotty Bowman decided to assemble the first all-Russian five-man team in NHL history. Despite Fetisov and Larionov both being well into their 30s by this point, the new version of the Green Five featuring Fedorov, Kozlov, and Konstantinov proved incredibly efficient for the Wings. The five players occasionally showed the brilliant finesse reminiscent of the original Green Five, but this group was different. This new unit was instead custom built for the NHL's considerably tougher game. Konstantinov's signature nastiness made the team very difficult to combat, while Fedorov and Kozlov shaped their still-developing two-way game within the confines of NHL arenas. With Larionov moved from center to wing, the unit may not have demonstrated the polish of its Russian predecessors, but there wasn't a crew in the NHL that could exceed their grit and toughness, qualities Soviet hockey players were always perceived as lacking. In the group's first full season as a unit in 1995–96, the Wings started an astonishing 24–7–2. After the Wings were eliminated in the 1996 conference final by Colorado, the Russian unit returned the next season, with the 38-year-old Fetisov enjoying his finest NHL season, thanks to a start that saw him register five goals and 14 assists in his first 35 games while posting a plus-25 rating, third best in the NHL. When the Red Wings won the Cup that season, the crew became the first Russian five-man unit to have their name inscribed on it.

On June 13, 1997, after a party celebrating the Wings' first
championship in 42 years, Fetisov, Konstantinov, and team mas-
seur Sergei Mnatsakanov left the festivities in a rented limousine.
Unbeknownst to all three men, the limousine driver, Richard
Gnida, was driving with a revoked license and had previously
been ticketed for speeding as well as operating a vehicle while
impaired. Tragically, the limousine hit a tree on the median, leaving both Konstantinov and Mnatsakanov in a coma. At age 30,
Konstantinov's career had abruptly ended, but when the Wings
repeated as Stanley Cup champions a year later, he was escorted
out onto the ice where, despite being restricted in his speech and
movement, he celebrated the championship alongside Larionov,
Fetisov, Fedorov, and Kozlov. Eleven years later, his legacy in
hockey already cemented, Konstantinov received a standing ovation when, with the aid of a walker and his former teammate
Larionov, he marched on stage to present the Lester B. Pearson
Award at the 2009 NHL Awards. With the crowd overjoyed by
his presence, Konstantinov leaned over to the microphone and
gently asked everyone, "How are you?"

Russia hasn't celebrated Olympic gold since the Unified
Team won in 1992. Ironically, in the time since that tournament
victory, there may not be a country that has more greatly influ-
enced the pace, look, and shape of the National Hockey League.
That Russian influence hasn't been lost on one of the men who
worked hardest to bring Eastern Europeans to the NHL before
leaving the Red Wings in 1993.

"The Russians as a culture, I think, have been beautiful for
our game," says Jim Lites. "They have been important for our
game. It's been a great thing."

7

The Last Defector

I had nothing. When I made the decision in Calgary that I was going to stay, I had 20 bucks in my pocket and that was it. That's what I had.

By 1989, 25 years after Vaclav Nedomansky's defection and with the Eastern Bloc experiencing sweeping political and social changes, the idea of a Czechoslovakian hockey player defecting to the West was no longer a completely alien concept. With over a dozen of its players now competing in the NHL, the Czechoslovakian government was actively selling its world-class hockey talent to NHL teams in the hopes it might curb future defections, or at least provide a new revenue stream. But when it came to their developing teenage players, there was no point in worrying about trying to keep them in Czechoslovakia. After all, the thought of a 16-year-old hockey player defecting to the West was too laughable to even contemplate. At least that's what Petr Nedved was counting on.

With a father and older brother who had been involved in a Czechoslovakian hockey program that was swiftly losing high-profile players to the NHL, Petr Nedved was developing into the future of his national team. But despite his impressive pedigree, Nedved felt contempt for the Communist government at a young age. "When I look back now, we're kind of happy that we grew up in this system. It was kind of an interesting lesson for the rest of your life," says Nedved. "Going on a vacation as a family for us was a headache. If you wanted to go to the Western countries, they wouldn't allow you. Or they would just allow my mom and me or my dad. We hardly went on a vacation to a Western country together. They always want to make sure they had somebody back there so you would come back home. So that was, if I may say, kind of fucked up."

Those frustrations over travel were somewhat resolved once Nedved became more deeply involved with the Czechoslovakian hockey program. Starting around age nine, Nedved began enjoying hockey trips outside Czechoslovakia. These tours helped him develop his game, but they also contributed to his mounting disdain for Communism. "That was a bonus that the other kids didn't have if they weren't playing sports. It was kind of nice that we could go. It was a big deal. We saw there was a different world," says Nedved. "On the TV or the news, they [the Communist government] were advertising what a bad world it was, and you would go there and say, 'Hey, this is something totally different from what they are telling us.' We would go to the shopping malls and you would see so much nice stuff. [Back in Czechoslovakia], we were waiting in line around Christmas to get food."

By the time 15-year-old Nedved was being fast-tracked through the Czechoslovakian hockey pipeline, the idea of defection, no matter how premature, started to come together. There was now a precedent set of Czechoslovakians who made their way to the NHL, either via defection or transferring legally after fulfilling their requisite time on the national team. Once Nedved began to think about playing in the NHL, making sure never to reveal these dreams to anyone, he soon decided that the latter option would be impossible. "I remember Jiri Hrdina. He was playing in Calgary, then in Pittsburgh, but that was [at] the end of his career. That is something I didn't want to do," says Nedved. "You can get injured when you're 22, then you never have the opportunity. Coming here at the end of your career, it's not an easy thing. By then you could have family. Then the language becomes a problem."

With Nedved's Litvinov squad invited to compete in Calgary's historic Mac's Midget tournament, the perfect opportunity for defection may have emerged. An annual showcase for the world's top 15-, 16-, and 17-year-old players since 1978, the tournament had seen the coronation of future NHL stars like Claude Lemieux, Mike Modano, Bill Ranford, and Mike Vernon. Having turned 17 in the weeks before the tournament, Nedved knew he might have an opportunity to add his name to that list. And that he did, leading the tournament in scoring and establishing himself as one of hockey's best junior-aged players. But this coming-out party wouldn't be abruptly spoiled by Nedved's return to the constraints of Czechoslovakian hockey. He didn't have much of a plan, but Petr Nedved wasn't coming back.

• • •

Many of Canada's first Czech and Slovak settlements had put down roots in Alberta, particularly Lethbridge, and by the time

Petr Nedved arrived at the Mac's Midget tournament, a vibrant Czech and Slovak community had grown throughout the province. Before long, Nedved met some local expats, striking up a conversation with a man in Calgary who became a fast friend. "He would say, 'Hey, you want to see this or that?' and then he would take us there. We would just go and see downtown and the high-rises and walk through the city," says Nedved. "We went to different restaurants, that kind of thing. We went to an NHL game too, when we were in Edmonton for a couple of days, so we saw the Oilers."

For Nedved, seeing the Edmonton Oilers had been a special experience. Despite the filtered Czechoslovakian media, he had grown up idolizing Wayne Gretzky. Although the Oilers had traded Gretzky to Los Angeles five months earlier, the Great One was still synonymous with his former team, and Nedved was thrilled to be in their presence. Nedved began to feel increasingly comfortable with his new friend and before long found the right time to express his intentions to defect. The man, whom Nedved refuses to identify to this day, was the first person he had ever shared his plan with. "I felt very comfortable with him. Because he defected too, so I was asking him about it. He was telling me how tough it was," says Nedved. "At the beginning, I don't think he thought I was serious. When I had some time alone, I was able to talk to him about it."

In the short history of Czechoslovakian hockey defections, a premium was put on inconspicuousness and silence. Nedved had learned from that precedent, never telling his parents about his plans, for fear they would not allow him to attend the tournament in Canada. Before long, the stranger understood that his new 17-year-old friend was serious about defecting and offered to do what he could to help. Of course, Nedved mentioned that he would likely do it with or without the man's help.

Nedved emerged from the Mac's Midget tournament an undeniable star. In his first trip to North America, he was named a tournament All-Star after leading Litvinov to the championship. At the conclusion of his three-week trip to Canada, with his place confirmed as one of the best young players on the planet, Nedved might never have a better opportunity to defect. For one thing, he was already in Canada and the team only had a single person tracking it through the tournament. Conventional wisdom said that one agent was all that was necessary for a group of teenagers traveling abroad.

Because he was only 17, Petr Nedved was too young to be drafted by an NHL club, meaning that if he did defect, he would start his new life without any of the financial security his predecessors enjoyed. Their professional rights belonged to an NHL team, so they had a proper contract signed and notarized by the time they arrived in North America. Petr Nedved would not have that if he defected. That big difference between him and other Czechoslovakian defectors was a major factor in Nedved's decision. "They [other defectors] made a huge decision too, and I'm sure it was very tough for them at the beginning as well. But for me it was really, really tough," says Nedved. "I didn't have any security. Those guys, when they came, they signed an NHL contract and they had security money-wise. I had nothing. When I made the decision in Calgary that I was going to stay, I had 20 bucks in my pocket and that was it. That's what I had."

With the tournament won and a 10 a.m. flight scheduled for the next morning, the victorious Litvinov team was enjoying a fairly nondescript final day in Canada when their star player out of the blue revealed that he wouldn't be returning to Czechoslovakia with them. Naturally, no one took him seriously. Nedved could only laugh nervously as he went from teammate to teammate, shaking hands and wishing them well.

"Listen, this is it. I'm going to stay here," he told them. "If you don't see me tomorrow on the plane, then I guess I'm not coming back."

That night, around 2 a.m., mere hours before he was expected to pack his things to meet his teammates at the airport for their return trip to Czechoslovakia, Nedved called his new friend. It was then that the man finally understood that Nedved's overtures for defection weren't simply the impulsive whims of a temperamental teenager. Shortly after their phone call, the man drove by the home of the billet family where Petr was staying and picked up the young hockey star in a scene shrouded in secrecy.

"Get me out of Calgary," Nedved demanded after getting in the car.

The pair drove to Banff, Alberta, where they immediately stopped by a police station and shared Petr's story. The RCMP officers were understandably shocked by the story of the teenage defector who couldn't speak a word of English. By now it was official: 17-year-old Petr Nedved was an international refugee. "The most important thing for me was if I would see my parents and my brother. I was really close with my brother, he was only two years older than me. We did everything together. If I was without him for a day or two, I was almost sick. That was the biggest thing," says Nedved. "Not being able to know when I'm going to see my parents and my brother, that was probably the toughest. Saying to myself that I might not see my brother again for another 15 years, I didn't even want to think about it. Because basically that was saying to myself, 'Don't stay here and go home.'"

After contacting local immigration officials, the police and the stranger helped iron out the details of Nedved's impending immigration hearing. Still unsure of exactly what was happening, Petr was escorted by police to a nearby hotel, where he was asked to keep the door locked and await word from police.

"Don't answer the door unless someone knocks three times," they said before leaving him alone in the room.

By now, Petr's billet family in Calgary had called his team to let them know that he would not be making his 10 a.m. flight. His whereabouts still a mystery to most of the hockey world, Nedved sat in the hotel room. "I was there for about a half hour and thought, 'This is not good,'" remembers Nedved. "I don't like this."

And like that, without so much as alerting hotel staff, Petr Nedved left. His friend lived a short drive from the Banff hotel and, after spending some time at his house over the previous several days, Nedved knew the route from memory. Of course, a drive of a few minutes between the man's home and the hotel turned into a 45-minute trip on foot. Referencing the map he had drawn in his mind, Nedved walked through the cold Alberta streets, in January no less, toward his friend, without the slightest assurance that Czechoslovakian officials weren't after him. "It was the strangest walk in my life. Because you're walking through downtown and it's almost like everybody I looked at, I felt that somebody was going to take me," says Nedved. "It wasn't a good day, that's for sure."

When the man opened his front door later that day, he was more than a little surprised to find the frazzled Petr standing on his doorstep. Even if he was scared, the teenager was assertive with his friend. He would not be staying at the hotel any longer. Whatever he would have to do to be cleared by Canadian immigration, Nedved would do it from the friendly confines of his friend's home. His friend immediately called Lubos Pesta, a

Calgary lawyer originally born in Czechoslovakia who had immigrated to Canada with his family at age 11. Pesta put together
Nedved's immigration case, compiling witnesses from Calgary
and Edmonton who could attest to the dangers the teenage hockey
star faced if he returned to Czechoslovakia. Even though he
hadn't yet been granted legal entry into Canada, speculation
had already started in the media as to whether Nedved was even
good enough to make it in the National Hockey League.

"Nedved is definitely far above average as a teenage hockey
player, but professional scouts who have seen him play say he is
a long way from being assured of even first-round draft status in
the NHL," Al Strachan wrote in the *Globe and Mail* in the days
following Nedved's defection. "As a result, he may never be able
to earn a job in the NHL, let alone be accorded superstar status."

Regardless of what his NHL future held, Nedved was immediately coveted by teams in the Western Hockey League (WHL),
a junior hockey league considered a direct gateway to the NHL.
Fears of international sanctions for signing Nedved had done
little to sway 9 of the league's 14 teams from attempting to sign
the young star. Because he was not yet eligible for the NHL Draft,
Nedved would have to play in the WHL, which did not have a
conventional prospect draft. Instead, WHL teams placed names
on their Player Protected List. If those players were not yet on
a WHL roster and still available, then they could become members of that team. By the time the WHL's Seattle Thunderbirds'
front office received a tip from scout Keith Wilson that Nedved
was defecting, they wasted no time placing him on their Player
Protected List.

"We were going to put in a claim and try to add him to our
list. Then we got worried that we weren't low enough in the
standings," says Thunderbirds president Russ Farwell. "So we

called another team and asked if they had plans to do things that day. They said they didn't. So we traded with them and got them to list the player for us. Then when the word came out who it was, they tried to bump up the price on us, so we ended up paying more."

After ironing out the details of the trade with the Moose Jaw Warriors, Nedved was the property of the Thunderbirds. But he wouldn't be arriving in Seattle anytime soon. Waiting for his immigration status to be resolved, Nedved stayed with his friend and trained in Alberta as the Thunderbirds completed a losing season in which they finished out of the play-offs. But the Thunderbirds' schedule would eventually bring them to Alberta, where they would finally meet their newest recruit, who by then had picked up a few helpful words of English. As soon as they saw Nedved practicing on the ice, the Thunderbirds needed no more convincing that the young defector was ready for the WHL game.

"We just knew that he was coming out to practice with us, and that's about it. Once he got out there, you could definitely see that he had enough talent to play in the league. But he didn't have the paperwork and everything to do that," says Turner Stevenson, who was then a 16-year-old T-Birds winger. "We saw this very skinny kid, definitely a very talented player. Still to this day one of the best pure wrist shots I've ever seen."

Nedved was soon declared a landed immigrant and received his visa, but there were still fears he would be ruled ineligible to play for the Thunderbirds because he hadn't received a formal release from his Czechoslovakian team. A temporary restraining order granted by a Seattle judge permitted Nedved to start the 1989–90 season with the Thunderbirds, although there remained the possibility that he might be forced to leave the team after one month.

On opening night, the Thunderbirds allowed seven unan-
swered goals to the Spokane Chiefs, losing 9–4 to one of the
league's worst teams from the previous season. But with Nedved
registering a goal and an assist in his first game, Farwell was
relieved to see the first European player in team history pay instant
dividends. Three nights later, Nedved scored twice more to lead
the Thunderbirds to an 11–2 win over the Victoria Cougars, their
first win of the season. By the time the Thunderbirds returned
to Seattle for their home opener, word had spread about their
emerging star. Nedved opened the scoring that night on the
power play, leading the Thunderbirds to a 4–3 win in front of
12,173 fans, the largest crowd in WHL history. With 19 points
in his first 11 games, Petr Nedved had arrived.

"He definitely had a swagger to him," says Stewart Malgunas, a
Thunderbirds defenseman who roomed with Nedved at a wealthy
billet family's home near Seattle. "Russ Farwell approached me
and asked if I would like to take the new guy in. So I was chosen
as a leader on the team to take Petr under my wing and show
him the sights of the Western Hockey League and Seattle."

By November, Petr Nedved was an established WHL star
with a legitimate shot at a fruitful NHL career. That great promise, coupled with his slight, wiry frame and Czechoslovakian
origins, made him the target of opposing teams, especially their
larger, rougher players, in what was by now a rite of passage
for European hockey players in North America. Fortunately
for Nedved, the Thunderbirds surrounded him with teammates who were more than happy to defend him against
oncoming on-ice traffic. There was Stevenson, who despite his
young age carried a massive six-foot three-inch frame, as well
as Darcy Simon, who collected more than 700 penalty minutes in his three seasons in Seattle. And, of course, there was

Stewart Malgunas, whose role as Nedved's protector extended far beyond the ice. "Petr didn't have a car, so it was my job to drive him to the rink every day. So we got to be pretty good friends. I was 19 at the time and he was 17," says Malgunas. "I started to teach him some words. Probably swear words, just to try to put us both at ease. We used to fight over the radio all the time. Petr's favorite band back then was Depeche Mode. I was into Motley Crue and Guns N' Roses. He hated that stuff, would pull his hair out. But I was the veteran so I got to listen to my stuff more often than not."

It wasn't long before Nedved invested in a Sony Walkman, a cutting-edge gadget for its time, that allowed him to listen to his own music whenever he wanted. All the while, he began to pick up English little by little, a developing skill that served him well as local and national sports media began to request more and more interviews with the burgeoning hockey star. Being able to communicate with his teammates had made things easier for the young winger, particularly considering how poorly his first few interactions over the phone with his parents had gone. "I remember calling my dad. He was coming to Prague to pick me up from the airport. At first he said, 'Hey, you already at the airport?' Then I told him the story. It wasn't a good conversation," says Nedved. "I hung up on him because it wasn't going anywhere. None of it was making sense, so I just said, 'Let's not talk.'"

The highlight of Nedved's time in Seattle came in December, when, on the day of his 18th birthday, Petr scored three goals in a six-point night against the Victoria Cougars, a team he was beginning to relish skating against. By then, Seattle was enjoying its best start in franchise history and Nedved was continuing to improve his stock for the upcoming NHL Draft.

The success and Nedved's eagerness to acclimate certainly served him well socially, making his experience in Seattle an enjoyable one. "He was one of the stars of the team and the team was doing well. American girls tend to gravitate toward that type of person. So Petr didn't have any problems with the girls. He seemed to be okay in that capacity," says Malgunas. "They always thought it was cute that he had this accent. They always wanted to know about Europe."

The accolades continued through the season for Nedved, who was named the West Conference team's MVP at the WHL All-Star Game before helping the Thunderbirds clinch a play-off spot with a hat trick in a 16–2 thrashing over, yes, the Victoria Cougars. All the while, the emerging superstar continued to endear himself to his North American teammates. "Petr was such a breath of fresh air once we got to know him. He was such a laid-back guy. Always smiling, always laughing. He fit right in with our crew," says Malgunas. "His big English word he learned early on was 'hang loose.' So he used to go around saying, 'Hang loose, buddy.' I don't know if he knew what it meant, but he liked 'hang loose.'"

Nedved would finish his incredible first season in Seattle with an astonishing 65 goals, his 145 points good for sixth in the league. More importantly, he led the Thunderbirds to a franchise-record 52 wins and a second-place finish in the West Conference, an impressive 19-win improvement from the previous season. And with highlight-reel plays to go with his impressive statistics, Nedved was being noticed in a city that already boasted three professional sports franchises. But it all ended abruptly come play-off time.

In a conference semifinal match against the Tri-City Americans, an errant slash broke a finger on Nedved's left hand.

Although the Thunderbirds would finish off Tri-City, Nedved had been rendered ineffective. With their star unable to unleash his feared shot, Seattle was matched up in the conference final against the Kamloops Blazers, the only team in the entire league to finish with a better record. Led by two of the league's leading scorers in Len Barrie and Phil Huber as well as one of the league's top young defensemen in Scott Niedermayer, Kamloops rolled over a Thunderbirds team that couldn't quite compete with their star player injured. The Blazers would go on to win the WHL championship, and Nedved's Thunderbird teammate, Glen Goodall, would win the Four Broncos Memorial Trophy as league Most Valuable Player. But it was clearly Nedved who had captured the spotlight that season, becoming one of the upcoming NHL Draft's top prospects. A few weeks after the end of his first WHL season, Petr Nedved was about to realize his hockey dream.

• • •

The season in Seattle certainly had some downs to go along with the mostly ups, but all in all, Petr Nedved had acclimated remarkably well. He had been surrounded by a team full of like-minded same-aged hockey prospects and embraced by a big city in a hockey league littered with small towns. Playing junior hockey had given Nedved an opportunity to develop his hockey skills, but it was playing in a city like Seattle that may have most helped the soon-to-be NHL star adapt to Western life. "I could have ended up in some little town in Canada. Those little towns are very supportive of the teams, and I'm sure it would work out nicely too. But for me personally, I like the bigger city," says Nedved. "Definitely for myself, I couldn't ask for a better team and a better city."

If the season in Seattle seemed to be a series of dream-like heroics, the 1990 NHL Draft was just as magical for the young Nedved. Staged just a short flight from Seattle in Vancouver, the 1990 draft boasted one of the best collections of young talent in recent NHL history. So it was a testament to Nedved's hard work and skill that he would be taken second overall by the home-town Canucks. Upon being selected by an emerging Canucks team that had welcomed Igor Larionov and Vladimir Krutov a year earlier, Nedved was showered with applause by the record crowd of 19,700 that attended the draft. Even Petr's formerly angered father, Jaroslav, was coming around.

"I would like to have seen how he played and developed. But I am pleased he did well and I am happy he succeeded in his dream," the elder Nedved, who traveled to Vancouver to be with Petr at the draft, told Bob Finnigan of the *Seattle Times*. "From age two, all he wanted to be was a hockey player and play for the biggest league he could. Of course, we did not realize he meant the NHL."

By the day of the NHL Draft, Nedved was also receiving news from his family about the sweeping changes in the country he had left 17 months earlier. After living their entire lives under a regime that had restricted their movements, Nedved's parents came to the draft speaking of a new era in Czechoslovakia in which it was suddenly much easier to visit most parts of Europe and the world. "The biggest thing was finally we were free. The Russian army was moving out of the country, because they had camps all over Czech," says Nedved. "For a lot of countries, it's just a normal thing [to be free]. But in our country it wasn't, to be able to breathe without somebody watching your back."

Despite the outright domination Nedved demonstrated with Seattle, his first NHL season in Vancouver would prove far more trying. His days weren't nearly as regimented, and the attention and stakes were much more intense. Instead of being assigned to a billeting family, Nedved would have to find his own living quarters, and Stewart Malgunas certainly wouldn't be around to drive him to and from practice. As a boy playing among men, Nedved was overwhelmed on the ice for the first time in his life. "The first year, as far as hockey [went], was frustrating. The first time in my hockey career I kind of felt a little like I didn't belong," says Nedved. "I wasn't producing as good as I thought I would. I'm not playing as much as I'm used to. It was a few things mixed together, and I wasn't totally happy about it."

A teenage player on a roster full of veterans, Nedved felt isolated and out of his element. Still sporting a thin, wiry frame, Nedved would try the same moves that had made him a star in Seattle, but the NHL's bigger, faster players could easily stifle his play. In an early-season game against the Los Angeles Kings, Nedved deked out an opponent and accelerated toward opposing goaltender Mario Gosselin. He appeared to have nothing but space to take a shot on goal when defenseman Rob Blake swooped in, knocking him off the puck. Later on in the game, he looked to take a pass on a two-on-two break and overskated the puck, killing the play. That extra second Nedved enjoyed with Seattle was gone forever. "He had this move. He would deke to his forehand and then go right to his backhand and just shelf it every single time up in the top of the net. The goalie knew he was going to do it but could not stop him," remembers Malgunas. "Then you get to the pros and everyone catches up."

As other rookies like Mike Ricci and Jaromir Jagr, himself recently arrived from Czechoslovakia, enjoyed superior seasons, the media began to speculate that the Canucks had selected the wrong player with the draft's second overall pick. The Canucks

defended Nedved publicly, but it was indeed a tough season for
the young player. With four points in his first 24 games with
the Canucks, Nedved had trouble finding consistency, and a difficult season was made even tougher in February when Canucks
coach Bob McCammon was fired and replaced by GM Pat Quinn
after a disappointing 19–30–5 start. The season became down-
right tragic following McCammon's firing when, shortly after
the team's flight landed at the Los Angeles airport for a game
against the Kings, USAIR 737-300 collided on the runway with a
commuter plane before skidding into an unoccupied fire station,
killing 33 people. Nedved and his Canucks teammates witnessed
the entire scene from their plane windows. The Canucks' pilot
braked hard upon landing, perhaps averting what could have
been an even greater tragedy.

Despite Nedved showing occasional flashes of his WHL
glory, the truth is he was overmatched in the NHL and could
have used another year of seasoning with the Thunderbirds. "I
needed to put on an extra 10 to 15 pounds. When I got drafted,
I was 170 pounds. So I was very lightweight for the NHL. As far
as skill goes, I definitely belonged in that league. But I needed
to get bigger and stronger," says Nedved. "There was a one-way
contract. So if I would go to the juniors, they [Vancouver] would
still have to pay me. They knew it was going to take me a little
time to get used to this league."

By his third season, Nedved would gain the muscle mass he
had lacked in his rookie season, giving him the strength necessary to compete against the world's best players. Now equipped
with some increased confidence to go along with his improved
physique, Nedved flourished for the Canucks, posting career
highs in goals (38), assists (33), points (71), penalty minutes (96),
and plus-minus (20). As great as his third season in Vancouver

had been, his play-off performance proved lackluster. With 5 points in 12 play-off games, Nedved's play was roundly criticized by media and fans alike. The criticism grew harsher when word began to spread that Nedved had asked his idol, Wayne Gretzky, for a game stick after the Kings' six-game ouster of the Canucks in the play-offs' second round.

Emboldened by his career year, Nedved would face off against the Canucks in a bitter contract dispute that came just one year after Michal Pivonka's first dispute with the Washington Capitals. Nedved's contract demands were maintained by his agent, Tony Kondel, another Czechoslovakian expat he met in Calgary shortly after his defection. Although Nedved was technically a free agent, his services would cost other NHL teams quite a haul were they to try to sign him. As a 21-year-old who had played fewer than five NHL seasons, Nedved was a Group 1 free agent, meaning that any team other than Vancouver that attempted to sign him would have to compensate the Canucks with either draft picks or players. Vancouver would also retain the right to match any offer Nedved received from another team. Making an offer for another club's Group 1 free agent proved exceedingly unpopular for NHL teams, especially after the St. Louis Blues signed Brendan Shanahan, formerly of the Devils, two years earlier.

In 1991, the Blues attempted to sign Shanahan away from the Devils, offering goaltender Curtis Joseph and forward Rod Brind'Amour as compensation. An independent arbitrator instead awarded the Devils St. Louis' defenseman and former team captain Scott Stevens. The drama surrounding the Shanahan signing made meddling in the Nedved affair an unsavory prospect for other NHL teams, meaning that it would be up to the Canucks and Petr Nedved to solve their contract standoff.

As Nedved's holdout looked as if it might wipe out his regular season altogether, an unexpected opportunity to play came from the unlikeliest of sources. With Nedved and Kondel standing by as the 1993–94 season ran its course, the fourth-year holdout and recent Canadian citizen eventually got in touch with the Canadian Olympic team, who were looking to fill out their roster in anticipation of the upcoming 1994 Olympics in Lillehammer, Norway.

Joined by Paul Kariya, another young NHL star engaged in his own lengthy holdout with the Anaheim Mighty Ducks, Nedved starred for a national team he had only recently become eligible to play for. He led the Canadians to the gold-medal game, where they would suffer a 3–2 shootout loss in one of the most dramatic championship games in Olympic history. But by his own admission, the star turn for the Canadian Olympic team wasn't borne entirely out of a newfound patriotism. "It was a funny situation. I had a contract dispute with the Canucks. That's when I became a Canadian citizen. Then this phone call came asking if I was interested to play for the national team. I thought about it for a little bit. It was kind of getting to the point where I had to go and start playing somewhere. It was a great experience, but it felt funny. I was very proud to represent Canada but the one game we played against the Czechs, that kind of felt weird," admits Nedved. "They understood, sports is business. They didn't feel that I betrayed them or anything like that. If the Czech team would have asked me to go play in the Olympic Games for them, I would. But they didn't. When this thing came up with Team Canada, I said, 'Okay, I'll do it.'"

• • •

Nedved's holdout ended shortly after the Olympics when the St. Louis Blues, willing to overlook their headaches in signing Shanahan, presented him with an offer sheet paying $4 million over three years. By signing Nedved, the Blues would simply have to compensate the Canucks and the whole matter would be over with. The Canucks asked for Shanahan in exchange, eliciting an outright refusal from St. Louis that led to an arbitration hearing at the NHL offices in New York. When it was over, arbitrator George Nicolau awarded the Canucks center Craig Janney, not the player they wanted but a young talent nonetheless.

Nedved would play only 19 games for St. Louis, registering 20 points, before being traded to the New York Rangers during the lockout-shortened 1994–95 season. In a bizarre bit of fate, the Nedved trade to the Rangers marked the end of another complicated hockey saga. In 1994, when coach Mike Keenan controversially signed with the Blues a month after leading the Rangers to their first Stanley Cup in 54 years, the Blues were required by the NHL to give the Rangers a player back in exchange. That player turned out to be Petr Nedved.

In what was developing into a nomadic career, after failing to adapt to the Rangers' style of play, Nedved was traded once again the next season, this time to Pittsburgh, where he enjoyed his best season, posting 45 goals and 99 points. But the statistical benchmarks would be soured by charges in British Columbia of sexual assault dating back to an alleged incident in 1994. Nedved willingly turned himself in to authorities, vigorously denying the charges. He entered a not-guilty plea, and the charges against him were dropped a year later after his lawyer claimed that Nedved wasn't even in Vancouver at the time of the alleged attack.

By then, at the last possible moment, Nedved signed a one-year extension with Pittsburgh. After waking up the morning of the 1996–97 season opener without a contract, Nedved and Kondel ironed out a last-second deal with the Penguins. With the ink barely dry on his new deal, Nedved boarded a flight from Vancouver that arrived in Pittsburgh at 4:30 p.m., giving him just enough time to convince the Penguins' brain trust to put him in the opening-night lineup. Although he was used only sporadically in the game, Nedved assisted on a Mario Lemieux goal with 3.6 seconds left that sent the game to overtime. Despite the Tampa Bay Lightning winning the game 4–3 in extra time, Petr Nedved was locked up and under contract for at least one more year.

Nedved had another successful season with the Penguins, scoring 33 goals, but, in what was now becoming a troubling trend, engaged in another lengthy contract dispute that off-season. Though his last contract had been signed in the nick of time, this holdout would eventually cost him a sizable portion of his NHL career.

After a late-season slump that saw him score one goal in his final 19 games before being held to three points in 5 games in the Penguins' first-round play-off loss to Philadelphia, Nedved found himself at odds with the Penguins once again. With Nedved listed as a Group 2 restricted free agent, the Penguins, like the Canucks before them, could match any offer for Nedved and would have to be compensated, potentially in the form of five first-round picks, if he signed with another team. As Nedved spent that summer back in the Czech Republic waiting for a new contract, there would be no eleventh-hour resolution this time around.

When it seemed apparent that he might miss the beginning of the 1997–98 season, Nedved opted to play a few games for the Novy Jicin club, a low-level franchise in the Czech leagues.

Unbeknownst to Nedved and Kondel, playing in what was now the Czech Republic would further complicate things, as the National Hockey League ruled that playing outside North America would force Nedved to go through waivers if he wished to return to the NHL. Ironically, Nedved's old Team Canada teammate, Paul Kariya, was simultaneously engaged in another holdout with the Mighty Ducks.

In January 1998, an independent arbitrator ruled that Nedved could reenter the NHL without clearing waivers after determining that Nedved never formally signed a contract with Novy Jicin. Despite the historic ruling, negotiations between Kondel and the Penguins failed to progress. Eventually, with the Penguins' posting multimillion dollar losses and experiencing deep ownership turmoil, Penguins' co-owner Howard Baldwin decided he had seen enough and finally lashed out publicly at Kondel. "What this guy should do is put up or shut up. With him, it's always the other guy's fault, always the Penguins' fault," Baldwin told Dejan Kovacevic of Pittsburgh's *Post-Gazette* in February 1998. "If he's so right and we're so wrong, why doesn't he have any other offers? Where are all the offers? I don't see them. There's no negotiating with him, and that's a shame because Petr's a good guy, a real good guy."

By the middle of the season, Paul Kariya finally resolved the second holdout of his career by signing a new contract with Anaheim. The Kariya signing left Nedved as one of only two players still battling their team for a new contract, the other being Sergei Fedorov of the Wings. When the Penguins started 18–11–8 and claimed their main roster priority was signing winger Jaromir Jagr to an extension, it became apparent that Nedved might not play a single game in the 1997–98 NHL season. Once Sergei Fedorov finally signed his contract with

Detroit in February, the prospect of Petr Nedved losing an entire season became increasingly likely. With little recourse and the season already lost, Nedved chose to play with Sparta Praha in his native Czech Republic. By the start of the NHL play-offs, the Czech team was eliminated from the Elite League play-offs, compelling the frustrated center to sign a contract with the Las Vegas Thunder of the International Hockey League, the same league Michal Pivonka and Peter Bondra played in during their extended holdout two years earlier. After playing three games with Las Vegas, Nedved was ruled ineligible by the International Hockey League because he had already played with Praha in the Czech league. By the fall of 1998, still without an NHL contract, Nedved signed another contract with the Thunder. But he also looked to finally resolve this seemingly endless standoff by making the difficult decision to fire Kondel in favor of established NHL agent Mike Barnett, whose clients included Wayne Gretzky and Jaromir Jagr.

"It was one of the toughest things I had to do, but I felt that I had to. Tony understood this. He didn't have a problem with that," says Nedved. "Obviously, he was disappointed that we couldn't get the deal done. But on the other hand, he was happy that he didn't have to have all this major stress on his back. We're still really good friends. I talk to him almost every week. That's the guy that had the biggest influence on me after Calgary."

After the most tumultuous season in his hockey career and with a new agent in tow, Nedved finally spoke out against the Penguins. "If one team offered me $20 million and Pittsburgh offered $25 million, I would go with the other team because this isn't about money anymore in Pittsburgh," Nedved told reporters. "[Penguins GM] Craig [Patrick] understands that, but his hands are tied."

On the eve of the 1998–99 NHL campaign, more than a year after the holdout began, the Penguins finally announced that they had abandoned any hopes of signing Nedved and would trade him before the beginning of the season. But there was a problem. In sitting out an entire season over a contract dispute, Nedved found that his stock had plummeted among NHL GMs. Kovacevic had covered the Nedved fiasco extensively at the *Post-Gazette* and described his eventual situation thusly: "Within the past few weeks, some NHL general managers made it clear they wanted no part of Nedved. George McPhee of the Washington Capitals questioned his integrity. Bob Clarke of the Philadelphia Flyers called him 'an idiot.' Harry Sinden of the Boston Bruins went so far as to create a new hockey term by referring to three of his own holdouts as 'a bunch of Nedveds.' The damage is done."

"I'm sure the managers weren't happy. For me it was business. For them, I'm sure it was business too," says Nedved when asked about the league backlash. "I was never asking for something that I think wasn't market value."

Nedved's rights were eventually traded two months after the start of the 1998–99 season to the Rangers, who signed him to a three-year, $10.5-million contract. The deal involved multiple players, though the Penguins' main acquisition was Alexei Kovalev, a Russian winger experiencing his own contract squabble, who also enjoyed the distinction of being, along with Sergei Nemchinov, the first Russian player to win the Stanley Cup. Nedved had earned plenty of negative publicity over the course of his holdout, but he had an instant impact with the Rangers, leading the team to a 3–1–1 record in his first five games with New York. If there was one positive in the entire saga, it was that Nedved was now in New York playing alongside his idol, Wayne Gretzky, in his final NHL season.

Petr Nedved played six mostly successful seasons with the Rangers, his longest stay with any of the seven NHL teams he played for. In a lengthy NHL career, Nedved isn't generally remembered as the youngest defector in hockey history or the last hockey player to defect during the Cold War. Instead, despite Nedved's teenage heroics, his career is at least partially clouded by his endless contract squabbles. As a result, he is characterized as stubborn by some of the people who worked with him.

"He would have little episodes and whatnot and we would say, 'Where is your head, kid?'" says Glen Ringdal, the Canucks' former vice president of communications and marketing, when asked about Nedved. "They would wonder about him, and it eventually led to him leaving town."

After splitting the 2006–07 season with the Philadelphia Flyers and the Edmonton Oilers, the team he had watched play in the days leading up to his defection, Nedved returned to the Czech Republic, where he continues to play in the Czech Elite League. Regardless of the varied opinions about his holdouts, Nedved says he has just one regret from what can only be characterized as a long and productive NHL career.

"I would probably do it differently with Pittsburgh. I should have signed for less than market value for one year and just dealt with the situation later. Not playing for one year was frustrating," he says, perhaps identifying the source of some of the contract issues other Czechoslovakian players dealt with. "I think that people sometimes were thinking, 'Oh, those guys coming from Eastern Europe, they should be happy. At home they're not going to make anything near this.' Which is absolutely correct. So why should I take this much less? Just because I'm from Czech Republic?

"I don't want to be putting words in anybody's mouth. I'm hesitant to say it aloud," he continues. "But sometimes I felt a lot of the guys from Eastern Europe had the same problems. Maybe they [NHL executives] thought, 'Why shouldn't they take it?' They probably thought, 'Where are they going to go anyway? They're not getting even half what we're giving them back home.'"

Even if the Cold War ended shortly after his defection, Nedved has no regrets about the fateful decision he made in Calgary. It did, after all, bring him one step closer to his NHL dreams.

"Let's put it this way. I'm not going to say I only made right decisions. I made mistakes throughout my career. No question about that. Sometimes I wish I had done this differently. But I think it's all about growing up. If you made only the right decisions, it would be no fun," he continues. "When I look back, I enjoyed every minute of it. I was very fortunate that I was able to play in the National Hockey League. In a way, I got rewarded for the risks I took."

In a bizarre way, Nedved's story is a fitting end to a historic period in sports that saw countless men and women risk their livelihood for an opportunity to go west. Of all the players who did make the brave decision to come to the National Hockey League against the wishes of their government, none embraced capitalist ideals more than Nedved. And for a group of athletes raised in a system that dictated many of the details of their daily lives, nobody demonstrated more outright defiance. Considering his response to authority both east and west of the Berlin Wall, it seems appropriate that Petr Nedved closed the final chapter in this unique era.

• • •

In 2011, 20 years after Nedved completed his first season in the NHL, Zdeno Chara of the Boston Bruins raised the Stanley Cup, becoming the first Eastern European to captain a team to hockey's grandest prize. Later that summer, Chara brought the Cup home to Trencin, the Slovakian town that, less than half a century earlier, saw the militaristic rules of Eastern Bloc forces posted on its walls and lampposts during the Soviet-led siege.

In the time since Vaclav Nedomansky first arrived in Toronto, players from Eastern Europe have only further expanded their NHL presence, developing from a taboo fascination into a vitally important part of the league fraternity. By the 2005–06 season, Czechs accounted for 6.9 percent of the NHL's players, with Russians making up 4.3 percent and Slovakians 3.2 percent. Even if today's international players face far fewer political hurdles in reaching the NHL, the road for all of them was paved by the brave athletes, from Nedomansky to Nedved, from Fetisov to Fedorov, willing to risk plenty for an opportunity to play in the world's most competitive hockey league. During a historic period of intense international turmoil, it was they who realized the dreams of millions behind the Iron Curtain—dreams of victory, dreams of greatness, dreams of freedom.

Index